CULTURE and SELF

CULTURE and SELF
Asian and Western Perspectives

Edited by
Anthony J. Marsella
George DeVos
and
Francis L. K. Hsu

Tavistock Publications
New York and London

First published in 1985 by
Tavistock Publications
in association with Methuen, Inc.
29 West 35th Street
New York, NY 10001
and Tavistock Publications Ltd
11 New Fetter Lane, London EC4P 4EE

© 1985 Anthony J. Marsella, George DeVos,
Francis L. K. Hsu

Printed in the USA

Library of Congress Cataloging in Publication Data
Culture and self.

Bibliography: p.
Includes index.
1. Self – Cross-cultural studies.   2. East and West.
I. Marsella, Anthony J.   II. DeVos, George A.
III. Hsu, Francis L. K., 1909–
BF697.C86   1985   155.2   85-2661
ISBN 0-422-79130-X
ISBN 0-422-79140-7 (pbk.)

British Library Cataloguing in Publication Data
Culture and self: Asian and Western perspectives.
1. Self perception
I. Marsella, Anthony J.   II. DeVos George
III. Hsu, Francis L-K
155.2   BF697

ISBN 0-422-79130-X
ISBN 0-422-79140-7 Pbk

Contents

In Memory of
Youngsook Kim Harvey
Teacher, Colleague, Friend

List of Contributors

Agehananda Bharati, PhD
Professor of Anthropology
Syracuse University
New York

Godwin C. Chu, PhD
Research Associate
Communications Institute
East-West Center
Honolulu, Hawaii

George DeVos, PhD
Professor of Anthropology
University of California
Berkeley, California

Francis L. K. Hsu, PhD
Professor Emeritus
Department of Anthropology
Northwestern University
Evanston, Illinois

Frank Johnson, MD
Professor of Psychiatry
School of Medicine
University of California
San Francisco, California

Anthony J. Marsella, PhD
Professor of Psychology
University of Hawaii
Honolulu, Hawaii

M. Brewster Smith
Professor
Adlai E. Stevenson College
University of California
Santa Cruz, California

Tu Wei-ming, PhD
Professor of East Asian Languages
  and Civilizations
Harvard University
Cambridge, Massachusetts

Preface

The self has returned! After almost seven decades, there has been
a resurgence of interest in the concept of self. At the turn of the
century, the self was a major tenet in many theories of human
behavior. William James, George Herbert Mead, Carl Jung, and a
score of other notable figures had elevated the self to a position
of primacy in their theories. But, by the 1920s, the influence of
logical positivism and other reductionistic movements had
significantly reduced the impact of the self on social science
theory, and the self had disappeared as a fundamental concept
among all but a few psychoanalytic and phenomenological
theories.

Today, social scientists, philosophers, and even theoretical
physicists are increasingly invoking the self as an explanatory
concept for understanding complex human behavior. The present volume is a contribution to the renaissance of interest in the
self.

The purpose of this volume is to provide teachers, students,
scholars, and professional practitioners with a comprehensive
resource for understanding the reciprocal relationships between
culture and self in western and Asian thought and the implications these relationships have for human adaptation and adjustment. All of the chapters proceed from the premise that the self is
a necessary construct for explaining those emergent qualities of
human behavior that proceed from person-context relationships;
it is these qualities that are most associated with meaning,

consciousness, and knowing in human experience. In illuminating the relationships between culture and self in western
and Asian thought, the chapters discuss both historical and
contemporary concepts in the scholarly literature. Readers
will find the chapters a fascinating journey across time and
culture in the search for understanding the roots of human
behavior.

The current volume is divided into four major sections.
Section I, "Introduction and Foundations," includes three
chapters. Chapter 1 is an overview and summary of the chapters
contained in the volume. It was written by the editors to provide
an integrated statement of the major themes and issues of the
various chapters. Chapter 2 was written by Francis L. K. Hsu.
Along with Chapter 3, prepared by M. Brewster Smith, these two
chapters offer a foundation for grasping the nature of the self
from a cross-cultural perspective.

Section II includes a chapter on western concepts of the self;
it was authored by Frank Johnson. Section III contains four
chapters on different Asian views on self. Chapter 5 is on the
self in Japanese culture; it was written by George DeVos.
Agehananda Bharati prepared Chapter 6, the self in Hindu
thought and action, and Chapter 7, the self in Confucian thought,
was authored by Tu Wei-ming. The concept of self in contemporary China is the topic of Chapter 8, written by Godwin
C. Chu. The fourth and final section of the volume consists
of Chapter 9, which was authored by Anthony J. Marsella. The
chapter discusses culture, self, and mental disorder.

The editors wish to express their appreciation to the
Department of Psychology, University of Hawaii, Honolulu,
Hawaii and The University of Hawaii Foundation for their
financial support in the preparation of the volume. Our appreciation is also extended to Gill Davies, editorial director of
Tavistock Publications Ltd, for her support throughout the
various stages of publication. We also owe much gratitude
to Freda Hellinger for typing many of the manuscripts and
to Bonnie Ozaki for preparing the index. Last, the editors
wish to thank the chapter authors for their cooperation,

patience, and scholarship, all of which reached extraordinary proportions.

Anthony J. Marsella
Honolulu, Hawaii   *George DeVos*
February, 1984   *Francis Hsu*

PART I

Introduction and Foundations

1

Introduction:
Approaches to Culture and Self

George DeVos, Anthony J. Marsella,
and Francis L. K. Hsu

The present volume attests to the confluence of several strong contemporary currents in social science today. Though out of fashion in psychology since the days of William James, there has been a resurgence of interest in the study of subjective experience as a valid approach to human behavior. The rabid logical positivism of the past has abated. Human behavior cannot be reduced to physiological explanations – or even to variance in personality structure. A consciousness of meaning must be considered as transcendant and not reducible to learned patterns of cognition and affect. Conversely, there is a rising discontent against a materialist reductionism that sees all of human behavior explainable as simply complex forms of ecological adaptation. Symbolic interactionism and "hermeneutic," or interpretive explanations, have achieved increasing prominence in sociology, psychology, and anthropology. These approaches emphasize both the necessity and the difficulty of including subjectivity as an essential ingredient in the social sciences, whether they are to be explored in those observed or as an essential characteristic of the observer.

In this volume we directly explore the "self" cross-culturally, specifically comparing this concept within the western tradition of thought with that developed so differently under Hinduism in India, Confucianism and Maoism in China and the unique blend of borrowed and indigenous representations found in Japan. What we seek to convey in the following chapters is how these differences in perception of the self relate to some remaining implicit ethnocentrisms in social scientific enquiry as well as in the art and literature of our increasingly interrelated world. Since further political and economic interrelation will continue to take place, it is vital to increase our mutual understanding of the different premises and perceptions that continue to underlie social behavior in different civilizations and cultural communities large and small.

The self as an experiential or "emic" concept in contemporary social science is to be distinguished from the "ego" as used in an "etic" or externally analytic approach to personality structure in western psychology. Similarly, the experience of the self is to be distinguished in a social structural analysis of man in society as perceived in the context of social "roles." There is some tendency in both psychological and sociological theory to fuse, if not to confuse, objective "etic" and experiential "emic" approaches to social behavior or even to ignore self-consciousness as a nonsignificant determinant of social behavior undeserving serious scientific study in its own right. The experience of selfhood – consciousness – that occurs in human beings in various cultures is *not* totally derivative of or reflective of personality structure, nor is it reducible to an analysis of the social structure in which an individual participates. The behavioral implications of this distinction between ego and self, self and social role, will become evident as we explore the self in European and Asian heritages of thought.

In this introduction, it may help to distinguish the various levels of approach on which contemporary social science takes place to better locate the focus of attention on the self. *Figure 1.1* serves to orient us depending on where we start, either by observing man in his natural environment or in the details of his physiological potential. Human behavior can be analyzed on a number of levels – but human consciousness as an emergent force cannot be subsumed or ignored.

If we start with a social ecological approach, the dynamic interaction is between the total ecological system and man's social system. A society will be observed to function more or less adequately in its adaptation to the environment. Seen diachronically, environments change and societies change, due either to

Figure 1.1 The self in culture: levels of scientific analysis in the study of human behavior

levels of analysis	mode of analysis	major behavioral concepts and governing concepts	positive versus negative functioning	diachronically historical dimension
ecological		the environment	ecological adaptations	environmental change
social structure as an aspect of culture	etic	social behavior as representations of social structure	organization – disorganization cohesion – anomie	social change; changes in technology
social role interaction	etic-emic	patterns of social interaction	social conflict – accommodation	patterns of conformity or deviancy
"self" in social interaction	emic	the self – the subjective experience; social or ethnic "identity"	adaptation – maladaptation; conflict between self and role expectations; belonging – alienation	changing perceptions of self and society – with changes in the life cycle or changes in social conditions
"personality" psychological structure	emic-etic	ego mechanisms; fixed patterns in behavior – expressive emotional styles	adjustment – maladjustment; "health" – pathology	psycho-sexual development; cognitive development
physiological		"instinctive" patterns or drive propensities	physiological functions	maturation

demographic or technological forces. This potential for change can be seen as a continuous tension. Complicating patterns of change still further is the fact that social systems are never in total isolation but in continuous contact with one another so that there will be complementary or destructive interaction to be considered through time.

We may choose to forego this macrotheoretical level of social vision to focus more sharply on the interaction between a continuing social structure and the social roles played by the participants in the system. Patterns of social interaction, status positions, and forms of interaction related to social stratification all can become a topic of observation. The conflicts and adaptations as societies slowly change or the influence of abrupt events changing the social order can be studied. These patterns can be observed from the outside but they also may be observed by understanding the experiences communicated by the participants. Social role theory can be both "emic" and "etic" depending upon the observer's emphasis.

Starting from a totally different concern with structure, theories of human behavior may be considered to begin out of a concern with man's biological heritage, the evolution of physiological systems that eventuate in the potentials of human behavior. The interaction observed scientifically from this vantage point relates biological structure to physiological functions that govern human behavior. One seeks out the mechanisms underlying an ego structure – the patterns of cognition and the expressive emotional styles which are relatively fixed and enduring, and therefore govern behavior. Looked at through time, there is an unfolding of a maturational pattern. One can assess differences among individuals in internally adjustive functioning.

Some behavior can be seen in concordance with maturational potential. Other resultant human behavior is assessed as partially deformed, and maladjustive structures are sought out to explain psychopathology. This point of view sees analogies between physical disease (or illness), and psychological malfunctioning. The effects of particular cultures on normative patterns of realization or non-realization of maturational potential is the study of the "personality" in culture. Ultimately such study is an etic analysis. The system of thought brought to bear in cross-cultural observation is ultimately external to the experience of the members of a particular social system or culture being observed.

What we have been describing as social structural or psychological etic systems in western science gained their relative independence from religious and/or philosophical systems that were built on premises of a man-centered moral universe with human experience as the starting point for explaining human behavior. It is not surprising, therefore, that there is considerable resistance among the scientifically dedicated to reconsidering how and to what degree human self-consciousness has to be reconciled in formulating the dimensions of a valid social science — a social science which has had such difficulty in the past in extricating itself from particularistic subjectivity. Only a century has passed since social science gained independence from the western philosophical premises as discussed by Frank Johnson in Chapter 4. Indeed, even today, anthropology, psychology and sociology are not free from ethnocentric biases.

This volume assumes, however, that there is a valid level of analysis located beneath "objective" approaches to how social structures and social roles are interrelated with given social role expectations. The self can and must be considered apart from one's social role. Behavior is often a result of continuous conflict between experiences of self and one's social role expectations. Moreover, the self changes through time. It changes in the life cycle and/or with social change occurring external to the individual. Such changes can cause new tensions in the experiential self, resulting in changing forms of behavior.

Turning from the direction of social structure to that coming from psychological structures, observation of the self as a central concept explaining behavior must be distinguished from underlying concepts of ego structure. This is particularly apparent in cross-cultural analysis. The principal argument of various chapters of this book is that cultural traditions of thought influence how the self perceives itself and, in turn, how this perception interacts with, rather than is determined by, the operation of underlying coping mechanisms that comprise personality struc-ture. In brief, as outlined in *Figure 1.1*, the analysis of the self in social interaction is a necessary intervening level of analysis between that concerned with social role interaction on the one hand, and personality structure on the other.

In considering this point of view, we stress the necessary distinction between the concepts of adaptation and of adjust-ment as complementary to one another in understanding human behavior. These concepts are based on explanatory systems that intersect but are not reducible into one another. Personality structure is not reducible to social structure, nor can social structure be conceptualized simply out of an interplay of internally motivated patterns of behavior. Adaptation is an interactive social concept. Behavior is often judged by the "self" as well as being socially judged by others with whom one is in interaction. Behavior is judged consciously as adaptive or maladaptive in reference to social expectations or in reference to such criteria as that of social success or failure. Socially visible maladaptive behavior can, for example, be attributed to internal tendencies or mental incapacities without necessarily exploring the underlying malfunctioning. Indeed, very often underlying structures are ignored or not considered in the evaluation of behavior.

By itself, any emic social judgment of maladaptive behavior may or may not actually relate directly to the underlying causal patterns in personality. The explanation for maladaptive behavior may be further sought by the sociologically oriented observer in reference to an etic explanatory system which is not part of the direct awareness of any social group. Alienation, for example, may be seen as having its origin in malfunctioning interaction within the social system. For instance, members of a low status group may or may not be aware that they are being economically exploited.

Conversely, the concepts of psychological adjustment or maladjustment are often etically conceived. They refer most frequently to the theoretical explanations of the psychologist, not to self-conscious or socially conscious attitudes. In western culture, a psychologist or psychiatrist, as Anthony Marsella discusses in Chapter 9, is sought out as a specialist who has developed an explanatory system about "personality" without reference to the "self" as a causal agent of behavior. A person judged "maladjusted" by the psychological specialist may be socially adaptive in that he or she manifests no visible maladaptive behavior externally, but is, nevertheless, experiencing internal disorder. Conversely, an internally "adjusted" person with no psychological structural problem may not fit in his social niche and so may be considered "maladapted" by his social group. Subjectively, on the level of the conscious self, a person may be aware of being maladaptive and therefore accept a diagnosis that he is maladjusted.

The interplay in any individual case between consciousness and unconsciously structured behavior is very complex. What is very apparent, however, in considering concepts of adaptation and adjustment, is that "consciousness" is interactively causal and therefore has to be taken into account as a determinant of behavior. For example, in the psychiatric realm, the conscious social attitudes of the group are a determinant of the course of psychiatric treatment. The attitudes of the individual and group may indeed influence the direction and course taken in any psychiatric intervention. Even further, the "self" may influence underlying psychophysiological structures as well as being influenced by them. The direction of changes in adjustment is influenced by changes in consciousness. Seen from the perspective of adaptation, the subjective sense of how one is in harmony with one's own expectations of self and those of the group have to be seen as a determinant of behavior, whatever the larger frame of analysis.

Francis Hsu, the author of Chapter 2, has long been a champion of the comparative, interactionist point of view in his own work in anthropology. Hsu's diagram of psychosocial homeostasis (PSH) with its concentric layers in the structuring of the self shifts us from a strictly psychoanalytic approach, which concentrates on the innermost areas of the psyche, to the sociocultural approach, in which his distinction between the unexpressed conscious and the expressible conscious is fundamental. From that point he moves outward toward the ever widening realms of the interpersonal. Closest to the physical individual is a realm where the self maintains affective links; next comes one characterized by role relations; followed by another where the humans, gods, ideas, and things belong to the same wider society as the self even though it has no connection with or knowledge of them.

Interestingly enough, in the light of Hsu's formulation, the Chinese form of self-consciousness proves to be more interactionist than those coming out of either western or Hindu thought. Hsu demonstrates how differing cultural patterns create divergent forms of selfhood as the individual strives to achieve a dynamic balance (homeostasis) between psychic demands and sociocultural requirements. Hsu's PSH formulation as a way of understanding the self is indeed most congruent with the level of theoretical analysis independently taken by the various contributors to this volume about the self and culture.

M. Brewster Smith, in Chapter 3, discusses the metaphorical basis of human thought generally. The question is, how is human consciousness in different cultures governed by the use of different forms of metaphor? Smith notes how in our own society a behavioral positivistic approach has precluded, for some time at least, an examination of consciousness itself as a valid variable to be studied. Yet one can point out how culture itself resides in what we can selectively find out about the human experience in particular environments. It is not simply a matter of how the environment in given socialization practices structures behavior in the light of underlying functioning mental mechanisms. We have to look further into how the "meaning" that the human being has conceived in his subjective experience is a direct determinant of all intentional behavior. Without such a construct, one cannot truly understand behavior in any culture. Behavior cannot be reduced, as a positivistic approach would have it, to levels of causality that are functioning beneath this level of consciousness. Consciousness cannot be reduced to unconscious mechanisms. Consciousness itself is a determinant of how intentionality interacts with underlying structures. This attempt at understanding the level of the self is presented differently among general systems theory and the work of other

contemporary philosophies which are breaking the stranglehold
of reductionism in philosophy as well as in the social sciences.
Smith discusses how recent developments in social psychology,
specifically, seek to free us from the impasse of positivism.

Smith makes another point which is central to the approach of
this volume, that the self is not a static concept, a reified entity,
but that selfhood is something that is continuously defined in
one's experience in interaction with others, and that it is this
interactional process that contains the meaning of social experience. It follows, therefore, Smith argues, that people's own
formulations and theories about themselves as personal and
social objects ought to play a larger part in our social science
conceptualizations of personality. Smith sees such formulations
or theories as constructions of organized processes, states, and
dispositions. This point of view emphasizes the symbolic which
is now of higher currency than previously in both psychological
and anthropological theory. Culture is partially, at least, a system
of patterned symbolic interaction which is perpetuated from one
generation to the next. The question raised in this volume is,
how do culturally contrasting peoples conceptualize their human
nature and their personal social processes? In this context, the
western cultural tradition is seen as only one of a number of
possible ways to conceptualize the person in society.

Smith traces the concept of the self as developed in the
tradition of symbolic interactionism most stimulated by the work
of George Herbert Mead. Once popular among social scientists
schooled at the University of Chicago, this tradition is being
rediscovered and extended both in social psychology and in
cultural anthropology. Smith asks the question, how do culturally provided symbol systems as well as normatively specified
patterns of socialization and family interaction affect people's
self conception and therefore their distinctive ways of relating
self to an interpreted world? He stresses how different approaches are needed to enrich our understanding of the content
of selfhood, this content being expressed in interactive behavior.
Finally, Smith examines in some detail the metaphorical bases of
self-conscious thought.

Frank Johnson, in Chapter 4, traces the western history of the concept of self. He points out how in both modern western philosophy and social science a functional concept of self presumes reflective human consciousness. Despite differences in disciplines and terminology, the differentiation of self is consistently related to the attainment of a degree of reflective awareness. Hence it is presumed that before a certain age selfhood does not exist; children's "selves" are incomplete since self demands a certain level of maturation. This is not to say that the experiences of infancy and childhood do not continue and influence later awareness, but that it is necessary for there to be some maturity in experiential depth for the self to interpret ongoing actions in the light of previous experience.

In symbolic interaction theory, the self is created in the context of communication and the sharing of interactive symbolic processes. Some existential descriptions attend to degrees of consciousness and reflection. In this sense they come closer to some Buddhist and Hindu conceptualizations. The interactionalist approach is very congenial to what Wei Ming Tu, in Chapter 7, and Francis Hsu, in Chapter 2, describe as the Chinese self existing in family and community interaction. Johnson points out how all western theories make important distinctions between the phenomena regarding "inner self" versus "outer self." The psychoanalytic western tradition is concentrated theoretically on the structural levels beneath the inner self. Francis Hsu's description of "self" takes the two inner circles of preconscious and unconscious experiences as givens and concentrates in his exposition on the interaction levels. Johnson points out how, in discussing Japan, DeVos concentrates on a distinction between the adaptive and adjustive levels of analyzing behavior. In general, Johnson categorizes the western concept of self, which he derives from an examination of the philosophical as well as the psychological literature, as having three levels. On the first level there are states of mind accompanying inner experiences in solitary communication, as in fantasy and introspection. These contrast with states of mind on another level associated with interpersonal experiences in dyadic or small groups which are encountered only in interaction. On the third level are experiences incurred in crowds or large groups in which the person is present among others but is not directly communicating.

Johnson also stresses that there is a bipolarity in the conceptualization of the self as subjective, or acting, and objective, or being acted upon. In contrasting western concepts to other models, he views the self as subject or actor as experienced primarily in internal states. The self as object is experienced primarily in external reciprocal social relatedness. There is an awareness of the difference between the inner and outer states. For instance, there is a difference in the concept of "sincerity" between Japanese and Americans. For Japanese, sincerity is expressed in behavior which is in accord with one's role expectations, while for Americans, it is behaving in accord with one's inner feelings.

Prior to modern times, European philosophy was concerned with mind and its relationship to soul. Johnson suggests that following the Enlightenment, questions related to the animation of the body were approached more positivistically in seeking out the physical, mechanical, biochemical explanations underlying mind. However, mind and body continued to be methodologically dissociated and independent in a good part of the western tradition. This dualism between mind and body remains both implicitly and explicitly in modern science.

A notable trend in modern psychology was to give up concern for mind and to turn to a study of the physiological functioning underlying sensation, perception, etc. in the exploration of the human psyche. Non-empirically resolvable questions related to the self were excluded as non-scientific and, as Johnson terms it, "The immeasurable abyss of subjectivity was to be avoided." Social science, generally, entered into a more positivistic phase in which reductionism was to unite mind and body by denying any functional autonomy to "immeasurable subjective concerns." Scientific determinism implied that ultimate explanations would be found in terms of a better understanding of the physiological-maturational functions to be found underlying human consciousness. Although he still continued to be read, William James was considered by some of his contemporaries to be a scientific embarrassment. He continued to espouse concern with consciousness of self and subjective experience.

One must note that these reductionist concepts are to be found in both psychology and anthropology. To a greater extent, functional anthropology is reductionist and is positivist in seeking to find understanding of human behavior only in social structural functioning rather than psychological experience. One notes, however, a recent trend toward a "semiotic anthropology," which in effect seeks to see behavior as interpretable simply on a phenomenological, experiential level. Our view is that the experiential level is not autonomous.

Johnson's general arguments are far too rich to paraphrase in this introduction. Suffice it to raise one last comment. The western concept of the self is to a large part influenced by a monotheistic tradition in western thought which may lead to a more individualistic perception of the world. Experience is considered either true or false. There are dichotomous definitions rather than the more amorphorous diverseness of thought which attends polytheism. Monotheistic normative systems are more narrowly bipolar and may enforce the necessity for judgment about qualities of existence which are directed also toward the self. These bipolarities are positively and negatively judgmental, such as good versus bad, beautiful versus ugly, love versus lust, God versus Satan, etc.

One cannot help but comment that the structuralist approach in anthropology espoused by Levi-Strauss appeals to many as an explanatory device in studying other cultures because it reflects so purely the thought patterns of those members of western society who become anthropologists. In contrast DeVos, in Chapter 5, proposes that Japanese thought puts emphasis on nuance rather than polarity. Shinto beliefs are exasperating to those seeking to understand and compare them with Christian doctrine. Indeed, Shinto thought is not considered a religion. Absolute and exclusive categories in thought are an imposition from outside that covers rather than reveals the patterns of thought embedded in the myths produced by other cultures.

In religious terms, a sense of alienation for many westerners was due to a loss of a positive state of "being." This negative status resulted from one's own negatively judged behavior. This state of "sinfulness" caused a more acute perception of possible ultimate damnation. More recently western philosophical thought has given acute attention to the sense of alienation and loneliness which are the counterparts or the pathological reciprocals of concern with freedom and individualism. Johnson also points out how in the western preoccupation with the self, one finds often a sense of encapsulation and isolation, not only in the form of an estrangement from God or from a system of stable values, but also from other persons. There is a sense of being distanced from the environment. There is, in sum, an emphasis in the western self of a concern with being "rational," exemplified in Aristolelian logic. Marsella reaches a similar conclusion in Chapter 9 when he differentiates between "objective" and "subjective" epistemologies.

Perhaps the most difficult concept of self to grasp cross-culturally is that posited in traditional Hindu thought. Agehananda Bharati, in Chapter 6, takes on this task and attempts to help us enter into the Hindu concept of self. Bharati insists we must first understand how it starts with a monistic concept of deity. The concept of the "real self" in Hindu thought is the *ātman*. The ātman is a non-material realization of the real self as opposed to the material, experiential forms of self involving sensations, desires and thought. This tradition leads to a totally different concept of the individual. The Hindu self is that of a "dividual" not an "individual." What would be seen as self-inconsistency in a westerner is perfectly understandable given the idea that Hindus do not see their situational behavior as a reflection of their true self, but as a reflection of a lesser entity. If one is truly religious, one will overcome the contradiction by transcending all social behavior, not merely by reconciling behavioral inconsistencies on the material plane of existence. Bharati states that all Hindu traditions talk about the self either in order to reject its metaphysical status, or to assimilate it to a theological and metaphysical construct which is an ultimate "self." When the Hindu traditions speak about an individual, it is not to analyze but to denigrate.

Bharati points out that one cannot really translate the western concept of "soul" easily into that found in the Sanskrit tradition because the most used cognates for the soul are implicitly negative manifestations such as lust, anger, avarice or egotism.

The self as the basis of important human achievements, such as scholarship, artistry, or technological invention is totally ignored in Indian philosophical texts.

In looking at Hsu's concentric circles, Bharati says that to consider the Indian model we would have to add another number at the absolute center as a point in a geometrical sense of the term, a location without extension. This would be the *ātman*, the absolute, which is the real self in the Hindu concept, indistinguishable and inseparable from deity itself. In this way the Freudian conscious and pre-conscious in Hsu's inner circles seven and six would correspond to the Hindu concept of *Jīva*, and circle five in Hsu's concept, the unexpressible, would correspond exactly to the construct of *māyā*, seen both as individual and cosmic delusion. Hsu's circles four and three, the core of the *jen* of Chinese thought, representing the expressible conscious and what is intimately communicated in society, would be equated with *sāmsarā*, that is, the individual and social realm of conscious interaction.

Thus, the empirical self in the Hindu tradition is interiorized as a state of being which is hierarchically lower than the self of the religious ultimate. For the Hindu, western man is perceived as the master of the empirical self and a mentor in worldliness. the west can be envied, mistrusted, but coveted at the same time. The seeking out of education, language, or travel, and even anti-western sentiments pronounced as part of India's elite culture, are some of the manifestations of a contrastive perception, an ambivalence with which the western concept of self and its behavioral manifestations is perceived. The westerner is seen as incapable of grasping the meaning of his true non-empirical self. The Hindu is supposed to "know" that human action and decision-making are prompted by Karmaic forces which are linked to a metaphysical notion of the self whatever his own particular knowledge of doctrine and offical Hindu philosophy.

To the Hindu, all notions of the "mind" or the "structural ego" or the underlying psychological apparatus which governs and determines human behavior are inferior "material" conceptions. Psychosomatic or mind-brain concepts are nonexistent in indigenous Indian thought. The "body" in Hindu thought is the crudest and thickest of material entities and the intellect the most subtle form, albeit still material. These are visualized or analogized as sheaths superimposed on one another. The self is defined as the gross body which ultimately surrounds the senses and the mind or intellect. These are successively less and less material in form and surround more and more closely the *ātman* – the ubiquitous absolute which has no form nor material. The *ātman* is the nucleus underlying all layers of thought since the true self is formless, immutable, absolute.

In trying to describe Hindu thought, Bharati points up the semantic slippage from the verbal into the nominative. That is to say, "to be" becomes metaphysically nominative in the concept of "being," so that empirical concepts are transformed into metaphysical categories. Empirical concepts are further causally explained by such nominative categories of thought.

There are some difficulties encountered by the westerner who searches for consistency in behavior related to Indian notions of self. If one believes in the single true "self" as immaterial, actual behavior, materially governed, is ephemeral, conventional, relative. As Bharati points out, an individual can be a Marxian, a fascist, and a Hindu at the same time, since these various manifestations of thought emanating from the material self are partial, situational, needing no reconciliation since they are all less than the true self. The present can be dismissed as ephemeral. One seeks to join the real "god" by finding oneself and one therefore can hope to attain a transcendental state in which concern with the situational present disappears. In effect, the "dividual" rises above human misery. Social consciousness, therefore, is not the ultimate aim for self-betterment. Anyone who is so concerned is too fixed into one manifestation of his more material, hence hierarchically lower, state of selfhood. This is the essence of what Hsu characterizes as diffuseness in the Hindu world where caste impediment is a necessary, almost inevitable, mechanism for social control.

Bharati points out that when one asks for a Hindu's identity, he will give you his caste and his village as well as his name. There is a Sanskrit formula which starts with lineage, family, house and ends with one's personal name. In this presentational formula, the empirical self comes last. Self-representation and empirical action is invariably social, then specifically occupational. This contrasts with many Americans and Europeans who will identify themselves primarily and immediately by their profession or special skill, or in the situational sense by their immediate action. The "immutable" self of the westerner is as an individual but the empirical self of the Hindu is mutable, for it is merely secondary to an immutable ideal.

These concepts of the material, spiritual plane and their hierarchy are best conceptualized as degrees of pollution and purity. The self, the *ātman*, the ideal self, is totally pure, whereas the more material one's being is, the more one represents pollution. Matter exuded from the body is the ultimate in pollution, hence one's experiential aim is toward the spiritual, the non-material, and the pure.

Bharati insightfully cites the fact that Indian interest in drama, whether in cinema or in traditional forms, is intrinsically stereotypic. Characters represent various degrees of beauty or other desirable traits, or conversely, evil and reprehensible ones. Complex characterization of individuals who are neither purely beautiful nor reprehensibly ugly are rejected with disinterest whether produced in films by Indian film-makers or by foreign sources. Bharati suggests that complex characterizations such as those by Woody Allen or Ingmar Bergman have little appeal even to the most sophisticated of Hindus.

Bharati demonstrates how Hinduism implicitly sanctifies a continuity of the caste system. It legitimizes, reflects, and reinforces role-stereotyping based on the status to which an individual is born. The concept of self-betterment does not involve betterment *within* society. That is beside the point. True betterment is outside of society, outside the material realm and toward the spiritual. Bharati raises interesting questions about the relationship of "oceanic experiences," whether in infancy or religious ecstasy, to our concept of self. Is the differentiation we experience in the development of selfhood in western psychological thought, of progressive separation of the inside self and the outside world, an illusion? We view such a lack of separation, or an inability to maintain it, as relative primitiveness in a developmental sense, or psychopathological in a psychiatric sense. By contrast, some glimpse of such a lack of differentiation is sought for in the experience of holiness within Hindu religious concepts.

The western striving is toward the development of a solid well-functioning ego. The inner experience of self should be clearly delineated from the outside. The Hindu striving goes in the opposite direction – to achieve union with the immutable self, which is ultimately indistinguishable from deity and the totality of the universe. Clearly this different conceptualization of goals about the self in the philosophic and religious tradition of India helps explain a great deal of Indian cultural behavior, and especially the inconsistencies found in Indian intellectuals when they are viewed from a western frame of reference.

In contrast to the Indian quest for an ultimate self which totally removes the person from society, Tu Wei-ming, in Chapter 7, describes a Chinese concept of self-development in which the realization of sagehood as an ultimate transformation is inherently communal. It aims at transforming the self into a totally social setting. The self, for the Chinese Confucianist, is envisaged both as a center of relationships and as a dynamic process of becoming or development. Development continues through a life-long process of learning, not only through books but through ritual practice.

In this sense, Chinese concepts of the learning process predate those of the western exponents of pragmatism. The Chinese idea of "ritualization" is that it is a means of self-cultivation in a spirit of filiality. The self, in essence, is a developing part of a continuing family lineage. It is a progressive continuity of the specific ancestry of one's family. It is to be realized neither in the transcendental *ātman* of Hindu thought with no earthly ties, nor in an individual ego, whose subjectively experienced existence continues for all eternity as is envisaged in western religion. Tu does not discuss the issue, but implies the differences between Buddhism, with its Indian-derived thoughts of self as illusion, and the Confucian self as part of ethnic continuity. The Confucian scholar, throughout Chinese history, was opposed to Buddhist philosophy and religious practices since they were in ultimate opposition with the principle of filiality. Belief in Buddhism was seen as antithetical to the Confucian sense of self.

Tu stresses that filiality does not imply simple obedience to the wishes and desires of the real father. Rather, one is obedient to the purposes of the ideal father. Ideally, the filial son guides his behavior so as to transcend the momentary imperfections of the real father's wishes when it would be harmful to obey them; whereas in the west, self-development implies bringing one's behavior into line with one's own "ego" ideal or ideal self. In western religious philosophy this implies bringing one's behavior into line with the wishes of a transcendental deity.

Rather than concerning oneself with such a far-off concept of heaven or deity, Confucian thought exhorts one to realize oneself by keeping one's behavior in accord specifically with the ideals of the family lineage. In essence, in seeking self-development one must, in turn, act in an exemplary fashion in the role of father once achieved. One develops inner constraints as an authority. All social harmony ultimately depends on self-regulation. One must note, as does Tu, that imbedded in the Confucian concept of self-development is the recognition of human frailty and fallibility. The individual seeking development alone, without the experiential support of a community, is inconceivable; hence, one must seek out supportive relationships in the human endeavor. This is a message contrary to that espoused in Buddhist retreat both from the world and ultimately from the self.

Tu touches upon but does not enter into an "etic" examination of underlying Oedipal problems viewed psychoanalytically. How the developmental problems of a Chinese child are resolved in the process of becoming an adult within Chinese culture is not essayed. That such unresolved problems do periodically arise in individual Chinese is attested to by the person of Mao Tse-tung who wrote intimately about his hostility toward his own father and how it was an instigation for his revolutionary ideology. The fact that negative experiences in childhood become part of the adult self is a human universal. However the conceptualizing of this process and what such past experiences mean to the adult vary from culture to culture. The

Chinese kinship configuration fosters a relational but not existential approach to life.

Mao used the concept of "Cultural Revolution" explicitly because he considered that continuity of culture is to be found in basic family relationships. Therefore he deliberately sought to change family life as well as other aspects of Chinese culture. He promoted conflict between the generations, and he encouraged attacks by workers and students on their superiors and teachers. He did this because he considered such unrest to be a prerequisite for change. However, as has become clear, the Cultural Revolution is now considered to be an aberration, due to the "evil" hands of the "Gang of Four," which slowed down the economic and social progress of the land.

Godwin Chu, in Chapter 8, attempts to trace out what has happened to the "self" as a result of the revolutionary changes sowed by Mao. What has happened to social authority? What has become of the nature of the self in relation to marriage partners? What has been the impact of thirty years of ideological insistence on change through governmental planning and deliberate attempts to inculcate new ideas and values?

Chu approaches this very difficult set of problems by focusing almost totally on role interaction. By so doing, he demonstrates some of the strengths as well as weaknesses of reducing the concept of the social self to that of role playing. As he sees it, self is a configuration of role relationships with significant others. He chooses to avoid the appreciable dynamic tensions between observable social behavior and the individual's subjective experience. Indeed, this is a difficult topic to consider. It may well be that the Chinese adult consciously perceives less family disharmony than is true for individuals living in other cultural settings. The interrelation between a deeply felt need to see the family in harmony and one's individual private perceptions is difficult to approach, let alone to document. As witnessed in many chapters, there seems to be a difference in the living out of the Confucian heritage when one compares the contemporary Japanese, Korean, and Chinese.

The Japanese younger generation is slowly, self-consciously shifting away from accepting parental directives in occupational and marital choice but the emotional bonds with parents forged in the primary family are still in force. Japanese do not today conceptualize their social obligations in formal Confucianist terms but one must note that the father's status as family head is still socially reinforced, although this reinforcement is no longer emphasized as part of a lineal family identity.

Chu considers the traditional Chinese self to be basically accommodating rather than assertive. It seeks to receive social support from family and kin. The other side of this coin is the ability to expect strength and support from these relationships in times of stress so that self–other relationships are built on networks supported by cultural ideas such as loyalty, filial piety, endurance, and courage. It was the attempt of the Cultural Revolution to direct loyalty to family toward loyalty to party and new collective groupings.

In discussing change in the Chinese self, Chu does not concern himself with the comparative cultural considerations that Hsu previously addressed in his volumes *Clan, Caste and Club* and *Iemoto: The Heart of Japan*. For example, differences between the Chinese and Japanese are to be found in the Japanese ability to transfer the affective experiences of the primary family out into other pseudo-family relationships. Such transfer out of primary group feelings to occupational goals has met with difficulty in China. A central question remains, can modern China transfer affective ties that had their origin in the primary family into other forms of relationships? (See Hsu, Chapter 2.) Moreover, the fact that Chinese in the past only periodically expressed themselves in protest cannot be as quickly interpreted as an existential or experiential difficulty with self-assertion. When the opportunity to express protest arose during the Cultural Revolution, it was seized and protests were made against corruption and against authority. Since younger generations were encouraged to protest, the question arises whether there is now more subjective experiential tension since protest has become more actively discouraged under tighter official social control.

Chu, in looking at relationships with marriage partners, cites a set of ten criteria distributed by the authorities to urban young women looking for a suitable mate. He reports that most of the considerations, in one way or another, are directed toward materialistic concerns rather than questions of emotion and intimacy. He points up the fact that this may be due to the Cultural Revolution and the increasing concern with material benefits. However, it may be that there were continuing concerns with material benefits in traditional Chinese culture. With the shift of marriage choice from the parents to the children themselves, it is possible that the materialistic approach has not changed. It was quite apparent among Chinese in the past that in making a marriage choice for their children, material considerations and economic concerns were very important in assessing suitable mates. Perhaps there has been little change in values concerning the relation of marriage to the acquisition of material wealth as a form of economic security in the younger generation.

In Chapter 5, DeVos discusses constancies in the Japanese self despite the social changes caused by modernization. William Caudill has carefully distinguished between such "social change" and more basic "culture change." Culture change in Mao's revolutionary experiment involved some basic changes in the early socialization of the child. Therefore, DeVos's approach to the discussion of the Japanese self attempts to combine psychoanalytic "etic" analysis of developmental processes in ego functions throughout the life cycle with discussions of enduring continuities in the interpersonal attitudes occurring inside the family and occupational groups outside it.

Examining the experiential level of selfhood cross-culturally should not be limited to a concern with what is normative in each group. Chapter 9, by Anthony Marsella, examines the psychopathological as also revealing something about the operation of the self in a culture.

By and large, the contemporary psychiatric model applied in psychiatric practice is western in origin. However, in a transcultural psychiatric approach, there is an attempt to examine the culture-specific understandings of disorder. Within western definitions of disorder, there is a conflict between those who advocate a universal conception based on biological similarities, versus those who contend that cultural variations result in differences in disorder.

Marsella suggests a framework for conceptualizing mental disorders which is based on the self. He notes that a culture-centered approach which considers distinct views of the self can provide an understanding of the patterning, classification, and causes of certain mental disorders. Based on research comparing western, Japanese, and Chinese symptom patterns associated with depression, he and his colleagues found western subjects evidenced a strong existential component in their depression, while Japanese subjects evidenced interpersonal components, and Chinese evidenced somatic components. These differences were related to unlike ways of experiencing the self. Marsella posits that selfhood, language, and modes of experiencing reality (e.g. imagery versus lexical) are interdependent phenomena which ultimately give rise to epistemological and ontological models of reality linked to self as a *process*. This, in turn, influences the patterning, experience, and etiology of mental disorders.

In brief, Marsella asserts that there is an intimate relationship between culture, self, and mental disorders. To the extent that cultures vary, we can expect differences in the structure and process of self. These variations in self ultimately reflect differences in the manifestation, experience, and etiology of mental disorders. To conclude otherwise would require a refutation of the critical role which subjective experience plays in human behavior. This would, in turn, demand a limited and ethnocentric view of human behavior. The self thus emerges as a fundamental concept for understanding, describing, predicting, and ultimately controlling disordered human behavior.

In summary, we hope the current volume will stimulate further thought regarding the role of the subjective as a vital determinant of human behavior. The various authors in this volume share the theoretical contention that the self in culture is a valid level of concern in seeking to develop a more integrated science of human behavior.

2

The Self in Cross-cultural Perspective

Francis L. K. Hsu

Introduction

The concept of personality

In old China the thinking scholars used to speak of *ta wo* (greater self) as distinguished from *hsiao wo* (smaller self). The latter referred to the individual's own desires and actions for him or herself, albeit they might encompass spouses and children. The former referred to the individual's concern for the wider society and even humanity as a whole.

This was a simplified description of the idea of the self, but it points its finger at the right place. What does self consist of? If not the individual, who or what else is involved? In the social, psychological, and clinical disciplines the study of self has centered in the concept of *personality*. When I was a college freshman in China I learned from a western text that this term came from the Greek word, *persona*, mask.

It is the contention of this paper that the concept of personality is an expression of the western ideal of individualism. It does not correspond even to the reality of how the western man lives in western culture, far less any man in any other culture. The stranglehold of the western ideal of individualism on our intellectual deliberations must at least be loosened. Many social scientists of non-western origin, like myself, have in this regard essentially acted like intellectual Uncle Toms. I am of the conviction that the time has come for us to replace this concept with something more serviceable and get off the demi-scientific carousel called culture and personality. An understanding of how self is defined or operates in different cultures is the basic means of unlocking the secrets of social and cultural stability and change.

The main problem created by the concept of personality is that we tend to see it as a separate entity, distinct from society and culture. It is not that students of personality ignore society and culture; they do not. In fact Kluckhohn, Mowrer, and Murray have even laid out a schematic view of personality formation, with its "constitutional," "group membership," "role," and "situational" determinants (Kluckhohn and Mowrer 1944: 35–48). All students of psychological anthropology have concerned themselves with how society and culture shape personality (see Honigman 1967), and less frequently how personality orientations have in turn affected society and culture. But the notion that "every society is composed of individuals and every culture is created by and expressed in the individual" remains at the foundation of all deliberations on the subject. Since personality is seen as a distinct entity, there is an inevitable failure to come to terms with the reality of man.

We have, for example, works which use depth psychology or psychoanalytic mechanisms to explain large social and cultural patterns or national affairs (Hsu 1952). We also have works which rely on data derived from projective techniques (such as TAT, Rorschach, sentence completion, children's books as a source for achievement motivation, etc.) for ascertaining the psychological characteristics of societies or subsocieties. Finally we have works which tend to highlight a sort of global cultural difference without reference to individuals, or which see individuals as being at the inevitable mercy of external forces. Alex Inkeles, a sociologist, emphasizes the convergence of outlook of all peoples under what he designates as "modernization," in which industrial development is an essential component (Inkeles 1960). The latest devotee to this line of thought is Heiliger, who said the Soviet and Chinese personalities are converging. In fact he grandly forecasts "a unification of technological knowhow, management abilities and personality qualities, and a general tendency towards equalization of societal characteristics throughout the world" (Heiliger 1980: 185).

There are even anthropologists who have opined that all "primitive" peoples (that old anthropological grab-bag of a term) suffer from the same sort of paranoia, due to their common failure to cope with or achieve mastery over their physical environment (Schwartz 1968). Along the same lines there are also some who have worked on agricultural villages in literate civilizations and who see "peasants" all over the world (or at least all over Asia and Latin America) in terms of another kind of psycho-cultural unity, distinct from the "moderns" and the "primitives."[1] (See, for example, Foster 1965.)

Reformulating the concept of personality

Some students, sensing the inadequacy of the concept of personality as a tool for understanding human behavior, have already begun some kind of reformulation. Talcott Parsons, in his attempt to link the insights of Freud and Durkheim, noted that the super-ego acquired through the process of social interaction is the bridge between personality and culture (Parsons 1964:31). Bert Kaplan coined the term *social personality*, with accent on the characteristic mode of cognition rather than the total personality of the individual, on the "realm of what the individual is doing" rather than on what "he has" (Kaplan 1954:244, 1961:249). Anthony Wallace advanced the theory of "Mazeway," emphasizing "the importance of [the] capacity to learn and to maintain a semantic equivalence, without a necessary uniformity of motivation" (Wallace 1961:157). These attempts are on the right track in so far as they reveal the inadequacy or misleading nature of the concept of personality. But they have not, in my view, gone far enough. We need to define, in the first place, not merely how the individual mobilizes the motivational organization to feed the "semantic equivalences" for performing the "cognitive tasks required by the culture," but the reasons why, and the pressures under which, the individual will select one line of "semantic equivalences" but not other lines of "semantic equivalences" (unless we make the unrealistic assumption that there is only one line of "semantic equivalences" open to the individual who has to act).

Second, we need a more precise delineation of the individual's relationship with his world of men, gods, and things, not merely in terms of "semantic organization" and "cognitive tasks," but also of the *intensity of affective involvement*. For intensity of affect can hardly be measured in terms of "equivalences." How far is a man's love for his mate equal or unequal to his desire for professional advancement?

The first step toward understanding our new formulation is to forget about the term "personality" and note that the meaning of being human is found in interpersonal relationships, since no human being exists alone, not even the Hindu holy men who often claim they have been up in the Himalayas for thirty-five years or so during which time they abstained from food and drink. My reply to that kind of claim is, why did they not remain in their preferred abode so that we would not have to hear so much about them? The fact is that to all humans, however great, solitary periods are either an intermission or a means to impress the public. Hindu holy men are not alone in this regard. Buddha, Jesus, Thoreau, and adolescent Kwakiutl Indians in search of personal guardian spirits are other examples.

Man, society and culture

Elements of man's existence

If everyone acts as individualized individuals, no society is possible. If everyone acts in complete conformity with others, there will be no differences between human beings and bees. Human ways of life are obviously somewhere in between these extremes. To avoid wild swings from one extreme to the other and the common failing of confounding psychology of the individual (including individual psychopathology) with the sociocultural orientation of the group (including its overall economic and political patterns and trends), we need to develop a more precise formulation of how man lives as a social and cultural being. For this purpose we must reexamine the elements of human existence. The schematic picture given in *Figure 2.1* will help us in this task.

Figure 2.1 Man, culture, and society

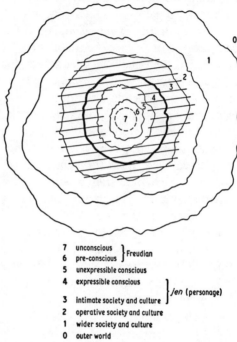

7 unconscious } Freudian
6 pre-conscious }
5 unexpressible conscious
4 expressible conscious
                                        } /en (personage)
3 intimate society and culture
2 operative society and culture
1 wider society and culture
0 outer world

Note: This figure and the two on later pages as well as the psychosocial homeostasis (PSH) formulation are given in another publication (HSU 1971c).

In the absence of a better way, I have represented the elements in irregular, concentric layers. Layers 7 and 6 are the "unconscious" and the "pre-conscious" according to Freud. They contain, respectively, repressed and semi-repressed psychic materials. These concepts are probably so well known among social scientists that they need no elaboration. Layer 5 is termed "unexpressible conscious" because its contents are generally kept to the individual himself. The mental materials are usually not communicated to his fellow human beings because:

(a) the individual is afraid to do so (as when a man does not speak up against his superior for fear of losing his job); or
(b) others will not understand even if he tries to do so since

the material is too privatized (such as certain deep aversions due to childhood experiences); or

(c) the individual can feel something but has trouble verbalizing it (such as the Japanese preference to pronounce the Chinese word tea as "sa" when it is used to designate the Tea Ceremony but "cha" in other connections; when pressed the Japanese answer is that saying "sa" sounds "more sophisticated" or "purer"); or

(d) the individual is ashamed to do so (most readers can appreciate this if we reflect on how we all have sinned according to the impossible standard set by Jesus when he said, "But I say unto you, that whosoever looketh on a woman to lust after her hath committed adultery with her already in his heart" (Matthew 5:28). Robert Louis Stevenson said the same thing: "We all have feelings that would shame hell."²).

Layer 4 is termed "expressible conscious" since it contains materials, ideas, and feelings which the individual does communicate to his fellow human beings and which are responded to by them, often as a matter of course. These may concern a variety of things such as love, greed, vision, hatred, and knowledge of the correct and incorrect ways (according to the moral, social, and technical standards of his culture) of doing things. On a personal level, examples of these include trivial matters such as table manners and important rules such as who should mate with whom. On a national level, examples of these include the expressions of patriotism, notions about keeping certain ethnic groups in their place, fear of communism, or ideals such as devotion to the emperor. The communicability of some of the materials of layer 4 may, of course, be restricted to members of the same society. For example, it will be difficult for most Chinese to understand why so many Americans should consider differences in religion to be a barrier to marriage or even employment. But all peoples in all cultures can readily appreciate some form of grief following the death of a dear one.

Layer 3 is that part of the external world with which each individual has strong feelings of attachment, which often seem to people of other cultures irrational. It contains, first, human beings with whom he stands in a relationship of intimacy. By intimacy I refer to a relationship in which the individuals concerned can afford to let their guards down, can communicate their worst troubles to each other without the fear of rejection, and can count on comfort, sympathy, and support without the onus of charity. There are three basic elements in a relationship of intimacy of which verbalized communication is but one. The other two are emotional support and mutual receptivity. The last may involve listening even when one does not understand what is being communicated and has no intelligent response to it. For any individual the inmates of his layer 3 are what Talcott Parsons might call his "significant alter." But our layer 3 contains also cultural usages (such as the Hindu's strong sense of caste pollution and the American male's aversion to physical intimacy with another male), artifacts (such as the Japanese seatless toilets which have contributed to the culture shock of many an American visitor to the Orient), pets (for which some owners have insisted on expensive coiffures and segregated cemeteries), and material collections (such as Silas Marner's money in George Eliot's celebrated novel). Changes in layer 3 are most upsetting to the individual and therefore likely to be strongly resisted.

Layer 2 is characterized by role relationships. That is to say, here are found humans, ideas, and things which the individual finds useful.[3] A teacher must have students. A merchant must have customers. An employer must have employees. A ruler must have subjects. A chess player must have at least one opponent. Each of these and other relationships have at least two or more role players. The performance of roles does not demand or imply intimacy or affect. The role occupants sometimes communicate with each other to such a limited extent that a crisis of communication is said to develop.[4] The cultural rules and artifacts in layer 2 are those with which the individual deals without strong, or even any, emotional attachment. Examples of rules in this layer are: traffic rules, taking tests and examinations, courtesy customs (such as presenting the hostess with a box of *manjū* in Japan or a bunch of flowers in the United States when visiting), patterns of greeting, ways of buying and selling (one price versus haggling), and methods of using machines. Examples of artifacts in this layer are: vehicles, ash trays, currency, fans, and utensils. We perform our roles in association with them, or act according to them, or use them, but are not greatly disturbed, or disturbed at all, by changes in them. In the normal course of events, the individual is less likely to resist changes in layer 2 than in layer 3.[5]

Of course, the same human beings, ideas, and materials may be in either layers 2 or 3 for members of different societies. Farmland is one such example. For most Chinese in traditional China, including those who lived in cities, a farm was a man's most important sign of success and security. It did not only concern him but it was also linked in his relationship with and feeling about his ancestors and his descendants. For this reason, sale of his land was to many a Chinese farmer like going through a funeral of a dear one, and he would therefore prefer to resort to uneconomic means of holding on to it rather than selling it. Land was definitely part of the traditional Chinese individual's layer 3. His attitude toward it contrasts sharply with that of the average American, which is to treat ownership of land as one form of investment – like buying shares in a company. It is, therefore, in the average American's layer 2. Similarly, grand-fathers are more likely to be in the American individual's layer 2 but in the Chinese individual's layer 3, while God is likely to be in the American individual's layer 3 but in the Chinese individual's layer 2. Hence death of one's grandfather is a more significant event for the Chinese individual than for his American counterpart, while differences in church affiliation may be an American barrier to marriage but are of no consequence at all in Chinese romances.

Layer 1 consists of human beings, cultural rules, knowledge, and artifacts which are present in the larger society but which may or may not have any connection with the individual. Until very recently American blacks were in this layer for a majority of American whites. Even now American Indians are still in this layer for nearly all white Americans, as are the Appalachian poor to most of their well-to-do brethren. The automobile is a common artifact to all Americans, but few Americans know or even care about the theory of the internal combustion engine, just as the average Japanese still worships his emperor without any idea as to the origin or the symbolic significance of the custom. Other examples are the Great Wall to a majority of the Chinese, the pyramids for modern Mayans, and the Tennessee Valley Authority, which brought electricity to much of rural America. In the normal course of events the individual has no role or affective relationship with these at all.

In layer 0 are people, customs, and artifacts belonging to other societies with which most members of a society have no contact and of which they have no idea or only erroneous ideas. For example, many Americans still think in some way that Chinese men wear pigtails and that Chinese women have bound feet. A recent TV western featured a Montana cowboy with a Chinese wife whose feet were so bound that she could not walk at all.

JEN: a "Galilean" view of man

The reader will already have noted that I have put a thicker circle around layer 4 than around the others (see *Figure 2.1*). This circle marks the outer boundary of the traditionally understood personality. When clinicians and psychological anthropologists speak of personality structure, personality adjustment, personality change, emerging personality, basic or modal personality, they refer to this entity. This is the boundary within which internalization of culture or moral values is supposed to take place. All kinds of psychological tests are designed to ascertain aspects of this entity, or its total organization and content.

I propose that we leave layers 6 and 7 alone, and instead we try to understand the shaded area in *Figure 2.1* which comprises layers 3 and 4, with the shading slightly running into layers 2 and 5. This shaded area is the central substance of man as a social and cultural being.

Borrowing a term from the Chinese, I should like to call the shaded area in the figure (with slight extensions into layers 2 and 5): *jen*. This is the Chinese word meaning "man." I suggest the term *jen* advisedly because the Chinese conception of man (also shared by the Japanese who pronounce the same Chinese word *jin*) is based on the *individual s transactions with his fellow human beings*. When the Chinese say of so-and-so *"ta pu shih jen"* (he is not a *jen*), they do not mean that this person is not a human animal; instead they mean that his behavior in relation to other human beings is not acceptable. Consequently terms like *"hao jen"* (good *jen*), *"huai jen"* (bad *jen*), etc., follow the same line of meaning. The difference is that the expression *"pu shih jen"* (not a *jen*) is stronger than *"huai jen"* (bad *jen*). For example, a man who abandons his parents is described as *"pu shih jen,"* but one who cheats his friend is better called *"huai jen"* (bad *jen*). Other uses of the concept are *"cho jen"* (endeavor to be *jen*) and *"hsueh cho jen"* (learn to be *jen*).[6] *Jen* contrasts sharply with the concept of personality, which refers primarily to what goes on inside the individual.

The central focus of the concept of personality is the individual's deep core of complexes and anxieties, while the nature of his interpersonal relationships is seen merely as indicators or expressions of these complexes and anxieties. But the central focus of the concept of *jen* is the place of the individual in a web of interpersonal relationships, while his wishes, predilections, and anxieties are judged according to whether they contribute to or destroy his interpersonal relationships. With real justification the *jen* approach is a "Galilean" view of man that sees him in terms of larger whole, as contrasted to the personality approach or a "Ptolemian" view that sees the individual human animal as the center of his world. I submit that the interpersonal concept *jen* is more useful as a basis for understanding human behavior with reference to social and cultural stability and change than the individualistic concept personality.

For every living human being *jen* is not a fixed entity. Like the human body it is in a state of dynamic equilibrium. It is a matrix or a framework within which every human individual seeks to maintain a satisfactory level of psychic and interpersonal equilibrium, in the same sense that every physical organism tends to maintain a uniform and beneficial physiological stability within and between its parts. We shall term the process *psychosocial homeostasis* (PSH).

The basic facts are as follows. In spite of the ever-changing human scene through birth and death as well as human movement and other external forces beyond one's control, every human being needs affective relationships with some elements of the world to make his existence meaningful. In the first instance he looks to other human beings for his affective relationships, which results in human intimacy. These human beings are part of everyone's layer 3. However, if human beings are not available for his layer 3, the individual is likely to fill it with gods or things or certain cultural rules (such as ideals) on which he will lavish his affect.

I suggest that man's need for layer 3 is literally as important as his requirement for food, water, and air. This is what basically gives the individual his sense of identity and fulfillment. Sudden loss of inhabitants in layer 3 may be so traumatic as to cause the individual to feel aimless. But even changes in certain cultural rules and artifacts in this layer are extremely difficult for the individual to tolerate. If the changes are forced on him over long periods of time, without acceptable alternatives, the individual is likely to develop psychological problems and even psychiatric symptoms. Consequently the secret of cultural change and stability, of resistance to change or insistence upon innovation, of the response of a majority of members in any society to stress, to oppression and conquest, to charity, to self-esteem, to learning, or to success cannot be unravelled without a knowledge of the nature of the individual's relationship with his layer 3 in that society.

On the other hand, every individual must maintain suitable levels and varieties of psychic output to make his layer 3 relationships satisfactory and continuous. For this purpose, every human being must rely more heavily on material from his layer 4 than on that from layer 5. He will not be able to mobilize that of layers 6 and 7 because they are repressed or semi-repressed; and because, even if he succeeds in mobilizing them, they will not be understood by others since the material tends to be so idiosyncratic.

Psychosocial homeostasis and social and cultural development

We are now ready to examine the operation of psychosocial homeostasis. In this task we shall explicate our views by examining relevant facts in three societies – China, the United States, and Japan.[7] Almost every human being in every culture begins life with parents (often siblings as well) who are the first occupants of his layer 3.[8]

(a) China: the supremacy of kinship For the Chinese whose culture says his self-esteem and future are tied to his first group, his parents, siblings, and other close relatives are permanent inhabitants in his layer 3. Even though a majority of Chinese households are not the giant structures emphasized by the traditional Chinese ideal and pictured in celebrated Chinese novels such as *The Dream of the Red Chamber*, the individual tends to have close relatives nearby, and to interact with them most frequently. They are likely to engage most of his attention, and command his respect or respect him, depending upon his place in the kinship organization. Since intimacy is readily and continuously accessible to him within the kinship network, the Chinese individual can maintain his psychosocial homeostasis without resorting to other elements such as gods or things, or going to the other layers.

Consequently, he tends to relate to people and things in layers 2, 1, and 0 (if he gets that far at all) in relatively impersonal terms befitting a variety of situations under which he and they meet. He can afford not to be curious or anxious about them; he is unlikely to have the urge to improve or help them; he can even afford to ignore them completely unless they threaten him physically. He can meet them or he can leave them. Hence the Chinese, throughout all of their history, have developed few secondary groups outside of their kinship boundary. China had some famous travellers and conquerors, but she had no Florence Nightingales, Lawrences of Arabia, or Carrie Nations.

In fact the Chinese approach to the supernatural can hardly be understood except in this light. For gods (as distinguished from one's own ancestors) are generally inhabitants of the Chinese individual's layer 2 and often layer 1. He relates to them in role terms, like doctors or suppliers of goods, who can come to his rescue or satisfy his wants if and when the need arises. But he is not likely to be committed to any one of them, any more than he needs to be committed to any one doctor or one merchant. The Chinese individual is not likely to feel he must rise or fall with his gods, defend his gods, spread the merits or messages of his gods, or make more converts for his gods. The Chinese, in contrast to westerners, have never related to their gods as fathers, mothers, brothers, or spouses. Hence the Chinese, in their long history of wars and civil disturbances, have developed no significant *religious* persecution, produced no St Francis Xaviers and St Thomas Aquinases, and left their Jews and Moslems alone (Hsu 1967). The few famous Chinese explorers were all imperial emissaries. And Chinese imperial conquests were neither followed by massive Chinese colonial settlements, nor Chinese proselytization of non-Chinese peoples (Hsu 1968). *Figure 2.2(A)* portrays the typical mode of the Chinese individual in his society and culture.

(b) The west: the most dynamic psychosocial homeostasis (PSH)
The westerner also begins his life with parents and siblings. These too are the first inhabitants of his layer 3. But since his culture says that his self-esteem and future depend upon how well he can stand on his own two feet, his parents and siblings are but its temporary occupants. As he grows up he may not always leave them or they him, but his relationship with them is a voluntary one, especially after he marries or reaches legal maturity. Consequently his layer 3 tends to be filled with individuals other than those with whom he began as a human being. Since these individuals are non-kin, he has to go out to search for them and establish some sort of link with them in order to secure his most precious commodity in life – intimacy.[9]

This necessity to search for his circle of intimacy makes the western individual's problem of life more complicated. For one thing, the new inhabitants of his layer 3 are likely to be his peers, while parents and other relations are relegated to his layer 2 and even 1. Having defined his grown-up status as one of freedom

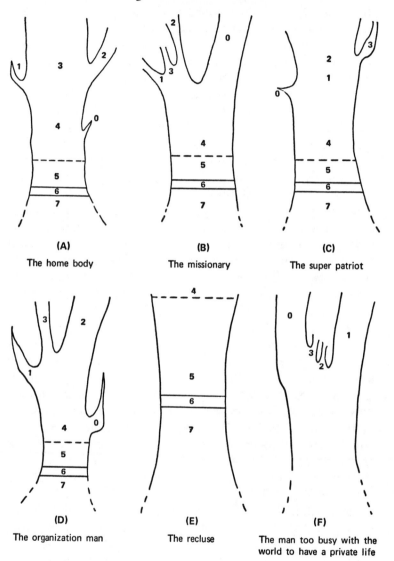

Figure 2.2 Varieties of *Jen*

(A)
The home body

(B)
The missionary

(C)
The super patriot

(D)
The organization man

(E)
The recluse

(F)
The man too busy with the world to have a private life

from his overpowering elders, he is not about to choose to be at the mercy of anyone like them. But relationship with unrelated peers is bound to be more unstable and require more constant fence-mending than that with his parents. Most parents are like dogs; one can kick them in the teeth and they will still come back for more. No one can take his peers for granted to that extent. He and they are likely to compete for the same things. His desire for mastery over them is matched by theirs over him. He has to satisfy his peers as much as they have to satisfy them.

Consequently the western individual has to work for his psychosocial homeostasis via a much larger variety of routes than his Chinese counterpart. He may have to search for his identity and personal fulfillment by expanding his human relationships through mastery of alien peoples and other worlds (his layers 2, 1, or even 0), so as to compensate for the precariousness in his layer 3 relationships. In this process he will try to relate himself in a more fervent way than his Chinese counterpart to those chosen for his attention – those who are seen as needing his help such as "savages," prisoners of war, the poor, the heathens, and the oppressed. He will want to love them, to improve them, or to make sacrifices for them.

Because of his emotional investment, he is likely to defend his "charges" vehemently against other possible influences or intruders and sternly impose his will on them to protect his investment; or hate and punish them because his feelings are hurt, or because his manhood is challenged, by their resistance or indifference to him. These are the psychological materials which most centrally fed and continue to feed the fires of crusades and proselytization or bigotry and persecution.

Or the western man may resort solely to his inner self for definition and guidance, with accent on exploration of his own inner world, his own anxiety, his own unconscious, with the aid of drugs if necessary. This finds expression in the western way of religion, in which the individual's conscience may be his sole guide to an absolute God, which view may be held so stubbornly that he is often willing to be put to the stake – or alternatively he may use his views as justification for putting others to the same fate; in the western way of psychoanalysis, in which sexuality occupies a central place and the individual is encouraged to work out and to express his own deep-seated anxieties and complexes (layers 6 and especially 7) regardless of custom and convention; and in the 1960s popularity of the hippie and yippie movements and soul singers like Janis Joplin, who was individual feeling personified and was said to "make more converts per capita than Bill Graham [sic]" (Newsweek, February 24, 1969: 84). In all of this, western man has truly achieved a degree of spiritual (psychological) depth unknown to the Chinese and Japanese.

Reaching outward and reaching inward for psychosocial homeostasis each have their own difficulties. They leave the need for interpersonal intimacy either in a precarious state of satisfaction or scarcely satisfied. By going to layers 2, 1, and 0, the individual often receives but the illusion of intimacy through intense but fleeting interactions with masses of other human beings. It was probably to overcome this very difficulty that Alexander the Great, having conquered what he thought was the end of the earth, took the following dramatic and extreme steps on his return from India:

> "After the ordeals of the retreat from the Beas and the terrible crossing of Gedrosia [the Baluchistan desert], on arrival in Susa he organized the marriage of ten thousand of his followers to Iranian maidens. And at Opis, in Mesopotamia, on his way to Babylon and his premature end, he gave one last, vast banquet, in which all joined him in a symposium and the drinking of a 'loving up' to the union of mankind and universal *amonia* (concord)."
>
> (Prince Peter 1965)

In the opposite direction, by going to his layers 5, 6, and 7 and defining his action as expansion of his inner consciousness, the western individual can indeed claim that he needs no one else. But just the same, his need for intimacy or for something tangible with which he can maintain an effective relationship remains unsatisfied.

The western individual tends to direct himself, therefore, to a third route to psychosocial homeostasis, the control of the physical universe which expresses itself in many ways. Business empires, exploration of hidden places and tribes, collections of antiques, stamps, or match covers, these are but a few of the myriad outlets for the westerner's desire for control. It is interesting that many of the famous Buddhist cave paintings in north-western China, neglected by the Chinese for centuries, were obtained and smuggled out of China by western scholars and travellers. It is also interesting that the Chinese kept pets, such as dogs and cats, principally for utilitarian purposes (dogs for guarding the home and cats for catching mice) but only in a minor way for companionship. Nearly all thoroughbred varieties of the world's canine population are of western origin.

Most dogs in China are mongrels of one sort or another. My inference is that since the Chinese individual is not likely to be short of human beings to inhabit his layer 3, he has little need to attach himself to pets. It is therefore natural that he would not be sufficiently attached to dogs as to wish to control their breeding. On the other hand, the need to lavish emotions on pets is more commensurate with the individual's scarcity of permanent inhabitants for his layer 3. Consequently some westerners support dog hotels, dog restaurants, dog psychoanalysts, phenomena which the average Chinese even today would regard as having come out of *Gulliver's Travels* rather than from reality.

Figures 2.2(B), 2.2(C), 2.2(D), 2.2(E), and *2.2(F)* schematically represent a few of the many possible psychosocial modes of the western individual in his society and culture. This diversity is rooted in the internal impetus to change inherent in the western kinship system. It expresses itself in western history as revolutions in many fields (political, religious, economic, cultural, artistic, social, and educational), and in the form of dispersion of dissidents from the mother country to set up independent societies. For example, European emigrants were not only proportionately numerous but have formed several independent nations elsewhere, including the United States, while Chinese emigrants were not only proportionately few but have never set themselves up as separate political entities, except once in northern Borneo for less than ten years. (Singapore is a modern phenomenon and a political accident.) Finally, it also expresses

itself in the form of massive and continuous missionary movements (nearly all the world's missionaries are of western
origin).[10] It also expresses itself in western literature through the
type of character whose chief source of personal fulfillment or
happiness (real or imagined) is to wage war against himself or
others: Holden Caulfield in *Catcher in the Rye*, "The Old Man" in
The Old Man and the Sea, or Captain Ahab in *Moby Dick*.[11]

(c) Japan: iemoto and industrial development   The Japanese
situation may be represented by *Figures 2.2(A)* and *2.2(C)* with
certain modifications. Detailed analyses of the similarities
between Japanese and Chinese kinship systems are available
elsewhere.[12] The following points are relevant to our present
presentation. Like its Chinese counterpart the Japanese culture
says to the individual that his self-esteem and future are tied to
his relationships with other human beings and not to himself; he
must find his appropriate station in life by insuring for himself
and his immediate family an appropriate place in such a human
network. However, here the Japanese and Chinese part ways. All
Chinese sons are tied to their first human group and their
common ancestors, but Japanese inheriting sons and non-
inheriting sons fare differently. For Japanese inheriting sons the
situation is quite similar to that of their Chinese brethren. But
Japanese non-inheriting sons must find their human network
elsewhere. In rural farm areas they may become heads of *bunke* to
some *honke*[13] (either that of their inheriting brother or someone
else) in a sort of *dōzoku*[14] arrangement. Or if they are in an urban
or trade or temple situation, they may become clients or disciples
in some *iemoto*[15] in the hope of eventually setting up their own
subordinate but separate *iemoto* with their own territory so that
each will be in a position to have subordinate *iemoto* under him.

But the differences between the Japanese and Chinese systems
go even further. The Japanese non-inheriting sons, once they
have joined a *honke-bunke* system other than the one of their
origin, tend to cut their relationship with the latter, including
obligations to the ancestors. Similarly, in contrast to the Chinese,
the Japanese household or *ie* is quite free and unconstrained in
accepting members unrelated to them by kinship or even

marriage – since *mukoyoshi*[16] and other forms of adoption are highly frequent.

In view of the fact that there are larger numbers of non-inheriting sons than inheriting ones, it is not unreasonable to assume that a majority of Japanese must move further away from their first group (kinship group) than do a majority of Chinese for their intimacy, though much less far than the majority of westerners. In our scheme this means that the Japanese individual may have to go to non-kin to occupy their layer 3, but (a) they do not have to move very far; (b) they can relate to their non-kin intimates under the kinship principle; (c) they can extend this linkage indefinitely if they are not tied to land; and (d) the people with whom they form their most crucial relationships in the human network are not peers. Therefore, the Japanese are less tied to the kinship base and they have a more adequate foundation for forming larger groupings than the Chinese; but they are less subject to the kind of precarious and highly competitive human relationships characteristic of the Americans.

To many a western observer, Japan is a prime example of a completely westernized society and culture in Asia. The observer can point to Japan's military capability, nuclear households in suburbia, parliamentary government, interest in western art, literature, and clothing, but especially her colossal industrial record. From the observer's economic determinist eye, the total westernization of Japan in the psychological, social, and cultural sense is a foregone conclusion.

I am of the opinion that all of this, but especially Japan's rapid industrialization before and after the Second World War are built on an infrastructure between the individual and the nation rooted in traditional Japanese social organization, not the western pattern of human relationships. And that pattern is found in the *iemoto* mentioned above. The core structure of *iemoto* is a master-disciple (client) relationship. Each master has several disciples (clients) with whom he maintains mutual dependence. He commands great authority over his disciples. He owes to them the best he has to offer (livelihood, instruction, justice, and social responsibility), and his disciples owe him allegiance, subordination, continuation of his art and skill, and most of whatever he requires. This relationship and its characteristic ideas are not economic, nor political, nor militaristic, nor religious. They can be applied to any field of endeavor, whether it be running a bean paste shop, an army, or a university.

The master-disciple relationship in China is somewhat similar to this core *iemoto* relationship. What differentiates the Japanese institution are the following features.

First, the master-disciple relationship in *iemoto* is more inclusive and is marked by a higher degree of continuing superordination and subordination than its counterpart in traditional China.

Second, each set of master-disciple relationships in *iemoto* tends to be linked with other sets forming a hierarchical organization, often of considerable magnitude. Where farms are the main source of livelihood, the spirit of *iemoto* tends to express itself in the form of *dōzoku*. In that case the total size of the *dōzoku* is, of course, limited by the available amount of land and its productivity. But where skills alone are involved (such as flower arranging, dance, *kabuki*, etc.), the resulting hierarchical organization may consist of millions of members and thousands of local chapters.

Third, an equally important feature is the fact that the spirit of *iemoto* prevails among businessmen, industrial workers, teachers, professors, and students in modern universities where *iemoto* does not exist in its traditional form. But its content (Hsu 1959) is pervasive and obvious in the all-inclusive and nearly unbreakable command–obedience, succoring–dependence relationship between the old and the young, the senior and the junior, the superior and the subordinate. It is well known, for example, that there is very little horizontal mobility among professors in different universities, and employees tend to remain for life in the same business firms in which each began his working career.

Finally, all ties in the *iemoto* are couched in pseudo-kinship terms. From this point of view each *iemoto* is a giant kinship establishment, with the closeness and the inclusiveness of its interpersonal links but without the kinship limitations on its size.

Therefore, although a majority of Japanese individuals have to move away from their first kinship base, their culture enables them to secure permanent circles of intimacy without moving far away from it. And the all-inclusive and interlinking mutual dependence between members of any two levels in a large hierarchical organization has the effect of extending the feeling of intimacy beyond those situated near each other. Under the circumstances, the individual can be interested and even involved in his layers 2 and 1 (though not 0) not because he needs to go that far to maintain his psychosocial homeostasis, but because he is linked to them through their links with his immediate circle of intimacy. On the highest level, the emperor becomes the head of a hierarchical organization embracing the entire nation. We may with real justification describe the Japanese *iemoto* and *iemoto*-like organizations as greatly expanded versions of Chinese kinship organizations, including links with deceased ancestors. In the widest extension of the *iemoto*, the Japanese emperor is comparable to the Chinese head of the living clan and the emperor's ancestors are those of his subjects as well.

The Chinese, on the other hand, were much more tied psychologically to their kinship base. Their rule of equal division of inheritance reinforced this tie from generation to generation. Over the centuries, for example, very rarely were Chinese males ever married matrilocally so that they had to change their kinship affiliations to those of their wives, while a very large percentage (perhaps in the neighborhood of 30 per cent) of Japanese marriages involve precisely this kind of arrangement. The ancestors of Chinese imperial lines were not the concern of the people at all.

Consequently, although the set of ideas of how human beings relate to each other (work, care, succoring, subordination and superordination, affiliation, competition, devotion, etc.) which are characteristic of Japanese *iemoto* was also present in China, the Chinese have largely restricted their application to those who were actually related through kinship bonds and their immediate extensions, in sharp contrast to the Japanese whose *iemoto* organization enabled them to live out these ideas far afield.

This difference in the Chinese and Japanese patterns of psychosocial homeostasis explains, it seems to me, how Japan responded to the challenge of the west by modernizing her government, industry, and armed forces so rapidly and so successfully, while China, caught in the same predicament, lagged so far behind. The traditional Japanese social organization gave the Japanese individual the psychosocial wherewithal to satisfy modernization requirements without having to seriously modify his PSH pattern. The traditional Chinese organization, on the other hand, did not offer comparable advantages.[17] The Chinese individual, in order to become an active and continuing participant in the modernizing process, must drastically modify his PSH pattern. The resistance to this change is so great that the task is far from complete thirty years after communist assumption of power (Hsu 1968, 1981, Chu and Hsu 1979). The modernization of Japan has not been based on any significant changes in the Japanese national character nor on changes in the psychology of the majority of individual Japanese. The Japanese society and culture happened to prescribe a kind of psychosocial homeostasis for the individual that is more easily adaptable than that of China to the organizational aspect of modernization.

However, although the institution of *iemoto* contributed greatly to Japan's rapid industrialization and technological excellence within the nation (layers 2 and 1), it could not enable the Japanese to be in tune with universalist aspirations (layer 0) on any egalitarian basis, such as preached by Jesus of Nazareth or envisaged by many western political idealists. In moving into layers 2 and 1 the Japanese has not really left the *iemoto* base of layer 3. He can conceptualize the wider world (layer 0) in an *iemoto* sort of organizing framework, distinguishing between we and they, between superior and inferior, between those who do business with him and those who don't, etc. This is why Japan is not a society in which the non-Japanese can ever achieve acceptance as a Japanese, no matter how well he commands the language, how well he has acculturated himself, or how many generations of his ancestors have resided in Japan. As evidence for this conclusion we need only to contrast, on the one hand, the Japanese non-acceptance of foreigners who are not physically different from them (such as the Chinese and the Koreans), and on the other hand, the white American acceptance of emigrant Europeans.

Previously I mentioned that the psychosocial homeostasis of Japanese non-inheriting sons is similar to that depicted in *Figures 2.2(A)* and *2.2(C)*. In view of this discussion I should modify it to look like the following:

Figure 2.3 Japanese non-inheriting sons

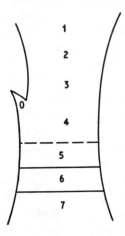

In contrast to the individual in China before western intrusion, and in Japan both before and after the Second World War, the American individual's PSH will always be more precarious. Lack of humans in his layer 3 has driven him to heavy and aggressive affective investments in things, in the supernatural, and in ideas and aspirations of global and intergalactic proportions. In that case his devotion to animals or ideas or gods tends not only to take precedence over any concern for human beings, but he often has no compunction in hating or even sacrificing the latter for the former. The anthropologists who are so absolutely opposed to national character studies that they refuse even to give a rational look at the merits and demerits of such endeavors fall into the same psychological pitfall. They share a great deal with the pope and his inquisitors who nearly put Galileo to the stake. They possess the same psychological materials which most centrally fed and still feed the fires of crusades and proselytism or bigotry and persecution.

Of course some of these ventures will involve other human beings, but they are human beings in his layer 2 or 1 or 0. The missionary will try to save as many souls as he can garner; the colonial doctor will try to save as many lives as he can treat; and the adventurer, like Steve Canyon of the comics, will try to save many natives from their "oppressive" or dictatorial government (usually communist). But it is unlikely that such western "saviors" have any friends, not to speak of intimate friends, among the peoples they have tried to help or have helped. The souls or lives they have saved or tried to save are but the realization of their own ideas or visions, exactly like some anthropologists who often speak of "my natives," or "I love my natives" – but some of them only remember "their natives" by nicknames or not at all (see Hsu 1979: 517–32). However, these affective investments for the western individual's PSH were and are the very source of the organizational, industrial, techno-logical, and ecclesiastical strength of the west in general and America in particular. Their ability to treat human beings im-personally as things is the secret.

This difference explains why Christianity, though it went to Asia (India) by way of its missionaries (Syrian) before its diffusion to Europe, achieved little following in China and Japan. Instead it caught fire at once in Europe. It was in Europe that it first aroused so much emotion that the Roman emperors threw their converts to the lions and then, after various European monarchs became converts, quite a few of them forced their subjects to espouse their newly-found faith.

Given the westerner's attraction to one God and one absolute truth, he was bound to suffer disappointments elsewhere. When Generalissimo Chiang Kai-shek was converted to Methodism in the early 1930s at the zenith of his popularity and power, western Methodist missionaries in particular were jubilant. Judging from the history of Europe, they expected most Chinese to turn Methodist, or at least Christian, soon. Nothing like that happened!

When Japan surrendered in 1945 and General Douglas

McArthur took over control of that island nation, western missionaries also entertained high hopes. And in view of the Japanese craze, even after the occupation ended, for American things from McDonald's hamburgers to Bernstein's music, many westerners thought the number of Japanese Christians would surely grow. They too were disappointed!

By 1949, less than one per cent of China's population was Christian. In 1945 only about one-tenth of one per cent of Japan's population was Christian and today the figure is not any higher. In fact, by some estimates it is lower. My prediction is that, in view of their PSH patterns, Christianity will not win many more future converts in the two Asian societies, in spite of the efforts of western evangelism.

Likewise, western psychoanalysis has not prevailed in Japan and China, and for the same reasons. Hong Kong has plenty of wealthy Chinese who can afford the analytic luxury. But to date there is not one practicing analyst in the Crown Colony. Instead *majong* is ubiquitous; it is even played in restaurants. In Japan, instead of Freudian analysis, Doi's concept of *amae* (Doi 1962) and Morita's quiet therapy (Reynolds 1980) have seemed to work much better among the Japanese. It is no accident that the Suzuki method of teaching the violin (now also piano) to children via group participation was developed in Japan.

It is important to recognize that layer 3 for the Chinese and Japanese is somewhat different from layer 3 for westerners. Clearly, the intimate relationships of both of the former group are characterized by more ritualization, role playing, hierarchical relationships, repression of negativity, and repression of personal spontaneity when compared to western ideals. These factors make it more difficult for intimacy, as westerners think of it, to occur. Family stability and security are maintained at the cost of the western concepts of intimacy and independence. But this is because the Chinese and the Japanese are not seeking a conceptually equivalent type of intimacy. For all groups, Chinese, Japanese, and westerners, intimacy is an important aspect of human experience and its absence or denial can result in many ills including delinquency and neuroses. The stability and reliability of intimate relationships with others are a source of strength for the individual and the society. The question is how and whether different cultures provide for this need and the tolerances and implications for differences in the experience of the need.

Conclusions

Once we substitute the PSH approach for the personality approach, we shall better be able to understand how the individual self differs drastically in unlike cultures, and how such differences bear on important problems such as social change, political stability, and economic development.

The Japanese learned all about Buddhism from China and Chinese masters. But Buddhism in Japan achieved a popularity and escalation in its organizational developments unknown to its counterpart in China. The *Soka Gakai* phenomenon is unthinkable in China. And an entire branch of Buddhism is known to the western world by its Japanese name *Zen*, not by its Chinese name *Ch'an*, simply because the Japanese elaborated its doctrine and its use way beyond what the Chinese did or cared to do.

The Japanese way in *Zen* is an outcome of the fact that the sustaining sources of PSH for the Japanese come from the *iemoto*. Relying far more on their immediate kinship ties and their extension, the Chinese have had no comparable affective needs to move away from them and seek life's meaning in some larger social arena.

Likewise, the fact the Chinese PSH is strongly rooted in their kinship system made them spectacularly different from their western brethren, whose sources of PSH are far more precarious, in their approach to religion as in other aspects of life. Tu in Chapter 7 makes clear, for example, the opposition of the Confucian scholar to Buddhist philosophy and practices because they are incommensurate with filial piety. Yet, despite the fact that Confucian officials had continuously been in power throughout dynastic China, the so-called religious persecution in China was limited to four occurrences in the tenth century AD. Even these occurrences were primarily attempts to *regulate* Buddhist functionaries and temples, not to *exterminate* them in the manner of the western inquisition. Furthermore, even such attempts to regulate them by limiting the numbers of temples and monks stopped after AD 955 (Hsu 1968:596–97).

The Chinese, unlike westerners, are too enmeshed in their kinship based PSH to give themselves to do-or-die situations involving distant causes. They go to deities and priests for specific problems such as illnesses and epidemics, or emergencies such as banditry or drought, but few if any of them find it necessary to resort to exclusive commitment to one god or creed, simply because supernaturals and priests are rarely part of their PSH needs (Hsu 1983).

Given the fact that patterns of PSH requirements of the self are closely linked to differing patterns of society and culture, it becomes clear that conversion of individuals into new faiths is futile unless the convertees can find in the new religious context alternative and more satisfying means of achieving PSH than were available in the old. By the same token, economic development cannot be induced and sustained until native laborers, technicians, and entrepreneurs can relate the old areas of intimacy to the new activities, or find new areas in which their need for intimacy and for lavishing their affect can be satisfied. It is simply beside the point for outsiders to decry, for example, the "irrational" or the "uneconomic" nature of the Hindu sacred cow.[18] Since the sacred cow is just as much a part of the Hindu individual's PSH as the Holy Bible is part of the Christian individual's PSH, exhortations or expositions, however rational or economically desirable from the outsider's point of view, are bound to fall on deaf ears.

Notes

1 Oscar Lewis's notion of "culture of poverty" (Lewis 1971: xxiv) is another variant of the same theme.

2 In other words, the individual's judgment of the likely effect of revealing materials will constrain him from communicating the contents of layer 5. However, under the guise of psychoanalysis, much of it may be divulged. For an illustration see *Portnoy's Complaint*, by Philip Roth (1969).

3 Sociologists have defined role as "a set of expectations which others share of the behavior an individual will exhibit as an occupant of a position, or status category" (Jacobson, Charters, and Lieberman 1951:18). In this paper we emphasize the "usefulness" component of role as contrasted to the "feeling" component of affect.

4 However, lack of communication may only be symptomatic of more basic difficulties or differences. For example, blacks will be turned away by some white churches no matter how well they communicate with each other. Nor can the mounting problems, e.g. between labor and management or between the generations, be solved merely by better communication. Better communication can reduce simple misunderstandings but cannot eliminate irreconcilable differences. An old Chinese proverb says: "You cannot consult with a tiger about getting its skin."

5 In saying layer 3 is characterized by affective relationships and layer 2 by role relationships we do not mean to imply that role relationships are absent in the former or that affect is absent in the latter. Instead, we insist that affective relationship is more common and important in layer 3 while role relationship is more common and important in layer 2.

6 The Yiddish word *mensch* seems to be close to *jen* in meaning. *Mensch* refers to a good human being who is, for example, kind, generous, decent, and upright. A *mensch* is "someone of consequence; someone to admire and emulate; someone of noble character." Leo Rosten (1968), on whose authority we rely, goes on to say that "it is hard to convey the special sense of respect, dignity, approbation that can be conveyed by calling someone a 'real mensch.' The most withering comment one might make on someone's character or conduct is: 'He is not (did not act like) a mensch.'" Even the following comments by Rosten fit the Chinese *jen*.

> "To be a *mensch* has nothing to do with success, wealth, status. A judge can be a *zhlob*; a millionaire can be a *momzer*; a professor can be a *shlemiel*, a doctor a *klutz*, a lawyer a *bulvon*. The key to being 'a real mensch' is nothing less than — character: rectitude, dignity, a sense of what is right, responsible, decorous. Many a poor man, many an ignorant man, is a *mensch*."
>
> (Rosten 1968:234)

7 There is a current tendency on the part of some of my fellow anthropologists to eschew or even to be derogatory toward the

concept of national character and researches into it. I firmly believe that this tendency, based on misguided views, is detrimental to the future of the discipline (see Hsu 1979:528–29).

However, as will become clear later in this chapter, the tendency to be *absolutely* negative about one approach to reality, just as its reverse (namely to hold another as absolutely true), is simply one of the manifestations of western ways in psychosocial homeostasis.

8 Most orphans are either adopted by parents or reared by foster parents. In matrilineal and matrilocal systems the mother's brother may figure prominently here instead of the father; but the ethnographic accounts I have seen would seem to indicate that the father is important nevertheless (see e.g. Malinowski 1929, a well-known account of the father among the Trobriand Islanders).

9 I am aware that the kinship system in various western cultures is not uniform. I am also aware that some students (sociologists in particular) maintain that the American type of kinship pattern, for example, is a result of the industrial revolution. In reply I wish to point out that the basis for the husband-wife type of kinship pattern was symbolized in the western Biblical legend of Noah and his sons, and is therefore very old. Even the generation gap was there. By contrast, the Chinese version of the Deluge symbolized cooperation between father and son, sacrifice of marital pleasure, and continuity between the generations (see Hsu 1969:446).

10 For documentation of these statements see Hsu (1967 and 1978).

11 One reviewer describes Philip Roth's *Portnoy's Complaint* as "a sort of Moby Dick" (Anatole Broyard in *The New Republic*, March 1, 1969:21).

12 See Francis L. K. Hsu, "Japanese Kinships and *Iemoto*" in *Nihon no Shinzoku to Iemoto* Tokyo: Baifukan, 1969 (Japanese translation of Hsu 1963, chapters XI, XII, and XIII); Hsu 1971b; and Hsu 1975.

13 *Honke* means chief household, and *bunke* means branch household. Each *bunke* is subordinate to some *honke*; each *honke* may have under it several *bunke*.

14 *Dōzoku* consists of a *honke* and one or more *bunke* in a superior–subordinate relationship.

15 *Iemoto* is a *dōzoku*-like arrangement except that it is not based on land.

16 *Mukoyoshi* is a son-in-law who assumes his wife's father's family name and who lives and works in her parents' household.

17 It may seem inappropriate to some but the only Chinese groups in traditional times similar to, but of course not identical with, the

Japanese *iemoto* were the secret gangster organizations such as the Blue Group (*Ch'ing Pang*) and the Red Group (*Hung Pang*). These groups existed outside the natural kinship boundaries but were organized along pseudo-kinship lines. Such groups were helpful now and then to anti-establishmentarian movements, and were of material assistance to Dr Sun Yat-sen's republican revolution which toppled the Manchu government in 1911. However, they remained *outside the established society* even after that.

18 An interesting article by Marvin Harris (1966) argues that the Hindu sacred cow is an economic necessity. This, too, is beside the point.

References

Chu, G. and Hsu, F. L. K. (1979) *Moving a Mountain*. Honolulu: University of Hawaii Press.

Doi, T. (1962) *Amae*: A Key Concept for Understanding Japanese Personality. In R. J. Smith and R. K. Beardsley (eds) *Japanese Culture*. Chicago: Aldine.

Foster, G. (1965) Peasant Society and the Image of the Limited Good. *American Anthropology* 67: 293–315.

Freud, S. and Bullitt, W. C. (1967) *Thomas Woodrow Wilson, 28th President of the United States: A Psychoanalytic Study*. Boston: Houghton-Mifflin.

Harris, M. (1966) The Cultural Ecology of India's Sacred Cattle. *Current Anthropology* 7: 51–66.

Heiliger, W. S. (1980) *Soviet and Chinese Personalities*. Lanham, MD: University Press of America.

Honigmann, J. (1967) *Personality in Culture*. New York: Harper & Row.

Hsu, F. L. K. (1952) Anthropology or Psychiatry: A Definition of Objectives and Their Implications. *Southwestern Journal of Anthropology* 8: 227–50.

____ (1953) *Americans and Chinese: Two Ways of Life*. New York: Henry Schuman.

____ (1959) Structure, Function, Content and Process. *American Anthropologist* 61: 790–805.

____ (1963) *Clan, Caste and Club*. Princeton, NJ: Van Nostrand.

____ (1967) Christianity and the Anthropologist. *International Journal of Comparative Sociology* 8: 1–19.

____ (1968) Chinese Kinship and Chinese Behavior. In T. Tsou and P.

Ho (eds), *China in Crisis*, vol. 1, book 2. Chicago: University of Chicago Press.

____ (1969) Eros, Affect and *Pao*. In F. L. K. Hsu (ed.) *Kinship and Culture*, chapter XIX. Chicago: Aldine.

____ (1970) *Americans and Chinese: Purpose and Fulfillment in Great Civilizations*. Garden City, NY: Doubleday.

____ (1971a) *Nihon no Shinzoku to Iemoto* ("Japanese Kinships and Iemoto"), chapters XI, XII, XIII of *Hikaku Bunmei Shakai Ron* (*Sociology of Comparative Cultures*), a Japanese translation of *Clan, Caste and Club* (1963, Princeton, NJ: Van Nostrand).

____ (1971b) Filial Piety in Japan and China: Borrowing, Variation and Significance. *Journal of Comparative Family Studies* Spring: 67–74.

____ (1971c) Psycho-Social Homeostasis and *Jen*: Conceptual Tools for Advancing Psychological Anthropology. *American Anthropologist* 73(1): 23–44.

____ (1975) *Iemoto: The Heart of Japan*. New York: Halstead Press.

____ (1978) The Myth of Chinese Expansionism. *Journal of Asian and African Studies* 8(3–4): 184–95.

____ (1979) The Cultural Problem of the Cultural Anthropologist. *Anerican Anthropologist* 81: 517–32.

____ (1981) *Americans and Chinese: Passage to Differences*, 3rd edition, greatly revised and augmented. Honolulu: University Press of Hawaii.

____ (1983) *Exorcising the Trouble Makers: Magic, Science and Culture*. Westport, Conn.: Greenwood Press.

Inkeles, A. (1960) Industrial Man: The Relation of Status to Experience, Perception and Value. *American Journal of Sociology* 66: 1–31.

Jacobson, E., Charters, W., Jr, and Lieberman, S. (1951) The Use of the Role Concept in the Study of Complex Organizations. *Journal of Social Issues* 7(3): 18–27.

Kaplan, B. (1954) A Study of Rorschach Responses in Four Cultures. *Papers of Peabody Museum of Archeology and Ethnology*, Harvard University, 24(2).

____ (1961) Cross-Cultural Use of Projective Techniques. In F. L. K. Hsu (ed.) *Psychological Anthropology*. Homewood, Ill.: Dorsey Press.

Kluckhohn, C. and Mowrer, O. H. (1944) Culture and Personality: A Conceptual Scheme. *American Anthropology* 46: 1–29.

Kluckhohn, C. and Murray, H. A. (1948) Personality Formulation: The Determinants. In C. Kluckhohn and H. A. Murray (eds) *Personality in Nature, Society and Culture*. New York: Alfred A. Knopf.

Lewis, O. (1961) *The Children of Sanchez* (autobiography of a Mexican family). New York: Vintage Books.

Malinowski, B. (1929) *The Sexual Life of Savages in Northwestern Melanesia*. London: Routledge & Kegan Paul.

Parsons, T. (1964) *Social Structure and Personality*. Glencoe, IU.: Free Press. (Chapter 1, "Superego and Theory of Social Systems," originally appeared in *Psychiatry* 15(1): 1952.)

Peter, Prince of Greece and Denmark (1965) The Importance of Alexander the Great's Expedition for the Relations between East and West. Lecture delivered at Amsterdam Institute of the Tropics, mimeo, pp. 1–18.

Reynolds, D. K. (1980) *The Quiet Therapies: Japanese Pathways to Personal Growth*. Honolulu: University of Hawaii Press.

Rosten, L. (1968) *The Joys of Yiddish*. New York: McGraw-Hill.

Roth, P. (1969) *Portnoy's Complaint*. New York: Random House.

Schwartz, T. (1968) Paper presented at International Congress of Anthropological Sciences, Kyoto, Japan. Later published as The Congo Cult: A Melanesian Type Response to Change. In *Responses to Change* edited by George DeVos, 1976, New York: Van Nostrand and World and Cult and Context: the Paranoid Ethos in Melanesia. *Ethos* 1: 153–173.

Tsou, T. and Ho, P. (eds) *China in Crisis*, vol. 1, book 2. Chicago: University of Chicago Press.

Wallace, W. F. C. (1961) The Psychic Unity of Human Groups. In B. Kaplan (ed.) *Studying Personality Cross-Culturally*. New York: Harper & Row.

3

The Metaphorical Basis
of Selfhood

M. Brewster Smith

Introduction

In this chapter, I take seriously the new label, displayed in the title of the present volume – "culture and self" – rather than "culture and personality," the label I grew up with in the 1930s to 1950s. As a culturally-oriented (but hardly cross-cultural) psychologist, I have always thought that mainstream social science deserted culture and personality before the full potential of the topic had at all been realized. It now seems to me that the general area is due for a renaissance of scholarly interest, catalyzed in part by the new semantic auspices. My contribution is intended to further the enterprise (to which this volume contributes in its entirety) by taking note of developments in the psychology of personality that favor it, and, particularly, by carrying forward my own treatment of selfhood (Smith 1978a, 1980) to make more explicit its symbolic grounding in culturally provided metaphor, and therefore the necessity of cross-cultural approaches if selfhood is to be dealt with satisfactorily, in ways that avoid the destructive charge of being culture-bound (or history-bound – an equivalent but much less recognized failing). The moral of my story will be: good *science* of personality or selfhood requires cross-cultural *hermeneutics*. If this be philosophical treason, make the most of it! In the realm of selfhood, I have come to believe, science does not clash with interpretation but requires it.

Culture and self/personality

What happened to "culture and personality"? As the movement thrived during the 1930s and 1940s, "culture and personality" was mainly a temporary marriage between cultural anthropology and neo-Freudian psychoanalysis. There were some extravagances and errors, particularly in the wartime study of national character at a distance, that began to bring the field into disrepute among more tough-minded behavioral scientists. By the 1960s and 1970s a cognitive focus had emerged in psychological anthropology as well as in psychology, which brought new issues to the fore. Academic interest in psychoanalysis crested, followed by a downward sweep that leaves its current scholarly reputation as undeservedly low as it was once faddishly high. In spite of some good work in continuity with the earlier tradition by scholars like LeVine (1973) and Spiro (1967), social scientists largely abandoned culture and personality just when more adequate methodological sophistication was beginning to prevail, before the major substantive problems of the area had been dealt with satisfactorily. The abandonment coincided, too, with the emergence of less dogmatically physicalistic, more interpretive psychoanalytic formulations.

The participants in this volume obviously have not given up on the old problems. But we are attacking them from a new angle. What denotations and connotations make the terminology of "culture and self" more auspicious than that of "culture and personality," and why, indeed, is the present time auspicious for a renaissance of interest in cross-cultural formulations of the relations between self and society?

The revival of personality

First a word about the auspiciousness of the time. In psychology, the 1960s and 1970s were a period of sterility and despair in personality psychology (Carlson 1971). The great academic personality theorists who were contemporaries of the culture-and-personality movement – Gordon Allport, Henry Murray, Gardner Murphy, and George Kelly – had envisioned a humane science of personality that aspired to be at once scientific and humanistic in traditional senses of both these words. In the academic psychology of personality, there ensued a period of laboratory experimentalism that emphasized experimental manipulations and situational influences rather than dispositions, and variables rather than people. The gospel of extreme situationism prevailed for almost two decades, if only because psychologists were mainly studying the impact of experimentally manipulated situational variables, encouraged by the grant system of project support that rewarded series of tightly designed studies that could readily be described in advance.

Shortly before the end of the 1970s, however, the tide had turned (see Magnusson and Endler 1977; and Epstein 1979, 1980). Person × Situation interactionism is once more acceptable and even fashionable, at least in principle. Personality structure or organization and traits or dispositions are no longer derided. New models are needed if the revived interactionism is to be pursued fruitfully, but armchair polemics are no longer called for. It is now respectable and even interesting to be talking about personality again.

The decline of positivism and rise of interpretation

Our choice of the term "self" or "selfhood" requires notice of an even broader set of developments. Relaxation of the stranglehold that situation-oriented laboratory experimentalism had on personality theory is part of a shift in the general atmosphere of enquiry in the human and social sciences. The heyday of culture and personality was also that of Vienna-style logical positivism (particularly exemplified in psychology by the neo-behaviorism of Clark Hull (1943), a major participant in interdisciplinary ventures of the culture-and-personality movement). As we all know, the dictatorial reign of logical positivism as a philosophy of science has ended. It never did constrain the self-confident physical scientists; now, in the human and behavioral sciences, it has become much easier to follow problems where they lead us, with fewer scientific restraints. As the credentials of positivism declined, those of a hermeneutic, interpretive perspective with roots in the humanities gained in attractiveness and credibility (see Bernstein 1976 and Geertz 1973). The terminology of self and selfhood fits naturally into this newer emphasis, as I will try to show more explicitly a little later on.

The broadening of our perspectives to include interpretive, symbolic considerations is critical in laying the basis for new advances in the study of personality. As I suggested earlier, the grand academic personality theorists who in their time were rebels against the behaviorist tradition saw their enterprise as both humanistic and scientific. Freud, too, had both his positivistic-mechanistic and his humanistic sides, which as Ricoeur (1970), Holt (1972), Loevinger (1976), Schafer (1976), and other recent interpreters of Freud in a more hermeneutic vein have made clear, got into considerable conflict with each other. During the 1960s and 1970s, when the positivists held the day in academic personality psychology, the attempt to sustain a humanistic psychology of personality got caught up in the irrationalist counterculture. So "humanistic psychology," as typified by the Esalen Institute and the Association for Humanistic Psychology, became more a social movement than an academic field (Smith 1984). That movement, too, has substantially faded. We can now try to reconstruct a psychology of personality that is interpretive and humanistic and historically anchored but shares the critical, corrigible, and conceptualizing aspirations of science.

The present need for a cross-cultural approach

A cross-cultural approach once more seems essential if the serious study of personality is to get back on track. Except for participants in the culture and personality movement, personality theorists have mostly been egregiously culture-bound. Maybe we can do better on this present round! It was easy enough for the generation of Karen Horney (1939) to criticize Freud for his lack of awareness of cultural influences. It is similarly easy – too easy – for contemporary feminists to reject Freud's thought out of hand because of his history-bound views of gender and sexual repression. Perhaps we are at last in a position to conceive that Freud's psychology of gender ana of the super-ego fits turn-of-the-century Vienna pretty well, but is much less apt for the men and women of today. If we are to build on this dawning insight into the inherently historical component in our formulations of personality, we obviously need all the help we can get from cross-cultural studies. Even though the methodological and conceptual relevance of historical and cross-cultural data are closely similar if not identical, we can pursue our questions more rigorously, with better evidence, in cross-cultural comparison than is ever possible in historical retrospect.

Some terminological issues

The time is opportune. And the term "self" does provide a useful change of semantic auspices, which has advantages beyond mere novelty. My own preference is for the term "selfhood," and for "self" in the many reflexive hyphenated contexts in which it is used in ordinary language. When a while ago I was addressing my colleagues in psychology about self-hood, I wrote:

"I am not talking at this point about *the* Self as a successor to the Soul, or even about the *self-concept*. Nothing that *thing-*like, substantive, or concrete can ground our consideration appropriately. I am talking, rather, about universal features of being a person, distinctive features that we find fascinating and, when we take them seriously, as mysterious as the frontiers of cosmology. So: Selfhood involves being *self-aware* or *reflective*; *being* or *having* a body (a large debate here); somehow taking into account the *boundaries of selfhood* at birth and death and feeling a *continuity of identity* in between; placing oneself in *a generational sequence and network of other connected selves* as forebears and descendants and relatives; being in partial *communication and communion with other contemporary selves* while experiencing an irreducible *separateness of experience and identity*; engaging in joint and individual *enterprises* in the world with some degree of *forethought and afterthought* (not just 'behaving'); *guiding* what one does and *appraising* what one has done at least partly through *reflection* on one's performance; feeling *responsible*, at least sometimes, for one's actions and holding others responsible for theirs. I could go on, but this already covers a lot of ground. These are features that a *human* psychology, let alone a humanistic one, has to take into account."

(Smith 1978a: 1053–054)

In that passage, I was trying to be evocative rather than definitive. However, in a paper written shortly thereafter for a somewhat more specialized audience, I ended by declaring more explicit preferences about usage. Reflexive self-awareness then seemed to me foremost among the criterial features of being human that warrant the term *selfhood*.

"There are a number of terms in the domain of selfhood that give me no trouble, or seem potentially useful. There is the *person*, the actual, concrete participant in symbolically construed and governed social relations. There is *personality*, the psychologist's formulation or construction of the person, a construction of organized processes, states, and dispositions. ... There is a set of terms in the reflexive mode – *self-perceptions* and *attributions*, *self-concepts*, *self-theories* (Epstein 1973) in which the prefix 'self-' implies reflexive reference but does *not* imply a surgically or conceptually separable object of reference – other than the *person*. People – persons – may reify 'I' and 'Me,' but psychologists shouldn't, except as they recognize the causal-functional importance of people's own reifications. ... I don't see a place for *the self* in such a list. It is not a term that designates an entity or agency, except in usages that treat it as synonymous with the *person* – in which case one or the other term is superfluous.

Yet there *are* contexts in which 'self' is employed in near synonymy with 'person' that seem to be more justifiable. We may talk about transformations of the Greek self from Homer to Euripedes, or of the Western self from Shakespeare to Proust, Pynchon, or R. D. Laing. We may talk of the fragmentation of self in role-differentiated modern society. When we use such locutions, we are emphasizing the symbolic, *self-referential* aspect of being a person (with the reflexive prefix having its usual sense as interpreted above), with the implied reminder that self-referential features in which we are interested are somehow constitutive of the person as social actor. We are not talking about an entity, conceptual or otherwise, that is distinguishable from the person. ... Self-hood, person, and personality remain my key terms."

(Smith 1980: 342–43)

But I do not revolt against "self" in the title of this volume. I take the implied contrast with "culture and personality" to suggest that people's own formulations and theories about themselves as personal and social objects ought to play a larger role in our conceptualizations of personality than heretofore. From such a perspective, it is immediately apparent that the symbolic ingredients of these formulations and theories are intrinsically cultural.

How people symbolize themselves to themselves and each other is important. Indeed, "ethnopsychology" (a term now employed rather differently) might become institutionalized as a special field analogous to ethnobotany or ethnoscience generally: how do culturally contrasting peoples conceptualize their human nature and their personal-social processes? The ontogenetic version of this question – "metacognition" – has recently opened up in developmental cognitive psychology, but the comparative cultural question seems still rather rare in the ethnographic literature. Some major examples are treated in other chapters in this volume. Among others, a fine example is Geertz's (1973, 1975) comparative treatment of naming as anchoring different modes of selfhood or identity in Bali, Java, and Morocco. (It was Geertz's provocative treatment of how the Balinese system of teknonomy minimizes the salience of individuality, taken together with Lionel Trilling's (1972) account of the historical vicissitudes of selfhood in European literature, that led me to see the strong parallel between historical and cross-cultural perspectives.) Another good example is Leenhardt's version of structures of the person in New Caledonia (Clifford 1982). Before her tragic death, Rosaldo (1984) was carrying Geertz's program forward in a provocative analysis very much along the lines I am asking for, focusing on her data on Ilongot ethnopsychology. A more systematic recent consideration of "the anthropology of self," with a number of contributed examples, is provided by Heelas and Lock (1981).

From classical symbolic interactionism to constitutive metaphor

For most contemporary social scientists, the terminology of self calls to mind the theoretical tradition extending from James (1890) through Cooley (1902) and Mead (1934) to contemporary symbolic interactionists, with a modern branching to include the phenomenological successors to Schutz (1967). As a deviant social psychologist (Smith 1983a), I enjoy watching my more experimentally oriented colleagues rediscover this tradition, as more and more of them are doing. One of its key features is the view that self-awareness and self-evaluation are social emergents.

The Meadian account

G. H. Mead (1934) held, as we know, that mind, self, and society emerge together both in the individual life and in the history of the human species. The attainment of language involves the acquired ability to emit signs that the emitter interprets in the same way as the receiver: "significant symbols." To acquire significant symbols, we must "take the role of the other," reacting to our own behavior as our partner in interaction does. From practice in a variety of such role-taking relationships, we generalize, and become able to take *ourselves* as objects, from the perspective of the "generalized other." By the same token, we can then orient our actions as well as our talk so as to participate effectively in the complexly organized expectation-and-rule systems of society. The "Me" is the product of generalization from the responses of others to us, and thought is inner dialogue between "I" and "Me". This armchair account, made the more difficult to grasp (and thus the more dogmatically received) because it was constructed posthumously from student notes on Mead's lectures, became the gospel of the so-called symbolic interactionists in sociological social psychology. For decades, it formed part of an orienting framework for research in a qualitative, participant-observer style, but it was not itself directly tested in research.

Needed revisions/extensions of Mead

Research is only now beginning to appear that requires us to correct or elaborate upon the Meadian formulation. The broader social science community is now becoming acquainted with Gallup's (1977) fascinating study of selfhood in chimpanzees. He raised chimpanzees in living quarters that were amply provided with mirrors. Then he anesthetized a test chimpanzee, painted a red patch on its forehead, and let the chimp come to in its own quarters provided with mirrors. Chimpanzees under these circumstances regularly grasped at their foreheads when looking in the mirror, evidently puzzled about the new red spot. Lower mammals did not show this behavior; neither did chimpanzees raised in isolation, even though mirrors were available. Appropriate understanding of one's mirror image may not reflect full-blown selfhood – say, that of a Kierkegaard or Sartre puzzled by the absurdity of existence – but it does suggest that socially raised chimps are capable of taking themselves as objects in a more conceptual way than is involved in scratching or self-grooming. This aspect of selfhood clearly does not depend upon language, though the fact that only the socially raised chimps showed this behavior agrees with Meadian assumptions.

Michael Lewis and his collaborators (Lewis and Brooks-Gunn 1979) are engaging in studies of mirror behavior among human infants, and Kagan (1981) infers the emergence of self-awareness, self-reference, and self-evaluation from the close observation of infants' and toddlers' behaviors in a variety of cognitive tasks in the laboratory. Selfhood, we now see, does not emerge suddenly, all-or-none; and the role of language and role-taking in its ontogenesis needs to be worked out in detail. Now that the details of how selfhood emerges have become problematic and methods have been devised for studying the problem, we can expect rapid progress in enriching the Meadian account.

The infant studies just cited were done in America (though Kagan incorporates Fijian data), but it seems likely that they concern developmental processes that are essentially pan-human. Language and self-reference are human universals. Cross-cultural studies are desirable to confirm this presumption, but I would be surprised if they showed much cultural variation in the steps toward attainment of selfhood in the first two years. The case should be different for later developments, especially with respect to what might be referred to as the *content* of selfhood: to use Kelly's (1955) language, how do persons in different cultures come to construe themselves? Competent reviews of the development of selfhood in infancy and childhood have recently been provided by Damon and Hart (1982) and by Harter (1983).

A focus on the symbolic content of selfhood

How do culturally provided symbol systems affect people's self-conceptions and therefore their distinctive ways of relating self to interpreted world? Currently fashionable miniature theories – "labeling theory" in sociology and "attribution theory" in psychology – have recently focused attention on some of the *processes* by which participants in society acquire interpretations of themselves, which therefore are likely to result in self-fulfilling prophecies. Labeling theory has mainly been used as a blunt instrument for cudgeling traditional accounts of deviant behavior (Murphy 1976, 1981), and attribution theory in the hands of experimental social psychologists has characteristically assumed a framework of causal explanation, not of intentional, meaningful interpretation (cf. Schotter 1981).

A prominent attribution theorist (Ross 1977) has called inappropriate attribution to personal dispositions "the funda-mental attribution error," a position that is readily misinterpreted as asserting that the error includes any attribution to personal dispositions whatsoever. Harvey, Town, and Yarkin (1981) have recently and I think appropriately questioned the "fundamental" label. There *are* problems in how attribution and labeling concepts have been deployed. All the same, attribution theory and labeling theory are focusing attention on social psychological processes that contribute to the content of selfhood.

I am particularly taken by how attribution theory has been used by Seligman and his colleagues (Abramson, Seligman, and Teasdale 1978) in extending and enriching his theory of learned helplessness (Seligman 1968) as a dynamic of depression and other self-defeating reaction patterns. As he and his colleagues have been saying, a vicious cycle of self-defeat can be sustained by the learned tendency to attribute failures to the self, the pernicious self-attributions being global rather than specific, and stable rather than temporary. That is, "I failed the math test not because the test was too hard but because of my own inadequacies, and it's not just a matter of my poor mathematical ability or the fact that I had a hangover – I am just stupid, so there is no point in trying."

This kind of dynamic, as formulated in attributional terms, goes well beyond the static and sterile work that predominated under the rubric of "self-concept" research (Wylie 1974, 1979). Psychologists do have a disciplinary bent toward preoccupation with abstract process, however, and different approaches are needed to enrich our understanding of the *content* of selfhood. In which respects is our experience of selfhood pan-human, and in which is it historically and culturally specific? This question is of great human interest in its own right, and we need at least an approximate answer before we can have any confidence in our strategies for developing personality theory. My hunch is that much theory in personality and social psychology, and related research, has been misdirected by the assumption that we are dealing with timeless human universals rather than with historically and culturally specific phenomena. I believe that psychology in its personal-social aspect will be more humanly useful, and also sounder science, if we give up the aspiration to an ahistorical, quasi-Newtonian science. (See Gergen 1973, 1982; Smith 1976, 1980.) But these issues are themselves pragmatic and historical, and cannot be settled from the armchair.

Enter constitutive metaphor

My own thinking about selfhood in historical/cultural perspective was much stimulated by Julian Jaynes's (1976) brilliant but extravagant speculations on *The Origins of Consciousness in the Breakdown of the Bicameral Mind*. Jaynes had the idea that consciousness as we know it originated rather recently. He drew on evidence from Egyptian and Sumerian inscriptions, some biblical writings, and Homer to suggest that people originally went through their lives unconsciously (un*self*-consciously?), unreflectively, receiving guidance when they were puzzled by hallucinating the voices of the gods – through some kind of right-left hemispheric shunt in the brain. He suggested that in the second millenium BC, the folk-wanderings and catastrophes in the eastern Mediterranean made this way of life untenable, giving rise to modern consciousness. The book is fun to read, both because of the outrageousness of the hypothesis, and because of its ability to integrate a wide range of phenomena including ancient oracles, modern mediumship, hypnosis, and schizophrenia!

I call upon Jaynes here not because I give credence to his main hypothesis: he is so centered on the traditions of western civilization that one immediately asks for better cross-cultural evidence. I am not persuaded that the ancient Sumerians and Achaeans were walking automata who continually hallucinated. But Jaynes's analysis of the language of the *Iliad* converges with independent analyses by the German classicist Snell (1953) and the English classicist Onians (1973) to suggest strongly that the Homeric bards conceived of self-consciousness in terms quite different from ours.

As we hear from Jaynes and from Snell and Onians, what at first glance seems to be the psychological language of the *Iliad* does not translate accurately into terms from our common language like spirit or soul, mind, thought, consciousness, emotion, will, or their reasonable equivalents in the Greek of classical times. Some of the words (like *psyche*) which later became explicitly psychological occur in contexts indicating that for the bards of the *Iliad*, they were not psychological at all. In the *Iliad*, they appear to stand rather for concrete bodily organs or functions – like the lungs, the breath, the blood, the stirrings of the gut, the movements of the limbs.

There seems to be little if any subjectivity or introspection in the *Iliad*. Passages that imply deceit and complexity of intention can be argued to represent later interpolations. Certainly, the voices of the gods are constantly intruding when courses of action are in doubt. At the very least, Lionel Trilling's remark seems well justified, that it would be quite meaningless to speak of Achilles as *sincere* (1972:2). Sincerity implies reflective scrutiny of intention and behavior – sophisticated but integral selfhood – that simply does not apply to the Homeric hero.

Snell and Jaynes converge in suggesting that modern self-consciousness depends upon the metaphors that people use to construe their experience. Snell goes so far as to entitle his book *The Discovery of Mind*, though he goes on to note the ambiguity as to whether one should speak of invention rather than discovery: mind as we know it requires our contemporary conceptualization to be what it is for us. To speak of the *discovery* of mind, says Snell, is to engage in metaphor, but he notes in passing that we must inevitably fall back on metaphor if we are to speak at all about the intellect or mind. This is a serious point which warrants elaboration.

The language of subjectivity *is* inherently metaphoric. The point is well recognized by the behaviorist critics of the older introspective psychology, who regarded subjectivity as a disqualification of any psychology of consciousness. It is a standard defense of objectivism in psychology that only when we are comparing each other's discriminations in the public world are we able to check our denotations by pointing – by ostensive definition. In the child's acquisition of language, no such check is available for the vocabulary of emotion or, for that matter, for the *qualities* of our experience of external stimuli. The language of phenomenological description stumbles at evoking qualities as such, and has to be satisfied with what the Gestalt psychologists called "isomorphism" – formal, structural correspondences. All of this was old hat in the heyday of behaviorism. Given the impossibility of direct denotation in the realm of the subjective, we inevitably fall back on metaphor, which is the language of isomorphism.

Jaynes (1977) bases his treatment of consciousness – with its "as-if" inner space, its serialized time, its narratively interpreted plot-structure of intentionality – on his own version of a theory of metaphor. One can agree with him that the substance and perhaps some aspects of the structure of our reflective consciousness are heavily metaphoric, without following him to his caricature of walking automata. His account of the metaphorical nature of mind is worth close consideration to which we will return. Here, however, I draw instead on the recent formulations of Lakoff and Johnson (1980). Metaphor is a complex and presently stylish topic, for which there are many competing treatments. (For a representative recent sampling, see Fernandez 1974; Sacks 1979; and Ortony 1979). In *Metaphors We Live By* (1980), however, Lakoff and Johnson provide a framework that seems to me ideally suited to my purposes. Encountering their book was a major intellectual discovery for me, so I sing its praises.

Lakoff and Johnson's treatment of metaphor

Here I must pause to expound and illustrate selectively what Lakoff and Johnson do with metaphor – in English: the possibilities of their approach for comparative treatment across languages and cultures remain implicit. It is difficult to be sufficiently selective, since their small book is a model of clear, efficient exposition. It demands to be read as a whole. "*The essence of metaphor is understanding and experiencing one thing in terms of another*" (Lakoff and Johnson 1980: 5; their italics). Like most of us, I was accustomed to think of metaphor as a "figure of speech," a linguistic phenomenon belonging to the minor ornaments of expression and not to the essential nature of thought. I was also educated to believe that our language is thickly sedimented with "dead metaphors" – expressions that were once vividly evocative but have mainly lost their connotative metaphorical meanings. The first novel idea with which Lakoff and Johnson confronted me was that although it may remain the case that literary metaphors lose their poetic vitality in common use (they do not discuss this), ordinary prosaic "human thought processes are largely metaphorical" and "the human conceptual system is metaphorically structured and defined." The metaphors are far from dead.

One extended example outside the realm of selfhood is essential to give meaning to their title, *Metaphors We Live By*.

"To get an idea of how metaphorical expressions in everyday language can give us insight into the metaphorical nature of the concepts that structure our everyday activities, let us consider the metaphorical concept TIME IS MONEY as it is reflected in contemporary English.

TIME IS MONEY
You're *wasting* my time.
This gadget will *save* you hours.
I don't *have* the time to *give* you.
How do you *spend* your time these days?
That flat tire *cost* me an hour.
I've *invested* a lot of time in her.
I don't *have enough* time to *spare* for that.
You're *running out* of time.
You need to *budget* your time.
Put aside some time for ping pong.
Is that *worth your while*?
Do you *have* much time *left*?
He's living on *borrowed* time.
You don't *use* your time *profitably*.
I *lost* a lot of time when I got sick.
Thank you for your time.

Time in our culture is a valuable commodity. It is a limited resource that we use to accomplish our goals. Because of the way that the concept of work has developed in modern Western culture, where work is typically associated with the time it takes and time is precisely quantified, it has become customary to pay people by the hour, week, or year. In our culture TIME IS MONEY in many ways: telephone message

units, hourly wages, hotel room rates, yearly budgets, interest
on loans, and paying your debt to society by serving time.'
These practices are relatively new in the history of the human
race, and by no means do they exist in all cultures. They have
arisen in modern industrialized societies and structure our
basic everyday activities in a very profound way.

Corresponding to the fact that we *act* as if time is a valuable
commodity − a limited resource, even money − we *conceive* of
time that way. Thus we understand and experience time as the
kind of thing that can be spent, wasted, budgeted, invested
wisely or poorly, saved, or squandered.

   TIME IS MONEY, TIME IS A LIMITED RESOURCE, and
TIME IS A VALUABLE COMMODITY are all metaphorical
concepts. They are metaphorical since we are using our
everyday experiences with money, limited resources, and
valuable commodities to conceptualize time. This isn't a
necessary way for human beings to conceptualize time; it is
tied to our culture. There are cultures where time is none of
these things.

   The metaphorical concepts TIME IS MONEY, TIME IS
A LIMITED RESOURCE, and TIME IS A VALUABLE
COMMODITY form a single system based on subcategoriz-
ation, since in our society money is a limited resource and
limited resources are valuable commodities. These sub-
categorization relationships characterize entailment relationships between the metaphors. TIME IS MONEY entails that
TIME IS A LIMITED RESOURCE, which entails that TIME IS
A VALUABLE COMMODITY."

                              (Lakoff and Johnson 1980: 7−9)

TIME IS MONEY is an example of what they call *structural*
metaphors, cases in which one concept is structured by another.
Another kind of metaphorical concept they refer to as *orient-
ational* metaphors, in which whole systems of concepts are
organized spatially, as in terms of up−down, in−out, on−off,
near−far, deep−shallow, central−peripheral. HAPPY IS UP,
SAD IS DOWN: MORE IS UP, LESS IS DOWN: GOOD IS UP, BAD
IS DOWN, and so on and on. Speculatively one can suggest in

each case a basis in physical and cultural experience. Even the concepts of scientific theory are often rooted in such metaphors. Thus, the *high* in "high energy particles" is based on MORE IS UP. Personality theory is full of such spatialization.

Still a further class are the *ontological metaphors*, which treat immaterial or unbounded aspects of our experience as entities or substances. Logical critics of human error decry many of these ways of thinking as "reification." Lakoff and Johnson point out, rather, how entity or container metaphors organize large stretches of our everyday thought. Another example, this time closer to ethnopsychology:

"Here are two examples of how the ontological metaphor THE MIND IS AN ENTITY is elaborated in our culture:

THE MIND IS A MACHINE
We're still trying to *grind* out
   the solution to this equation.
My mind just isn't *operating* today.
Boy, the *wheels are turning* now!
I'm a *little rusty* today.
We've been working on this problem all
   day and now we're *running out of steam*.

THE MIND IS A BRITTLE OBJECT
Her ego is very *fragile*.
You have to *handle him with care* since
   his wife's death.
He *broke* under cross-examination.
She is *easily crushed*.
The experience *shattered* him.
I'm *going to pieces*.
His mind *snapped*.

These metaphors specify different kinds of objects. They give us different metaphorical models for what the mind is and thereby allow us to focus on different aspects of mental experience. The MACHINE metaphor gives us a conception of the mind as having an on-off state, a level of efficiency, a productive capacity, an internal mechanism, a source of

energy, and an operating condition. The BRITTLE OBJECT
metaphor is not nearly as rich. It allows us to talk only about
psychological strength. However, there is a range of mental
experience that can be conceived of in terms of either
metaphor. The examples we have in mind are these:

He broke down. (THE MIND IS A MACHINE)
He cracked up. (THE MIND IS A BRITTLE OBJECT)."

(Lakoff and Johnson 1980: 27–8)

As they point out, we take such statements as "He cracked
under pressure" as entirely factual, true or false, not as metaphorical. Ontological metaphors pervade our thought.

Metaphors, the authors assert, enable us to understand one
domain of experience in terms of another. The domains organized by metaphoric relations comprise "experiential gestalts"
that are "natural kinds of experience" such as products of our
bodies, our interactions with the physical environment, and our
interactions with other people. Some of these kinds of experience
may be universal; others will vary across cultures. The concepts
that are used metaphorically to characterize other concepts also
are asserted to correspond to kinds of experience that are natural
in this sense. The meaning of some basic concepts, like that of
love in our culture, inheres primarily in the network of its
metaphorical affinities, which characteristically can be described
as connotationally coherent rather than logically consistent.
Since metaphors organize our experience through their entail-
ments, they thus create social realities for us, and become guides
to action. In this sense (congruent with my conception of the
consequences of our self-understandings), metaphors can involve self-fulfilling prophecies.

To be fair to Lakoff and Johnson, I should add that they are
careful not to overwork their central concept of metaphor. In
their usage, metaphor does do double duty to include what
would otherwise be labeled *analogy*. But they give explicit
treatment to *metonymy*, the general case in which one entity is
used to refer to another, as in letting the part stand for the whole
(*synechdoche* in traditional rhetoric), the producer for the product, the institution for the people responsible, etc. In their

view, metaphor and metonymy are different kinds of processes: "Metaphor is principally a way of conceiving one thing in terms of another, and its primary function is understanding. Metonymy, on the other hand, has primarily a referential function, that is, it allows us to use one entity to *stand for* another" (p. 36). Yet in the relationship chosen for metonymic reference, understanding is also involved, and, as in the case of metaphor, metonymic concepts are systematic and contribute to the coherence of thought and action within the framework of the cultural symbol system. A historically minded commentator cannot help noting that, between them, metaphor and metonymy cover the ground of the old psychological principles of association – similarity and contiguity – and of Frazer's (1951) conceptualization of "primitive" thought and action in terms of homeopathic and contagious magic.

Lakoff and Johnson embed their view of the basic concepts with which metaphor and metonymy operate in terms of prototypical instances, rather than neatly bounded logical sets. At a more complex level, metaphor merges with myth in giving meaningful structure to self and world.

I hope this brief selection conveys some of the persuasive attractiveness of Lakoff and Johnson's exposition. In the present context, it is essential to note that they are only incidentally concerned with the role of metaphor in framing concepts of selfhood, and hardly at all with the comparison of metaphorical constructions across languages and cultures. In a word, they do not do *our* job for us. But they provide us with powerful tools that can be adapted to our purposes. Further, by their insistence, well-exemplified, that the entire texture of human conceptualization is inherently metaphorical, they demystify what now in a sense appears to be the smaller claim that consciousness is metaphorical (Jaynes) or that metaphorical thinking is constitutive of our selfhood, as I have been asserting. The metaphorical texture of our views of self is part and parcel of our metaphorical construction of the world – necessarily so, since our interpretations of self and world emerge together in individual infancy. Presumably cultural interpretations of self and world have been linked in tandem ever since they emerged in human prehistory.

Metaphoric consciousness further considered

With the conceptual equipment provided by Lakoff and Johnson, we can now return to Jaynes's (1976) treatment of the metaphoric nature of our self-consciousness. Spatialization metaphors are central, for the mind-space of our experience has no literal location in geography; its spatiality is entailed by metaphoric linkages to such things as seeing with the eyes or moving along on the road. Thus we talk, and find ourselves thinking, in such terms as "the mind's eye" and "seeing the solution clearly." And we assume a mind-space in which these metaphorical events occur – for us, somewhere "inside our heads," though not for Aristotle, who thought the brain served to cool the blood, and put the mind-space somewhere near the heart. As Jaynes observes, we do use our brains in thinking and being conscious, but we also use them in riding a bicycle. No more than our bicycle riding is our consciousness "really" located inside our heads.

Consciousness is an especially complex metaphoric construction, which, once attained, provides a framework for interpreting our remembered past, our anticipated future, and the world around us. Jaynes proposes several key features of consciousness as metaphorically structured: among them, spatialization – very widely applied, even to temporal relationships; narratization – the interpretation of our own activity in the plot structure of intentionality; and the presence of a metaphoric "I" and "Me" in this spatialized and narratized construction of experience. Such a grandly ambitious view of reflective consciousness seems in tune with modern rejections of traditional dualism like Gregory Bateson's (1972) "ecology of mind" and the radical functionalism of Egon Brunswik's (1956) and James Gibson's (1950) different interpretations of perception.

It hinges on a *respectful* view of metaphor, in which "as if" is not regarded pejoratively as a reason for debunking. Our value-laden human world is richly metaphoric; therein lies its tragedy, comedy, and glory. It is not to be disparaged as "merely" metaphoric. Locke's doctrine of "primary" and "secondary" qualities, filtered down to become part of our common sense,

involves just such disparagement. The Lockean distinction is
itself a preemptive metaphor.

The metaphorically constructed microcosm of reflective selfhood and the linked, constructed macrocosm of an interpreted
world have presumably been supportively congruent throughout the previous course of human history and prehistory. One
interpretation of the underlying crisis of modernity is that the
accelerating trajectory of scientific culture and technology with
its preemptive metaphors has produced a dehumanized macrocosm for most people – not just for scientists – that seems
incompatible with the metaphoric microcosm of intentionality
and value in which most of us still live our lives (see Smith 1978a).

Second thoughts about metaphor and science

Having gone so far toward making salient, even celebrating, the
role of metaphor in human thought and in the constitution of
selfhood, I had best draw back momentarily. Is *everything*
metaphorical? Is even science metaphorical? If so, the term loses
meaning. This is not the place for a thorough discussion of
matters that concern the most fundamental issues of epistemology and philosophy of science, but it may be helpful to
sketch briefly the context in which I understand *constitutive*
metaphor.

There is a sense in which even scientific concepts are
metaphorical. They impose coherence upon the plenum from
which they select; they interpret "similarities" within an observed "reality." But they are distinctive from the metaphors of
everyday life and of literature in regard to the discipline of
evidence, logic, and public scrutiny that has arisen in the
scientific subculture to make them as corrigible and cumulative
as possible. Scientific concepts and laws are a special case, a
spectacular cultural emergent, the ideal goals of which inspire
the present enterprise.

At the most encompassing level I would place *generative*
metaphors, what Stephen Pepper (1942) called "world hypotheses": frameworks like mechanism, organicism, and contextu-
alism for "modelling" the macrocosm and microcosm, and – in a

world dominated by science and technology – for providing the metatheories within which scientific paradigms are nested. Generative metaphors are never tested directly, but whole structures of thought and evidential formulation that are based on them may continue to grow in empirical power and human relevance, or may become sterile and peter out; there is a long-run pragmatic control over their fate.

Constitutive metaphors that contribute to the composition of human consciousness and selfhood would be the next in comprehensive import. Here is where my concern has been primarily focused. These metaphors participate in the formation of emergent human nature. This is the special realm of self-fulfilling prophecy.

Then I would add, with some ambiguity, a class of *expository* metaphors: those embedded in the continually reconstructed narratives of our own lives (Gergen and Gergen 1983), and in the continually reconstructed formulations of personality theory. Narratives are more complex structures than metaphors, and merge into theory and myth. We all have our own theories and myths about ourselves, our "self-understanding," which is under continual revision. The general import of this chapter is that our expository metaphors about ourselves tend to become constitutive metaphors: there is no clean line between the two classes. The case is similar, I think, for the expository metaphors of personality theory. In this respect, psychoanalysis has been particularly rich. The metaphorical institutions of the person – id, ego, and super-ego, in the Latinate perversion of Freud's good German – became for a while more identifiable functionally in people at large, one can speculate, *because* psychoanalysis reified them metaphorically.

These considerations pose complex problems for personality theory. Within our chosen generative metaphorical frame – for most of us, mostly contextual or organicist (systems theory) – we aspire to formulations that meet the tests of science. But because people's and psychologist's narrative metaphors may become constitutive metaphors, the formulations we can arrive at which seem to meet the scientific test may lack the stability and transcultural validity of formulations in the natural sciences.

Culture and the content of selfhood

What, then, of the cultural content of metaphors of mind and selfhood? Jaynes suggests that symbolic culture is radically constitutive of consciousness, but he relies too exclusively on the written records of Mediterranean civilization. The challenge is clearly to pursue the question in cultures that have remained distinct from the modern western model. Of course, the "psychic unity of mankind" may be far greater than Jaynes's radical view assumes: an important conclusion if it is sustained. Our experience a quarter century ago in trying to break out of the closed circle of language in attempts to test the Whorfian hypothesis should leave us warned of the methodological traps and difficulties likely to beset such research.

Whatever the outcome with respect to basic psychic unity, we can be sure that differences in how people are culturally disposed to interpret themselves make a difference in their lives. Consider, for example, the cultural analogue to a concept popular among personality psychologists, "implicit personality theories."

Implicit theories of personality and psychology

During the dismal recent period when psychologists were skeptical of the very notion of personality dispositions, yet found that when they asked people to rate other persons on a series of adjectival traits they got stable predictable patterns of correlation, it became fashionable to attribute such patterns not to possible real personality structures in the persons rated but to the implicit personality theories held by the raters (see Schneider 1973). Implicit personality theories include the basis for "halo effects," the assumption that good qualities go together, likewise bad ones. They include assumptions about the relations between physique and temperament – the jolly fat man, the lean and hungry look – which have the possibility of becoming self-confirming.

People's implicit personality theories are obviously partly idiosyncratic, but there must also be strong historical and cultural components. For a recent example, as Freudian psychology permeated western culture, common-sense theory about the interpretation of human action was clearly affected. For another, stereotypic conceptions of male and female personality have obviously undergone changes in the past in our society, and are presently under strong feminist attack that is producing further rapid change.

George Miller's (1969) often cited remarks about how psychologists contribute to human welfare by "giving psychology away" bear on the diffusion of *explicit* psychological theory into the general culture. I am more skeptical than Miller about the social value of psychology's contribution thus far: we would be hard put to demonstrate a favorable cost − benefit balance for this indirect impact of contemporary psychology. In this connection, Hannah Arendt's (1958: 322) passing comment comes to mind, that the danger in the positivistic/behavioristic view of human nature is not that it is true as a description of the empirical world, but that it might *become* true in the mode of self-fulfilling prophecy if people were to come to believe in it consensually!

In general, once we escape from the dogmatic situationism that dictated an empty personality, the question becomes pertinent once again as to how, and to what extent, culturally shared implicit personality theories may actually be formative of personality. The narrower scope implied by "implicit personality theory" and the broader concerns suggested by Miller and Arendt both fall short of Jaynes' grand speculations about how metaphoric thought is constitutive of the entire realm of self-consciousness. The full range of relationships suggested by these examples would be encompassed in the kind of ethnopsychology that I am calling for.

Transformations of selfhood and transformative metaphors

Under the influence of contemporary cognitive psychology, there is a danger of overemphasizing conscious interpretations of selfhood, of who we are as persons. Less conscious, more tacit and affect-laden aspects are evoked in a literary critic's classic of western ethnopsychology: Lionel Trilling's *Sincerity and Authenticity* (1972) to which I have already referred. In this memorable book, Trilling traced the trajectory of selfhood as reflected in western European literature since the Renaissance. He started with the ideal of *sincerity* in Shakespeare's poetic formulation:

> This above all: to thy own self be true
> And it must follow, as the night the day,
> Thou canst not then be false to any man.

Through literary sources, Trilling followed the subsequent course of selfhood toward a skeptical view, in which sincerity, as an attribute of the well-integrated person, becomes hard to conceive, and gets replaced by authenticity to the possibly chaotic impulse. Trilling's account is supplemented by the recent critic Bersoni (1976), who celebrates the fragmented selfhood that Trilling deplored. I see Gergen (1971) as taking a similar position, in theoretical social psychology, as does Lifton (1976) in his concept of the Protean self. The very concept of integral selfhood underlying the ideal of sincerity is coming to seem an illusion. The old, metaphoric concept of the Christian soul is being replaced by less integral concepts – I fear to our considerable loss.

Although integral selfhood is important and good in my personal scheme of values, as a social-cultural scientist I cannot propose *the* self as a central concept. It is one of the problems of modern life in contemporary western society that integral selfhood is relatively rare and difficult to attain. With Trilling as a guide, I find it attractive to believe that sensed unity of selfhood may have been more accessible by persons of the advantaged classes in the Renaissance. The cult of the individual in Montaigne, Cellini, Rembrandt, Dürer, and Shakespeare is strongly persuasive. But Trilling and Laing are obviously right: many features of modern society make integral selfhood harder to attain today.

Any review of the treatment by psychology of metaphoric ingredients in the constitution of selfhood must attend to the mythopoeic writings of Carl Jung (e.g. 1966). Jung was not a scientist, and his writings need to be read in the interpretive humanistic vein rather than in a scientifically critical one. All the same, Jung gave a sensitive meta-metaphorical formulation to metaphorical processes that a science of persons must eventually come to terms with. As I try to read Jung, I find myself reformulating one set of his "archetypes of the collective unconscious" as proposals for relatively pan-human metaphors of recurrent experiences and relationships in the human condition, including metaphors provided by the seasonal cycle of the natural and agricultural world and by the life cycle inherent in the lives of individual persons and families. These archetypes are the stuff of thematic recurrences in world folklore. Another set of Jungian archetypes – Animus, Anima, Persona, Shadow – are presented as dynamic symbols of aspects of being a person that he claims are formative of personhood. His archetype of the Self appears as a metaphoric ideal that supposedly provides a template for "individuation" – the emergence of personal integrity. Is such a Self archetype a human universal, as Jung implies? What indeed are the cultural limits to his formulations?

Selfhood and culture change

From the standpoint of cross-cultural studies, change in culturally shared self-conceptions should be an interesting ingredient in the study of acculturation and modernization. In the classic study of *Becoming Modern* by Inkeles and Smith (1974), the sense of efficacy and the belief that the world is benign and supportive of human effort emerged as parts of the syndrome of modernity. In spite of the limitations in value perspectives that follow from the rootedness of this work in the development policies of the 1950s and 1960s, it still makes sense to regard self-conception as *agent* rather than *patient* as an aspect of modernity, and, indeed, as an attribute likely in the long run to be valued in a way that transcends cultures. It is involved in Levi-Strauss's contrast between "hot" and "cold" cultures. To study how culturally supported self-conceptions result from and mediate transitions into the modern homogenized world is a large agenda. For those who worry about the very fact of homogenization from either a principled or a nostalgic standpoint, a close look at how peoples

in transition actually conceive themselves should be very
relevant.

Conclusions and summary

When as a staff member of the Social Science Research Council a
generation ago I assisted in launching Whiting's cross-cultural
studies of child-rearing and of socialization, we liked to view the
array of still surviving nonliterate cultures as a natural laboratory. (That rhetoric would get aspirants to cross-cultural
research nowhere today!) Our stance was objective and positivistic. Cross-cultural comparison allowed the consequences of a
wide range of child-rearing practices to be studied under
conditions in which even the extremes of the distribution were
normative. Many of the old problems linking socialization,
modal personality, and cultural coherence remain interesting
today, but they are bound to look different from the new
perspective in which meanings as well as causes require consideration, and in which the "subjects" of our research require a
different kind of respect. Our present stance, embarking on the
study of "culture and self," is different from that of participants
in the "culture and personality" movement – toward the task of
the human sciences, toward the nature and significance of data,
and toward ourselves.

We are all too aware of problems in the modern world that put
at risk the future of humanity, and indeed of life on earth. How
we construe ourselves and one another is a crucial aspect of
determining what we will make of our future, complementary to
the more obvious issue of how we construe the world.

Like our predecessors in human history and prehistory and
our contemporaries in other cultures, we live as metaphoric
actors in a metaphoric reality, a reality of *as if*. Yet this is the
only world we know; it is not a pseudo-world. Our interpretation of it undergoes continual change as its relation to our
enterprises alters; the changes in our interpretations are constrained and disciplined by feedback from our actions, and to
some extent by the special discipline of scientific enquiry. Our
cultural interpretations of our human nature also change, and

here the constraint of ineluctable fact is looser, or at least different, because our assumptions about ourselves and each other have some of the causal force of fact in a way that is different from our assumptions about the physical world. Comparative cross-cultural studies should illuminate how people's views of themselves interact with their concepts of the world, and deeper knowledge of these relationships might inform our own attempts to find a new footing in a world that has increasingly come to seem unfriendly.

In summary: the study of "culture and self" on which this volume embarks furthers a renaissance of interest in problems abandoned with the demise of the "culture and personality" movement of a generation ago, with differences in metatheoretical orientation, especially involving new concern with reflexive self-regard in terms of cultural symbol systems. I have argued the need for a better-developed "ethnopsychology" displaying and analyzing how culturally contrasting peoples conceptualize their human nature and their personal-social processes.

The standard Meadian account of the emergence of selfhood in symbolic interaction needs correction and refinement in terms of psychological research now in progress, and it needs supplementation with respect to how culturally transmitted symbol systems inform the content of selfhood. We need richer data on people's self-understanding – the self-concepts, self-formulations, and self-theories upon which they draw – and on how these aspects of self-interpretation affect the terms and content of personality organization, as inferentially constructed by the outside observer. Progress on this front is essential if we are to advance in our intendedly general theories of personality beyond the collection of disparate and culture-bound theories bequeathed us by the theorists of a generation ago.

I drew on Lakoff and Johnson's (1980) recent conceptualization of metaphor to provide what seem to me promising underpinnings for the analysis of symbolic culture as constitutive of selfhood. Lakoff and Johnson illustrate richly and systematically how, for speakers of English, metaphorical linkage provides the coherent structure of thought in everyday life, whether in conceptualization of self or of world. I referred also to

Jaynes's (1976) analysis of the metaphoric basis of consciousness as posing the most extreme version of a view that strongly demands cross-cultural testing. At a more modest level, compatible with conventional assumptions about the "psychic unity" of humankind, culturally provided "implicit personality theories" call for study.

How people construe themselves and how their constructions are culturally phrased should interest us not only because they are humanly interesting for their own sake, and scientifically interesting for their bearing on general personality theory, but also because as reflexively conscious creatures people are influenced by their self-conceptions. Their metaphors of selfhood become in part self-fulfilling prophecies. A fuller understanding of this process would seem to be high in priority as knowledge that potentially contributes to human liberation.

References

Abramson, L. Y., Seligman, M. E. P., and Teasdale, J. D. (1978) Learned Helplessness in Humans: Critique and Reformulation. *Journal of Abnormal Psychology* 87:49–74.

Arendt, H. (1958) *The Human condition.* Chicago: University of Chicago Press.

Bateson, G. (1972) *Steps to an Ecology of Mind.* New York: Chandler.

Bernstein, R. J. (1976) *The Restructuring of Political and Social Theory.* New York: Harcourt Brace Jovanovich.

Bersoni, L. (1976) *A Future for Astynax: Character and Desire in Literature.* Boston: Little, Brown.

Brunswik, E. (1956) *Perception and the Representative Design of Psychological Experiments.* Berkeley, Calif.: University of California Press.

Carlson, R. (1971) Where is the Person in Personality Research? *Psychological Bulletin* 75:203–19.

Clifford, J. (1982) *Person and Myth: Maurice Leenhardt in the Melanesian World.* Berkeley, Calif.: University of California Press.

Cooley, C. H. (1902) *Human Nature and the Social Order.* New York: Scribners.

Damon, W. and Hart, D. (1982) The Development of Self-Understanding from Infancy through Adolescence. *Child Development* 53:841–64.

Epstein, S. (1973) The Self-Concept Revisited: Or a Theory of a Theory. *American Psychologist* 28:404–16.

_____ (1979) The Stability of Behavior: I. On Predicting Most of the People Much of the Time. *Journal of Personality and Social Psychology* 37:1097–126.

_____ (1980) The Stability of Behavior: II. Implications for Psychological Research. *American Psychologist* 35:790–806.

Fernandez, J. (1974) The Mission of Metaphor in Expressive Culture. *Current Anthropology* 15:119–33.

Frank, L. K. (1939) Projective Methods for the Study of Personality. *Journal of Psychology* 8:389–413.

Frazer, J. G. (1951) *The Golden Bough: A Study in Magic and Religion*, third edn, 13 vols. New York: Macmillan.

Gallup, G. C., Jr. (1977) Self-Recognition in Primates: A Comparative Approach to the Bi-Directional Properties of Consciousness. *American Psychologist* 32:329–38.

Geertz, C. (1973) *The Interpretation of Cultures*. New York: Basic Books.

_____ (1975) On the Nature of Anthropological Understanding. *American Scientist* 63:47–53.

Gergen, K. (1971) *The Concept of Self*. New York: Holt, Rinehart & Winston.

_____ (1973) Social Psychology as History. *Journal of Personality and Social Psychology* 26:390–420.

_____ (1982) *Toward Transformation in Social Knowledge*. New York: Springer Verlag.

Gergen, K. J. and Gergen, M. (1983) Narratives of the Self. In T. R. Sarbin and K. E. Scheibe (eds) *Studies in Social Identity*. New York: Praeger.

Gibson, J. J. (1950) *The Perception of the Visual World*. Boston: Houghton-Mifflin.

Hallowell, A. I. (1955) *Culture and Experience*. Philadelphia, PA: University of Pennsylvania Press.

Harter, S. (1983) Developmental Perspectives on the Self-System. In M. Hetherington (ed.) *Carmichael's Manual of Child Psychology*. vol. 4, *Social and Personality Development*. New York: Wiley.

Harvey, J. H., Town, J. P., and Yarkin, K. L. (1981) How Fundamental Is "The Fundamental Attribution Error?" *Journal of Personality and Social Psychology* 40:346–49.

Heelas, P. L. F. and Lock, A. J. (eds) (1981) *Indigenous Psychologies: The Anthropology of the Self*. New York and London: Academic Press.

Holt, R. R. (1972) Freud's Mechanistic and Humanistic Images of Man. *Psychoanalysis and Contemporary Science* 1:3–24.

Horney, K. (1939) *New Ways in Psychoanalysis*. New York: W. W. Norton.

Hull, C. L. (1943) *Principles of behavior*. New York: Appleton-Century.

Inkeles, A. and Smith, D. H. (1974) *Becoming Modern*. Cambridge, Mass.: Harvard University Press.

James, W. (1890) The Consciousness of Self. In *Principles of Psychology*, vol. 1. New York: Holt, Rinehart & Winston.

Jaynes, J. (1976) *The Origin of Consciousness in the Breakdown of the Bicameral Mind*. Boston: Houghton-Mifflin.

Jung, C. G. (1966) *Two Essays on Analytical Psychology*, second edn. Princeton, NJ: Princeton University Press.

Kagan, J. (1981) *The Second Year*. Cambridge, Mass.: Harvard University Press.

Kelly, G. A. (1955) *The Psychology of Personal Constructs*, (2 vols). New York: W. W. Norton.

Kluckhohn, C., Murray, H. A., and Schneider, D. M. (eds) (1953) *Personality in Nature, Society, and Culture*, second edn. New York: Alfred A. Knopf.

Koffka, K. (1935) *Principles of Gestalt Psychology*. New York: Harcourt, Brace Jovanovich.

Lakoff, G. and Johnson, M. (1980) *Metaphors We Live By*. Chicago: University of Chicago Press.

LeVine, R. (1973) *Culture, Behavior, and Personality*. Chicago: Aldine.

Lewis, M. and Brooks-Gunn, J. (1979) *Social Cognition and the Acquisition of Self*. New York: Plenum Press.

Lifton, R. J. (1976) *The Life of the Self: Toward a New Psychology*. New York: Simon & Schuster.

Lindzey, G. (1961) *Projective Techniques and Cross-Cultural Research*. New York: Appleton-Century-Crofts.

Loevinger, J. (1976) *Ego Development*. San Francisco: Jossey-Bass.

Magnusson, D. and Endler, N. S. (eds) (1977) *Personality at the Crossroads: Current Issues in Interactional Psychology*. Hillsdale, NJ: Erlbaum.

Mead, G. H. (1934) *Mind, Self, and Society*. Chicago: University of Chicago Press.

Miller, G. A. (1969) Psychology as a Means of Promoting Human Welfare. *American Psychologist* 24: 1063–075.

Murphy, J. M. (1976) Psychiatric Labeling in Cross-Cultural Perspective. *Science* 191: 1019–028.

——— (1981) Abnormal Behavior in Traditional Societies: Labels, Explanations, and Social Reactions. In R. H. Monroe, R. L. Monroe, and B. B. Whiting (eds) *Handbook of Cross-Cultural Human Development*. New York: Garland.

Onians, R. B. (1973) *The Origins of European Thought*. New York: Arno Press. First published in 1951.

Ortony, A. (ed.) (1979) *Metaphor and Thought*. New York: Cambridge University Press.

Pepper, S. C. (1942) *World Hypotheses*. Berkeley, Calif.: University of California Press.

Ricoeur, P. (1970) *Freud and Philosophy: An Essay on Interpretation*. New Haven, Conn. Yale University Press.

Rosaldo, M. Z. (1984) Toward an Anthropology of Self and Feeling. In R. S. and R. Levine (eds) *Culture Theory: Essays on Mind, Self, and Emotion*. New York: Cambridge University Press.

Ross, L. (1977) The Intuitive Psychologist and His Shortcomings: Distortions in the Attribution Process. In L. Berkowitz (ed.) *Advances in Experimental Social Psychology*. New York: Academic Press.

Sacks, S. (ed.) (1979) *On Metaphor*. Chicago: University of Chicago Press.

Schafer, R. (1976) *A New Language for Psychoanalysis*. New Haven, Conn.: Yale University Press.

Schneider, D. J. (1973) Implicit Personality Theory: A Review. *Psychological Bulletin* 79: 294–309.

Schotter, J. (1981) Telling and Reporting: Prospective and Retrospective Uses of Self-Ascriptions. In C. Antaki (ed.) *The Psychology of Ordinary Explanations of Social Behavior*. New York: Academic Press.

Schutz, A. (1967) *Phenomenology of the Social World*. Evanston, Ill.: Northwestern University Press.

Seligman, M. (1968) *Helplessness: On Depression, Development, and Death*. San Francisco: W. H. Freeman.

Schweder, R. A. and Bourne, E. J. (1982) Does the Concept of the Person Vary Cross-Culturally? In A. J. Marsella and G. M. White (eds) *Cultural Conceptions of Mental Health and Therapy*. Dodrecht, Netherlands and Boston, Mass.: D. Reidel.

Smith, M. B. (1976) Social Psychology, Science, and History: So What? *Personality and Social Psychology Bulletin* 2: 438–44.

―――― (1978a) Perspectives on Selfhood. *American Psychologist* 33: 1053–063.

―――― (1978b) What It Means to Be Human. In R. Fitzgerald (ed.) *What It Means to Be Human*. Rushcutters' Bay, NSW: Pergamon (Australia).

―――― (1980) Attitudes, Values, and Selfhood. In H. E. Howe and M. M. Page (eds) *Nebraska Symposium on Motivation 1979*. Lincoln: University of Nebraska Press.

―――― (1983a) The Shaping of American Social Psychology: A Personal

Perspective from the Periphery. *Personality and Social Psychology Bulletin* 9: 165–80.

—— (1983b) Hope and Despair: Keys to the Socio-Psychodynamics of Youth. *American Journal of Orthopsychiatry* 53: 388–99.

—— (1984) Humanistic Psychology. In R. Corsini (ed.) *Encyclopedia of Psychology*. New York: Wiley.

Snell, B. (1953) *The Discovery of Mind: The Greek Origins of European Thought*. Oxford: Basil Blackwell.

Spiro, M. (1967) *Burmese Supernaturalism: A Study in the Explanation and Reduction of Suffering*. Englewood Cliffs, NJ: Prentice-Hall.

Trilling, L. (1972) *Sincerity and Authenticity*. Cambridge, Mass.: Harvard University Press.

Whiting, J. (1966) *Field Guide for a Study of Socialization. Six Cultures: Studies in Child-Rearing*, vol. 1. New York: Wiley.

Wylie, R. C. (vol. 1 1974; vol. 2 1979) *The Self Concept*, rev. edn. Lincoln, Nebraska: University of Nebraska Press.

PART II

Western Perspectives
on Self

4

The Western Concept
of Self

Frank Johnson

Introduction

This chapter has two purposes which parallel the design of the present volume, *Culture and Self*. The first purpose is concerned with a review of historical and contemporary western contributions to the concept of self. The second purpose is to describe qualitative features of subjective experience held to be prominent in persons living in European, Commonwealth, and American cultures. Expositions of these traits will use textual, cultural, and situational commentary, contributing to an impression of western ways of thinking, particularly in their North American version. Some of this latter description will make cross-cultural comparison to accounts of Japanese subjectivity.

Comparisons of eastern and western ways of thinking exploit literary, scientific, philosophic, and cultural documentaries deriving from eastern and western nations and civilizations – past and present. Arthur Wright (1964) has summarized the problems inherent in attempting systematic comparisons between "east" and "west." He properly cautions that "false antitheses" and "monolithic comparisons" can readily slip into the cliché generalization and overstatement of the obvious. This risk is particularly high in condensed versions of cross-cultural comparison and is accepted as inevitable by the present author.

Two reservations deserve mention. First, generalizations stressing differences between east and west gloss over the diversity within both eastern and western traditions themselves

– over different eras, among different cultures, and as these traditions are differentially experienced by individuals. Second, such comparisons between east and west necessarily set aside civilizations and nations whose traditions have not been recorded in a manner permitting equivalent representation. Also, any description of the *self* in western societies may be seen as a play within a play. The conceptual threads from philosophy, theology, psychology, and social science assembled in this chapter not only constitute an historical record, but simultaneously are part of a cultural record within which westerners have inevitably *enacted* self in the process of *explaining* self. In that sense, this chapter is partly an "emic" statement about western world views, as well as an "etic" selection of scholarly viewpoints which scientifically examine the western self. It is important to bear in mind that a résumé of writings on the concept of the western self summarizes a compendium of selected viewpoints that intrinsically emphasize Aristotelian logic, Cartesian perspective, and (primarily) Christian orthodox insistence (Miller 1981).

Definitions and uses of the concept of self in the west

The word *self* is a noun whose primary definition is "the entire person of an individual" (Webster 1966). Its use as a prefix is extravagant: a recent unabridged dictionary has 415 self-referants denoting human existential states and personal actions (Webster 1966: 2059–061). Grammatically, such terms are reflexive nouns and adjectives which relate an extensive range of cognitive states, temperaments, emotions, and personal actions to the self. Its use as a suffix is narrower and occurs in the important but limited number of reflexive pronouns: "myself," "himself," "herself," "itself," "ourselves," and "themselves." (The self-referential possessives "my" and ' mine," although emphasized in some developmental theories as coterminous with *self*, are not systematically included in theories of the adult self.) Concepts and descriptions relating to self extend across many disciplines over a long history in various cultures, religions, and scholarly communities.

Despite this extensiveness over time and among disciplines, several salient consistencies in definition and conception are recurrent. For example, the concept of self is ordinarily defined as a *unitary phenomenon*; it is used to refer to a particular, individual person (or person-system) and not to a "personality" or to an aggregate of factors which "add up" to a person. The concept of self is typically separated into a nominative ("I") *self-as-subject*, and an accusative ("me") *self-as-object*. *Self-as-object* includes both the idea of *self as a social object to others* and that of *self as a social (and psychological) object unto itself*. Various disciplines address the *self* across both subjective and objective dimensions, although emphasisis is often applied to one rather than both dimensions. For example, the self-as-subject (or agent) which "initiates action" is a common research construction in psychology and social psychology. In contrast, research in the social sciences has focused on the self as a social object defined and determined by actions occurring within a collectivity of "others." Research and descriptions enquiring into the self as a reflective psychological object unto itself have been prominent in phenomenology as well as within psychoanalysis. As noted by both English and English (1958) and Wylie (1961), the self as "object known to itself" has been the subject of much social psychological research concerned with validating measures of reflective states of self-perception and self-esteem. A comprehensive review of this latter research has been recently updated by Wylie (1974, 1979). Constructions relating to "self-concept" have been clarified by Rosenberg (1979).

In various disciplines, self theory may include a description of *loss of self* in two general ways: as an intentional, mystical transcendence (e.g. through trance, meditation, or dedication to an ideology or "cause") and as a loss of self encountered in the face of personal disorganization, existential crisis, unexpected loss of control, or psychological disability In virtually all systematic explanations of self, the concept of *bodily self* is prominent and is connected to a complex ontogeny of growth, development, experience of injury, and aging. Various reviews of bodily self or "body image" (Schilder 1935; Piaget 1952; Fisher and Cleveland 1958) document the importance of tactile, kinesthetic, and motoric self-referrants as they become progressively differentiated during infancy and early childhood. These pre-reflective, sensory-motor experiences – involved in orientation, cognition, and action – are acknowledged to be connected to later symbolical representations, particularly to the self-concept. In terms of development, any functional concept of self presupposes either evidence or strong inference of *reflective* awareness. In this sense, infants and pre-reflective children are held not to demonstrate manifest or complete selves. In fact, the nascent development of self (or reflective *ego*) in various personality systems is depicted as first becoming apparent through a series of discriminations made by the infant between experiences differentially perceived as internal, external, and social-environmental. Despite differences in disciplines and terminologies, the differentiation of self is consistently connected to the attainment of a degree of reflective awareness, as described in James (1950), Peirce (1934), Mead (1913), Werner (1948), Freud (1923), and Piaget (1952).

This agreement concerning the development of self (as reflective ego) among theorists from separate disciplines belies the salient differences in methods, terms, and explanations respectively used in philosophy, social psychology, psychoanalysis, and developmental psychology. For example, the terms "self" and "ego" are defined and used in many different ways within, as well as between, disciplines. This present chapter will be confined to conventional descriptions of the self, primarily within psychology and social science. A detailed consideration of the historical, conceptual differences in multiple definitions of "self," "ego," "persona," "role," etc. is not possible in this present essay.

As another generalization, the concept of self refers to the characterization of a particular person persistent over time. Alternatively, the term is used to characterize the immediate situational presentations of a particular person during specific encounters within shifting contexts. In the latter, the self is seen as an actor or performer, consciously interpreting ongoing action in the light of previous experience, and calculating responses to achieve both immediate and remote objectives. This "past – present" duality is intrinsic. The existence of an expectant, contemporaneous self presupposes the prior existence of a developmental, experiential self. Thus in various systems the current self is systematically described as an accretion of behaviors or performances over time, through a variety of contexts and experiences, continuities and discontinuities. Self-in-action, therefore, implicates dynamic change as well as continuity. Self is seen as situational, and yet as something which transcends the ebb and flow of transitory encounters and reflections.

A number of theoretical explanations of the self characterize the concept by using models of "external" and "internal" communication. Social interactionists, for example, stress that the self is a "creation," like any other symbolical object; that it is a social, communicative construction interactionally emerging through a symbolical process (as in Mead 1922, or Berger and Luckman 1966). In phenomenological and existential descriptions, self is depicted as a waxing and waning focus of consciousness. Closer to eastern models, these descriptions emphasize that awareness of self takes the form of a fluctuating state featuring varying degrees of alertness, concentration, emotion, fantasy, and purposeful reflection – these various states being cued by the situational contexts in which the self is engaged as a participant.

Whether depicted in solitary reflection or in reciprocal interaction, the surface characteristics of self are described by some theorists as linguistic and paralinguistic constructions, constituted of words and gestures which convey complex ideas, feelings, intentions, values, and interpretations – both to self and to other interactants.

Many theoretical descriptions of the self utilize both functional and graphic divisions of self separated into a number of different "levels" (or "layers") representing relatively distinctive states of consciousness, perception and/or anticipation of action corresponding to differing social-psychological conditions encountered by the person. Such divisions are germane to virtually all systems of self (and personality) but vary in their elegance, complexity, and comprehensiveness. These divisions also vary in the specific ways in which these "levels" of experience are ascribed and given significance. All theories make distinctions between phenomena relating to *inner self* and those relating to *outer self*. Freudian psychoanalysis, for example, has concentrated on an elaborate structuralization of what other theorists would term "inner self." Hsu's description of self (see Chapter 2) applies Freudian metapsychology to his two innermost cores of pre-conscious and unconscious functioning ordinarily inapparent in the social-psychological interactions with family, friends, and general society (see pp. 28–9). Similarly, George DeVos (Chapter 5) has heuristically divided self-functioning into operational categories examined against both *adaptive* and *adjustive* criteria.

The purpose of this chapter is to review a number of systematic western descriptions of self. To facilitate this, a rudimentary separation of the phenomenology of self into three divisions of personal consciousness (and related experience) will be used – specifically the categories of *inner self, interpersonal self,* and *social self*. Overlap among these divisions is, of course, presumed. However, the designations "inner," "interpersonal," and "social" levels of self acknowledge those characteristics of consciousness (or "psychological sets") that inhere in:

(a) states of mind accompanying *inner experiences* involving solitary communication (as in fantasy, trance, reverie, introspection, prayer, concentrated problem solving, etc.);

(b) states of mind associated with *interpersonal experiences* featuring explicit communication in dyadic and small groups involving direct, reciprocal interaction (as in conversations, encounters, small group meetings, etc.);

(c) states of mind attending more diffuse *social experiences* characterized by vague, nonreciprocal interaction within larger groups and congregations of individuals (as in crowds, attending a theatre, performing repetitive mechanical work in a factory, etc.).

Obviously, the range of distinctive states of awareness and specialized concentration is vast within each of these three general levels. Also, fluctuations between these general states of consciousness occur in a fluid manner, as the individual experiences a variety of situations, and either lapses into or consciously chooses a mode of awareness appropriate and adaptive to the encounter. Many theories of personality are devoted to the detailed description of reflective and actional operations within one or more of these levels, usually at the expense of not accounting for actions and "psychological sets" connected to other levels. Unlike theories of personality, theories of self necessarily undertake the formidable responsibility of describing behaviors and psychological states relating to *all three levels*. Some of the difficult definitional and methodological problems inherent in systematic research on the self have been capably reviewed by Wylie (1961, 1974, 1979) and Rosenberg (1979).

In concluding this introduction, two generalities deserve mention. In both eastern and western concepts of the self, the *bipolar* quality of the term, self, is conspicuous. Self is both subjective (nominative) and objective (accusative). A number of paired terms are used to accentuate the division between these bipolar qualities of self. As Murphy stated, "[The self] is a thing perceived, and it is also a thing conceived; in both senses it is constantly responded to" (Murphy 1947:479). Eastern models of self deal more with the conception as simultaneously subjective and objective. Heuristically, it is a common (western) emphasis to relegate *self-as-subject* primarily to internal states of decision and control, and to relegate *self-as-object* (to others) to external and reciprocal social relatedness. However, so-called internal states are, in a number of systematic ways, objectifiable, and communicable to others. In the opposite direction, observation of the social performances of others involves the interpretive processes of the observer inevitably implicating the subjectivity of the "outside" interpreters.

Descriptions and formulations of self also tend toward division into "self-as-process" versus "self-as-state" – the former accentuating transactional, situational, and contextual variables, the latter emphasizing internal, structural, and biological factors. These differences in emphasis (and others already cited) testify to some of the confusion and complexity inherent in the attempt to define the self conceptually. Some of the apparent paradoxes relate to differences in methodology and emphasis among various researchers from psychology, psychoanalysis, and the social sciences. Other factors influencing the conception of self will be addressed later.

Historical background of the western concept of self

Recent western theories of the self are historically traced to descriptions of individual existence refined within the disciplines of theology, philosophy, and psychology during the late nineteenth and early twentieth centuries. Prior to the mid-1900s, concepts and theories regarding individual perception, cognition, memory, action, etc., were deliberated by a series of Middle Eastern, European, and British philosophers. Until the 1800s, attempts at collective and systematic descriptions of self remained the province of theology and philosophy. Operational questions concerning the functions of the self were described as inherent organizations of faculties of *mind* held to underlie (i.e. "cause") observed speech and action. Parallel questions regarding the faculties of *soul* were independently raised to account for those functions which monitored intentionality and responsibility governing purposive actions. Following the Enlightenment, questions relating to the animation of the body sought physical, mechanical, and biochemical explanations. In the western world, particularly, questions about the body were methodically dissociated from questions of the mind and/or soul. Although most commonly described as "Cartesian," such dissociation derived support from other philosophical, theological, and folk traditions in the west. Such traditions supported naturalistic observations that phenomena could be rudimentarily divided into categories involving natural and preternatural causation – ultimately reflecting the distinctive qualities of material "things" versus immaterial "things." Mind/body distinctions enjoyed a relative ascendency in the western world as describing methodically and philosophically different forms of reality. As repeatedly noted, the western emphasis on dualism left its imprint on science, psychology, and ordinary "ways of thinking"(see Ryle 1949).

Some of the historical connections among western psychology, philosophy, and theology have been reviewed and condensed by Murphy and Murphy (1968). Their summary and others (Allport 1943; Boring 1950; Sahakian 1975) emphasize the connections through scholastic philosophy derived from pre-Christian theologies and philosophies associated with Greek, Roman, Judaic, and Islamic sources. The significance of this lineage for the present chapter lies in the relative preponderance of montheism and monistic explanations of "being" in western societies, over pluralistic and polytheistic conceptions (Hillman 1971; Niebuhr 1970; Miller 1974). The implications of this ascendance for western descriptions of self will be discussed later.

At mid-nineteenth century, the formal discipline of psychology emerged as independent of philosophy, shifting from abstract concerns with faculties of "soul" and "mind," to an experimental focus on explanations of bodily perception (e.g. the works of Wundt and Helmholtz). Using methodologies from the physical sciences and physiology, hypotheses were raised and tested regarding sensation, perception, and neural function leading to explanations of these "faculties" in terms of the topographical anatomy of the peripheral and central nervous systems. Sensation, perception, and motor actions were explained through the characteristics of measurable electrical, neurochemical, and physical processes. In an understandable reaction against centuries of philosophical psychology, non-empirical questions relating to the "mind" and "self" were avoided as the discipline of experimental psychology turned away from teleological formulations and the apparently immeasurable abyss of subjectivity. This led to seventy years of partial moratorium (1870 – 1940) within mainstream western psychology which essentially ignored the "self" as a useful construct. As Allport commented:

"One of the oddest events in the history of modern psychology is the manner in which the ego – or self – became sidetracked and lost from view. I say it is odd because the existence of one's own self is the one fact of which every mortal person – every psychologist included – is perfectly convinced."

(Allport 1943: 71)

As traced by Gardner and Lois Murphy (1969), the Continental Associationist tradition eventually flowered in Great Britain and America in the works of Royce, Dewey, Peirce, and James, only to go underground during the next forty years. William James's (1950) comprehensive formulations, synthesized in 1890, placed the self continuously in both the foreground and background of other functions and faculties of mental organization. Despite his influence the scientific study of self yielded to the more efficient construct of *personality*, in its various measurable components reflecting intelligence, memory, perception, etc. Although denied prominence in psychology itself, the concept of self re-emerged in the philosophical, social psychology of George Herbert Mead (1913, 1922), eventually branching into a social-interactionist perspective (Baldwin, Cooley) and, much later, into the phenomenological and ethnomethodological positions in sociology (Schutz, Garfinkle). Historically related to the social-interactionist tradition, a psychiatric version of the self emerged through the interpersonal perspectives of Harry Stack Sullivan (1937, 1956) and later through a number of interactional and transactional theorists (Grinker *et al.* 1956; Berne 1967; Spiegel 1971). Another important contribution to self theory comes from Erving Goffman, who had described contemporaneous interactions on the basis of "presentation of self" in the context of "strips" and "frames" of action exemplified in a number of mundane and significant life situations (Goffman 1959, 1967, 1974).

As noted by Allport (1943), an important body of theory explicitly concentrating on subjectivity began to be elaborated at the turn of the century through Freudian psychoanalysis. Building on the French Associationist tradition (Charcot) and using the insights of clinical practice, a complex metapsychology was constructed over a period of thirty years, emphasizing unconscious, determinative forces held to underlie normal and abnormal personal functioning. Historically and institutionally distinct from academic psychology, Freud and his followers have implicitly clarified portions of a concept of self through an unconscious, causal – motivational explanation of human functioning. In this body of theory, a topological system originally identified the *ego* as a defensive agent negotiating between an internal need system (the *id*) and an external reality system (internally represented as the *super-ego*). However, within Freudian psychoanalysis, the term *self* has had a curious career. In the evolution of Freud's writings, the structural and dynamic formulations of the *id* and *super-ego* chronologically preceded detailed descriptions of the *ego* – a topological area in which functions relating to the self might be compared. Also a series of early defections and challenges to orthodoxy (Jung, Adler, Binswanger) made any "self-psychology" politically and conceptually destabilizing to the then thirty-year-old metapsychology. Freud's introduction of object-relations theory in 1923 eventually led a series of writers from the orthodox tradition to expand the ego beyond its defensive definition to include adaptive, developmental, and executive functions, more directly homologous to some conscious (and unconscious) aspects of self defined in other systems of personality (Reich, Hartman, Freud, etc.). A second wave of revisionists (e.g. Horney and Sullivan) during the 1930s again stressed individual (or self) concepts, stimulating an avoidance by the mainstream community. Recently the controversy has surfaced in the popular response to the writings of Kohut (1971, 1977) whose theoretical accentuation of *self* has seriously challenged orthodox positions. In contrast, Kernberg (1976) has carefully traced ego-functions through a genealogy of object-relations theorists (Jacobsen, Fairbairn, Kernberg) and has extended the importance of "drive-objects" using refined interpretation within the orthodox tradition. Although not defined as "self," the internal structures and ego-functions closely approximate properties and actions attributable to other systems to the self.

In yet another direction the concept of self also maintained a foothold during the early twentieth century through the phenomenologists, both in philosophy and psychology. The Act psychologists and (later) the Gestalt school of psychology continued to deal with the global, organismic factors of "self," visualized as operating in a context of "fields" or "wholes" representing a social psychological "theatre" in which individual action took place.

Within western theology and philosophy, concepts of the self were largely unaffected by the directions of experimental psychology and continued to deal with the self as a locus of personal responsibility centering on the explicit moral and ethical connotations of human conduct. The works of Charles Peirce (1958) are seminal and will be discussed later. More recently, the American theologian, H. Richard Niebuhr (1970), has focused on the psychological concomitants of immanent, on-going consciousness (i.e. the *self*) in defining responsibility from an interactional, situational perspective (as reviewed by Miller 1974 and Kliever 1977). Niebuhr's concerns have been simultaneously moral and ethical, as well as psychological. His depictions of self and interaction are comparable to some eastern philosophical systems which include implications of responsibility and ethics in the description of self-in-action (Inada 1979). Both Peirce (1958) and Niebuhr (1970) deal with situational (i.e. "contextual") descriptions of personal reality which are structurally similar to some contemporary theories of action in psychology, anthropology, and sociology (Harre 1977; Singer 1980; Schweder 1980; Heap and Roth 1973). Other philosophies of action have focused on the question of individual "agency" but have avoided the concept of self. Robert Nozick (1981) has recently reintroduced the self in the context of an exposition of metaphysics, epistomology, and value.

As yet another emergence, Jungian analytical psychology has consistently dealt with collective, social variables using descriptive terminology and theory concerning the *persona* or self. Also, writers from Adlerian and existential analytic traditions (e.g. Ansbacher, Binswanger) explicitly identified the conscious, social self as the epicenter of personal functioning.

In contrast to these disciplines, contributions from the field of anthropology to the theory of self have been indirect. These contributions derive from extensive ethnographic findings accumulated during the past hundred years. In the examination of human diversity, anthropologists have provided a counterpoint to clinical and research studies conducted by psychologists which have sought to define prototypical and universal personality elements which transcend cultures, nations and eras. In its documentation of cultural relativism, anthropology has laid bare the extensiveness of variation based upon custom, language, kinship, belief system, etc. Paradigmatically stated in the Whorf-Sapir hypothesis, this variation has revealed significant differences in the subjective experience of self contingent on culturally specified norms and socialization practices affecting perception, cognition, communication, and action. During the past ten years, a growing interest in cognitive anthropology has tended to supplant the more traditional psychological anthropology in the study of subjective culture, stressing ethnomethodological principles of investigation.

Parallel to anthropology, the field of linguistics has moved from interests in comparative philology and structure of language to concerns with structural characteristics of actual speech, including psychological and contextual features regulating "to-and-fro" communication. Representing a confluence of cognitive anthropology and linguistics, Singer (1980) has proposed a synthesis of elements from linguistics (Saussure 1959) and pragmatic philosophy (Peirce 1934) in the development of a design for a "semiotic anthropology." He has outlined the use of combined semantic and semiological methodologies leading to explanations of the self.

In academic psychology, as reviewed by Walter Mischel (1968), behavioristic researchers have turned to an examination of situational frames and contextual variables connected to action (behavior). Theodore Mischel (1977) has reflected on this change in orientation in regard to internationalism in psychology:

"[P]sychologists often talk as if one had to decide between the following alternatives: Either (1) behavior is controlled by underlying (inner) mental structures . . . which are relatively stable and exert a generalized, enduring effect on behavior across diverse situations; or (2) behavior is controlled by outer stimulus conditions and changes in response to environmental stimulus changes.

On the first alternative, 'control' is supposed to reside in mental structures in a way that makes situations relatively unimportant. . . . On the second alternative, 'environment' is supposed to exert control in a way that makes mental structures largely irrelevant. . . . Now if these are the alternatives between which one has to decide, then a behaviorist approach, even a radical behaviorism, may become attractive . . . but the counter-intuitive notion that people behave in pretty much the same way regardless of the situation confronting them is easily buried under massive empirical evidence for the situation specific character of behavior."

(Mischel 1977:12)

Mischel predicts that questions concerning a factorial/trait description of personality growing out of controlled, experimental settings will in the future yield to questions relating to the study of real *selves* in actual, multivariate, situational contexts. Exemplary of this, Pervin and Lewis have devised transactional methodologies where the units of study consist of *systematic components* (interactions, transactions) occurring in a *context* which itself is simultaneously a part (i.e. a "variable") within the transaction (Pervin 1979; Pervin and Lewis 1979).

Some structural models of the self

A comprehensive review of theoretical descriptions of self will not be assembled here. Detailed lists of various systems can prove more confounding than illuminating. In the author's opinion it is more instructive to keep three simple divisions of consciousness in mind in examining a selected number of systems. Stated again, these divisions are what can be loosely termed *inner*, *interpersonal*, and *social* states of consciousness, corresponding to three broad categories of awareness involving the self. As a general orientation to theories of the self, Gordon Allport's (1943) eight "categories of self" are useful. Appearing in an article in the early forties which attempted to rehabilitate the concept of self, these categories consist of *self as knower*, as *object of knowledge*, as *primitive selfishness*, as *dominance drive*, as *passive organization of mental processes*, as *"fighter for ends,"* and as the *subjective organization of culture*. In a review of psychoanalytic conceptions of self and ego, Rinsley (1962) employed a functional division of self into "self-as-process" and "self-as-object." Quoting Hall and Lindzey (1957), the "self-as-process" was defined as "...a doer, in the sense that it consists of an active group of processes such as thinking, remembering, and perceiving." Within traditional psychoanalysis, however, those self-as-process functions have continued to emphasize the intrapsychic and unconscious determinants of ego functioning as separated from the external social reality. Concepts concerned with "self-as-object" (unto itself) within psychoanalysis have been dealt with in an even more complicated manner. Within psychoanalysis, some early object relations theorists (Klein, Fairbairn, Guntrip) suggested a compromise of the classical position by introducing the concept of partial internalizations ("partial objects"). Such incomplete or partial incorporations of external reality were seen by them as due to the immaturity of the organism or as a result of a pathological need to defend against unacceptable external or internal threats. As mentioned before, Kohut (1971, 1977) has recently introduced the explicit concept of self into consideration for increased significance in psychoanalytic theory, but in a manner which runs counter to prior theorization.

In contrast to the controversy within psychoanalysis, those within the existential analytic group (Binswanger, Ellenberger, May) have taken the phenomenological position that descriptions of subjective reality can be seen as arbitrary and artificial. Hence, sharp distinctions between what is called "primary process" versus "secondary process" thinking or pre-reflective versus reflective ego states are not accentuated. Similarly, the concepts of self-as-process and self-as-object to itself comfortably fit into the perspective of *Eigenwelt*, as it deals with *welt* and *umwelt*.

Mischel (1977) proposed a categorization of self dividing the concept into terms of *self-knowledge, self-control, self-development*, and *self-intervention*. Another common differentiation is to regard the concept as composed of *cognitive, perceptive, integrative, executive, corporeal*, and *emotional* elements. Social psychology has conventionally divided self functions and states into an extensive list of operational categories, depicting self as an agent examined in a series of attributions concerning *causation, internal states, disposition toward others, monitoring of interaction, impression management*, and so on. Methodologically, the self has been treated as an object (or system) acted upon by other selves (or by larger systems) which produce changes in attitude, mood, opinion, or action. As Wylie (1979) has noted, an extensive empirical research into the concept of self has primarily looked into what she terms *phenomenal concepts* (i.e. conscious and behavioral) rather than *nonphenomenal concepts* (i.e. relating to unconscious aspects of self). She has also commented on the curious neglect of behavioral or contextual variables among investigators in their preoccupation with *attitudinal* dimensions of self.

Clearly, additional systems which address the operationalizing of self-concept might be listed here. However, the purpose of this chapter is to provide some general models, plus a "feel" for the various ways in which western philosophy, psychology, and social science has structured and operationalized the concept, rather than to provide a compendium of all theories. Before describing the "factors" and "parts" applicable to self-theory in general, an observation about phenomenal levels in theory construction will be considered. Both within western theories of self as well as cross-culturally, systematic descriptions vary according to the terms and methodologies used by the theorists, especially as they involve varying *phenomenal levels* through which the system is "explained" or described (Marx 1963; Johnson 1973). Psychological theorizing may be viewed as being based on three different levels of observation: *phenomenal, epiphenomenal*, and *metaphenomenal*.

(a) *Phenomenal descriptions* are those which relate to directly observed actions and where the units of study are quantifiable and replicable. Phenomenal terms are standardized and conventional; they refer to particular objects or actions which are measurable and validatable. Observations may be made of phenomena occurring in both experimental or naturalistic contexts. Clearly, the *self* as a global concept is not phenomenally observable, although behaviors or actions representing functions of self are observable and measurable.

(b) *Epiphenomenal descriptions* are those which define actions through the use of "explanatory" (indexical) terms that abstractly relate to specific, directly measurable events. For example, "self-consciousness," as an epiphenomenal abstraction, might be studied through certain measurable phenomena, e.g. changes in facial expression, galvanic skin response, etc. The epiphenomenal term "self-consciousness" would then function as a *construct*, i.e. "a term which can be defined by operations on symbols" (Rapaport 1953: 238, 266).

(c) *Metaphenomenal descriptions* are at the next level and have a less direct connection between a constructional term and its referant. Such a connection is at a yet higher degree of abstraction and is less formally − i.e. categorically or logically − related to those phenomena which it purports to subsume. Thus metaphenomenal terms are not immediately referable to the behaviors which they attempt to categorize. Such terms utilize a higher degree of generality concerning the consistency between the term and its referant. (An example of this could be an attempt to relate the epiphenomenal construct of "self-consciousness" to a metaphenomenal explanation of "genital shame" or "repressed exhibitionism.") This is not to say that blushing or self-consciousness may not be related to shame or repressed exhibitionism; merely that such connections involve a metapsychological leap.

Confusion occurs when these different phenomenal levels of descriptive terms are ignored. The tendency to concretize ("reify") both constructs and metaphenomenal terms is apparently universal. The danger is that metapsychological terms − including such a term as "self" − may become reified as if it were a particular, static, delimited *thing*, like a "face" or a particular facial expression. Similarly, epiphenomenal terms, such as "self-consciousness" or "intelligence," may irresistably become "objectified" and concretized as if they were philosophically equivalent to phenomenal attributes of (bodily) weight and height. It is well to bear some of these problems in mind as various terminologies relating to self theory are listed and discussed in this chapter and others in this same volume.

Categories and terms relating to self

The preceding introduction and historical survey have been concerned with a definition of the concept of self and providing a résumé of the treatment of the concept in western philosophy, psychology, and social science. This present section will briefly list and describe structural categories and mechanisms which apply to theory building contained in attempts at systematic explanations of self. Such a model can provide an outline for comparisons between systems both ideally and cross-culturally – including this present volume. Models may be seen as made up of the following categories and terms:

(a) terms relating to *components*;
(b) terms and mechanisms relating to *boundaries* (and to the topographical and dynamic relationship between parts);
(c) terms relating to *valence* (or weighting) of components;
(d) terms and mechanisms relating to *energic* aspects of the system (including "ends" and "goals");
(e) terms relating to *chronology and timing*; and,
(f) terms and mechanisms relating to *dynamic interplay of parts*.

Components

In self theory, the components of *inner*, *interpersonal*, and *social* have been suggested as constituting a useful division into three modes of psychological awareness.

Within each of these general divisions, subdivisions of components and processes are described in various systematic explanations of self and personality from the fields of psychology, social psychology, psychoanalysis, and sociology.

In these systems, components may be termed "elements," "attributes," "qualities," "faculties," "functions," "instincts," "traits," or "properties." These are held to have special significance as entities, and are identified with integral functions occurring within the system.

A comparative review of structural, energic, and boundary aspects of a group of theories cannot be undertaken here. A number of classic and recent summaries are available, including Murphy (1947), Snugg and Combs (1949), Hall and Lindzey (1957), Wepman and Heine (1963), Wyss (1966), Meissner (1978), and Wylie (1974, 1979). In regard to psychological theory building in general, an edited volume by Marx (1963) offers a comprehensive and thorough discussion.

Boundaries

The conceptualization of components within a system of self requires a description of both the interrelationship of these components and their separateness from each other. Psychological components are not materially objectified; instead, they are discriminated through nominal and logical differentiations which define the parts as structurally and operationally separate. The notion of boundary, then, is intrinsic to both the semantic and operational definitions of a component. The definition of a boundary is crucial in explaining how particular components are simultaneously distinct and interrelated to other components which are contiguous in time, frame of action, context, or shared function. For example, Hall and Lindzey (1957) in discussing Lewin's field theory, described boundaries as dynamically established, permeable "membranes" rather than rigid barriers. Mechanisms which define the relationships between and among components are at the very heart of all theories of self and personality. Whether defined in terms of conflicts or by way of identifying coordinated activities, mechanics are used to explain psychological activity involving memory, learning, perception, integration, and so on. Theories concerning the self focus on the *inner self* as the epicenter of consciousness (containing both self-as-process and self-as-object to itself) and relate outward across the boundary of *interpersonal self* into the arena of relationships with other selves, and the physical environment. Conflicts are depicted as occurring between components and across boundaries, e.g. in ego − super-ego conflicts in psychoanalysis. Boundaries are also critical in differentiating among various theories of personality relative to the degrees of permeability assigned to the separate components. Of equal significance are the cross-cultural implications of differences assigned to permeability of boundaries within personality or self systems. These will be discussed later in the portrayal of western subjective self in contrast to concepts regarding Japanese perceptions of self.

Valence

Gradations in the intensities of parts or components relate to the significance (or weighting) assigned to these various parts. Valence, then, affects the importance given to a particular component, e.g. the "super-ego" in psychoanalytic theory. Valence also applies to functional parts ("psychological objects") through establishing relative degrees of importance, e.g. the significance of behaviors attributable to "extinction" in theories explaining deconditioning in behavioral modification. Valence may be dealt with overtly (as in the term "cathexis" used in psychoanalysis), or may be present implicitly. In cross-cultural work, valence becomes explicit in accounting for differential meanings given to similar behaviors occurring in different ethnic settings. Some of the methodological problems associated with accounting for cross-cultural differences have been outlined in Marsella, Tharp, and Ciborowski (1979). Content analytic techniques can be employed to demonstrate valence empirically, as in the application of semantic differential techniques in the scaling of meaning of bipolar categories ("good−bad," "hard−soft," etc.). Szalay and Maday (1978) have used a cross-cultural methodology which permits examination of connotational differences in meaning among persons from different cultural or national groups, permitting a comparative quantification of "weighting."

Valence is also connected to an implicit scaling of values

inherent in behavioral research but often unacknowledged. For example, research into psychological *alienation* may implicitly regard "isolation," "normlessness," "anomie," etc. as undesirable conditions. The fault is not that such conditions are not usually undesirable, but that the presupposition of undesirability is not explicitly acknowledged (Feuer 1963; Johnson 1973). In systems of personality or self, the tendency to identify certain modes of functioning (or "presentations of self") on a desirable – undesirable axis may ignore the implicit, normative presuppositions which contribute to this polarity. Explications of this sort are crucial to cross-cultural work.

Energy

Energic aspects are essential to systematic psychological explanations of self; they attempt to account for the force and direction of actions occurring within the system. Energic concepts concerned with self theory are metapsychological and can be either descriptively parsimonious or complex. Terms such as "motivation," "drive," "libido," "life-force," "need," are tautological. These terms often borrow their explanatory power through metaphorical or analogical references to physical, biological, or physiological systems, e.g. "entropy," "atrophy," "reinforcement." Energic terms are also expressed in a rhetorical connection to their goals, e.g. "self-preservation," "pleasure principle," "object-hunger," "will-to-power." Energic factors are also explicit in systematic explanations of drive-reduction accounting for states of neutrality or "resting" – again borrowing metaphorically from physical systems, e.g. "homeostasis" or "death instinct."

"Goals" and "ends" connected to energic explanations of self-systems also are implicitly involved with "good–bad" distinctions. It is impossible to conceal that certain goals and ends are desirable for selves as opposed to others that are less desirable.

Chronology and timing

Issues involving chronology and timing influence the explanation of systems of self as described by various theorists. The commonest temporal consideration is that of diachronic comparison between past and present, where actions at time "A" are studied in relation to actions at time "B." Behavioral psychology is fastidiously concerned with the precise measurement of pre- and post-testing situations to examine for the effects of specific stimuli following a controlled period of study. Interactional studies also employ a careful analysis of change taking place during short-term "frames" and action sequences. As in the physical sciences, exact measurements of time in psychological research have been fundamental in the precise control of duration of test stimuli, length of observed response and conclusions concerning effects of stimuli. Different from the factor of siderial (i.e. real) time, ethnographic studies have illustrated the wide variation in the perception and meaning of time in different cultures. Work in phenomenology and in the study of psychological disability (e.g. in depression) add to the understanding of the importance of subjective temporal factors in models of self or personality.

The dimension of time is also connected to the significance of "stagings" or developmental "phases" through which the self is differentially expressed during periods of the life cycle. A theological predecessor of the "life cycle" was inherent in western "Natural Law" which stipulated times and conditions under which humans were held to be responsible for their actions and defined relatively exacting (normative) ranges of expectations for these phases and conditions. Western psychological versions of the life cycle have at times implicitly (and unwittingly) carried over the morally normative connotations of "natural law" (Hoffman 1960). Ethnographic reports of various cultural definitions of the life cycle reflect mixtures of biological stagings (e.g. puberty and aging) and symbolisms connected to physical adaptations or magical beliefs. Western social psychological versions of the life cycle have been androcentric, reflecting, in the main, the gender of their authors and the propensity to describe femaleness as derivative of maleness. As an additional bias, these stagings have been based on special populations. Ethnographic evidence documenting significant cross-cultural variation in the timing of continuities and discontinuities in the life cycle have, in general, been ignored (Benedict 1937; Pavenstadt 1965).

Dynamic interplay

Conventionally, various western systematic descriptions of self ultimately define action in terms of a dynamic interplay of forces operating among these components and mechanisms within the system. It is as if western psychologists were composer-conductors who step to the podium to direct their scientific ensemble in an orchestration of all these *components, boundaries, valances, energies,* and *time factors* as a *dynamic rendition of reality*. However well done, such a rendition is inevitably and noticeably less than the reality which it simulates. The western scientific community has seemed particularly prone to believing that a systematic description of phenomena *is* reality itself, rather than an epistemologically contrived version of reality. Attempts to narrow the distance between epistemic reality and ontological reality in terms of self-theory will be discussed subsequently.

Some qualities imparted to the western subjective self

The section which follows is concerned with creating a sketch of some features acknowledged to reflect the subjectivity and "ways of thinking" of western persons (Nakamura 1964). This is included here as a counterpoint to later chapters in this volume where distinctive features of eastern subjectivity will be illuminated. This sketch will provide an impressionistic profile through the use of a few "brush strokes" characterizing some of the ways of being and thinking prototypical of many western persons. The categories selected will describe some aspects of the western self as *analytic, monotheistic, individualistic,* and, finally, *materialistic and rationalistic*.

Western self as analytic

Analytic and inductive modes of thinking are reported as prominent in persons residing in western cultures. Perhaps foremost is the tendency to see reality as an aggregation of parts: that is, to see objects as potentially divisible combinations of yet smaller objects. Such parts are not only present in visualized, "real" things (e.g. trees, persons, stars), but are presumed to constitute the structure of immaterial "things" (e.g. thoughts, ideas, memories). Long before confirmation through the physical sciences, philosophical support was present for the conviction that material reality – although not visible to the material eye – also was structuralized and particulate. The belief was that parts could be divided into yet smaller parts and pieces – molecules, atoms, elementary particles. This endorsement of a particulate universe of material objects is important given the western tendency toward an emphasis on "taking things apart" – i.e. analysis – and on the consequent process – *deduction*. A tendency accompanying the analytic mode is toward the objectification of "external" objects as existing separately from the observer. Observation and measurement of external reality categorizes these objects as "out there somewhere" rather than simultaneously "out there" and (internally and perceptually) "in here." In contrast to various eastern philosophies and religions (Nakamura 1964), western differentiations between "inside" and "outside" versions of reality tend to accentuate the differences and separation between external objects and their internal representations. Western personality theories have also tended to accentuate the boundary between the domains of intrapsychic and extrapsychic realities – most prominently in traditional psychoanalysis.

An important corollary of the analytic mode is the intellectual method of *deduction* which, following the process of teasing things apart, thereupon "deduces" the nature of their inherent part-to-whole relationships. In terms of the comparative natures of eastern and western people, Gregory-Smith (1979) recently summarized Porkert (1974):

"Of particular interest to the philosopher is [Porkert's] brief and provocative discussion on the differences between Western and Chinese scientific thought. Western modes of cognition are deductive and analytic, emphasizing causal

relationships and the perception of substrata. Chinese epistemology, its logical complement, is inductive and synthetic,
emphasizing temporally defined dynamic relations and the
systematic perception of functions."

(Gregory-Smith 1979:228)

Porkert's comment goes beyond a cliché contrast between
eastern and western thinking to emphasize that the *goal* of the
analytic-deductive mode is to pursue *cause*, and to associate such
cause to mechanics involving structural, particulate entities. The
significance for this current essay is that a pursuit of cause in
understanding the self may be misdirected in looking for
ultimate causes in the increasingly microanalytic study of
behavior.

Since the 1940s, the hazards of psychological reductionism
have been repeatedly raised. The use of the analytic-deductive
mode, ingenuous in many ways, may unintentionally reify a
system of observation into a system of reality. The tendency for
static, structural models of "self as subject" to risk reification has
been well publicized. However, phenomenological models, in
the "bracketing-off" of structural considerations, hazard a
similar risk. As discussed by Toulmin (1977) this is exemplified
by Kant, who claimed that "any philosophically-acceptable *self*
must be the *transcendental subject* of any possible experience,
rather than as an *empirical object* discovered in particular, actual
experience" (Toulmin 1977:302). In Kant's view, therefore,
the self could be seen as a rather static part or entity – a "hidden
thread" linking all of the individual's sense impressions over
time – perhaps unseen, but none the less *ontologically there all the
time*. A contrasting possibility for the transcendence of subjective self will be mentioned subsequently.

Western self as monotheistic

The psychological and normative consequences of monotheism
have recently received interpretation, by Niebuhr (1970) and
Miller (1974). Miller quotes Nietzsche in an acerbic observation
on monotheism:

"Monotheism – the rigid consequence of the doctrine of one
normal human being – consequently, the belief in a normal
God, beside whom there are only false, spurious Gods – has
perhaps been the greatest danger of mankind in the past. ...
[In] polytheism man's free-thinking and many-sided thinking
has a prototype set up: the power to create for himself new and
individual eyes, always newer and more individualized."

(Nietzsche 1974: 91)

Arguments from theologians for the advantages of polytheism
are complex. These attempt to make the case that the creation of
a pluralistic (mythic) supernatural world permits an objectification of a broader range of "powers" which can represent
projections of potential human behavior. Monotheism, on the
other hand, is seen as forcing a constricted concentration of
supernatural (and hence human) capabilities through confining
and normative considerations within a perimeter of monotheistic
wholeness. As Miller (1974) has observed, pluralistic forms of
gods and goddesses permitted the personification of diverse
autonomous powers and forces which took on a persistent
normative significance.

Miller's lament about the loss of this pluralism has application
to western psychology and theories of self:

"In Western culture the polytheistic theology that would
enable us to 'name' our plurality ... died with the collapse of
the Greek culture. From then on our explanation systems,
whether theological, sociological, political, historical, philosophical, or psychological have in the main been monotheistic.
That is, they have been operating according to fixed concepts
and categories which were controlled by a logic that demanded a rigorous and decisive 'either/or': either true or false,
either this or that, either beautiful or ugly, either good or
evil."

(Miller 1974: 7)

Miller also cites H. Richard Niebuhr in his attempt to reconcile
a polytheistic western theology within a doctrine of monotheism
(in *Radical Monotheism and Western Culture*, 1970). Niebuhr's

synthesis is complex; he defines "gods" in normative terms as "value centers" which function toward regularizing the relativistic limits of behavior and standardizing the attachment of worth, significance, and meaning to human actions.

In contrast to Niebuhr's "theocentric relativism," Charles Peirce, in a philosophical essay on pragmatism written in 1903, described the normative sciences as incorporating three essential and universal categories. As cited in Potter (1967), Peirce characterized the normative sciences as: "those which distinguish good and bad in the representations of truth, in the efforts of the will, and in objects regarded simply in their presentation" (p.39). Potter comments:

> "After a good deal of hesitation, Peirce's final opinion was that there are three normative sciences: esthetics, ethics (practice), and logic. The trio relates to feeling, action, and thought. ...
> Thus esthetics sets up norms concerning qualities of feeling ... ethics (or practice) sets up norms for judging conduct ... [and] logic sets up norms for deciding what thoughts we should entertain and what arguments we should accept [and] what procedures we should adopt."
>
> (Potter 1967:19)

Although Peirce does not deal with monotheism versus polytheism, he indirectly reflects on the potential narrowness of dealing with normative phenomena on the basis of a restrictive and overly judgmental "ethics."

However, as stated by Miller, monotheistic normative systems have a potential for being narrowly bipolar, and, thus, for placing extreme judgments onto both *qualities of existence* (e.g. good/bad, beautiful/ugly, sacred/profane, etc.), and *categories of identity* or experience (e.g. God/Satan, mind/matter, love/lust, etc.).

For example, the bipolar (moral) extremes of "love" and "lust" might be mellowed in a polytheistic community where the *range* of behaviors connected to sentimental, passionate, affectionate, and sexual activities were not condensed into a generic normative category, but were recognized (in *praxis*) as having varying valences and significance depending upon the context, the nature of the participants, and the symbolical meaning of the activity. With such relativistic broadening into more versatile "value centers" – on different poles and spectra – love would not be so readily juxtaposed (and polarized) to lust; infantile sensuality and tenderness would not be so readily interpreted as adultomorphic sexuality. Thus, Niebuhr's suggestion of "theocentric relativism" and Peirce's categories of normative sciences both suggest that expanded value systems (whether "polytheistic" or not) have the potential for more authentic understandings of everyday, pragmatic life experiences, and provide a broader and more felicitous range of valences for the judgment of human behavior. In very direct ways, these deductive views reinforce the now universally accepted ethos derived from cultural relativism, which essentially argues this same case – although based upon the *empirical* study of diverse cultures through various eras.

Additionally, in western Judeo-Christian traditions, the relation of the self to a monotheistic God has been complicated by the experience of separation as a tragic "species condition," i.e. the inherent loss of "grace" (for all mankind) through the consequences of ancestral "original sin." This sense of anxiety, separation, and longing has been suggested as a central concomitant of western alienation experience (Johnson 1973). Benjamin Nelson (1965) has also emphasized the implications of the concept of "original sin" (and separation) on the western experience of alienation. Nelson described the development of the *forum of conscience* during the Middle Ages, which theologically placed an extraordinary emphasis on the individual's responsibility to (one) God in terms of personal, human actions. Such awareness of conscience was *proximate* and not *remote*. The sense of ultimate morality affecting here-and-now actions was oppressive not only in that there was only *one* rule and regulation, but also because such a regulation was immediately binding upon all persons in Christendom. Given such circumstances, redemption was only possible by way of a formal relation to the temporal Christian Church through the Forum of Conscience and the sacrament of Penance.

Another corollary of monotheism is the tendency to support a closed-system cosmology whose limits are coterminous with a singular, all-encompassing deity. Such encapsulation of reality, modeled after a unitary, omnipotent power, has tended to reinforce the description of a closed-system *personology* as well as a closed-system theology.

The often-stated western proclivity toward the experience of guilt needs only brief mention here. The works of Piers and Singer (1953) Ausubel (1955), and Lewis (1971) have discussed the psychological and cultural concomitants of shame and pathological guilt. Centering on observations in Japan, George DeVos (1960) has described guilt toward parents among the Japanese in the more interpersonalized context of achievement and expectation for arranged marriage. Ausubel (1955), DeVos (1960), and Caudill and Plath (1966) have independently concluded that the Japanese are culturally not as susceptible to guilt over physical pleasures as are westerners; nor is the conception of "original sin" and the need for redemption felt as a proximately experienced, normative pressure. As DeVos states: "From a sociological standpoint, Japanese culture can be considered as manifesting a ... situational ethic as opposed to the more universal ethic built around moral absolutes found in Western Christian thought" (DeVos 1960: 288). This is not to suggest that Japanese experience of guilt is quantitatively *less*, but rather that it is qualitatively not related to the monotheistic value center so prominent in cultures affected by Judeo-Christian traditions.

Western self as individualistic

From a comparative standpoint the experience of individualism is acknowledged to be psychologically more prominent in western persons than among modal representatives from eastern communities. Although the psychological and presentational features of this difference are well publicized, the theological, philosophical, and political correlates of individualism are not so commonly understood. Theologically, a relatively inflated concern with self has been explained as a consequence of the personal anxiety connected to the cultural belief in ontological separation and estrangement from a Judeo-Christian God (Nelson 1965). This anxiety may be seen as connected to a series of polarities. The political accentuation of individual freedom and rights within some western communities is seen as a license for positive fulfillment, but also as a negative potential for the experience of isolation and frustration. The positive heightened significance given to self-determination and self-actualization is accompanied by a personal sense of heightened responsibility and an inflated propensity for guilt, self-recrimination, and self-doubt. The acknowledgment of individual, unique existence is at the same time an invitation to a defensive, narcissistic self-infatuation.

Loneliness and alienation have been suggested as the pathologic reciprocals of freedom and individualism by a series of western writers. German and French existentialist philosophers and novelists have concentrated on the architecture of loneliness and void (Heidegger, Kierkegaard, Sartre, Camus). American versions have dealt with the combination of excessive feelings of loneliness and isolation (alienation) coexisting with the unprecedented opportunity for material goods and services. Representative of these latter commentators are De Tocqueville (1965), Reisman, Denny, and Glazer (1950), Henry (1963), Fromm (1955), Slater (1970), Bensman and Vidich (1971), and Lasch (1979).

In the United States, a virtual cottage industry of cultural criticism has developed at the folk, popular media, literary, and scholarly levels. Some particularly creative observations on the loss of meaning in western life have been made by Ernest Becker through a series of publications (1962, 1967, 1973). Becker has gone beyond the description of contemporary alienation experience to suggest ways of restoring meaning and modes of consequential action through existing cultural and institutional forms. Becker's identification of certain aspects of contemporary anxiety with the denial of death is particularly insightful.

Somewhat in caricature, the "pathological" western self is depicted as being in a state of narcissism which is portrayed in terms of unhappy social orientations by Lasch (1979), or, alternatively, in clinical portraits by Kohut (1971) and Kernberg (1976). The display of such abnormal states of narcissism is common in fictional characterizations of western heroes and heroines. Taviss (1969) has reviewed alienation themes in novels from 1900 – 50. Gelfant (1973) and Coles (1981) have commented on the experience of estrangement portrayed in more recent American and British novels. The combined documentary from literary, clinical, and social-historical commentary suggests that the experience of dread and unhappiness is apparently a high risk for individuals residing in western communities.

Looked at positively, western individualism has consistently espoused rights for personal freedom and enhancement – politically, theologically, and legally. The belief in individualism is an endorsement of the dignity and entitlement of ordinary persons before God, the law, and with other citizens. Obviously, there are broad differences in the actual manifestations and expressions of individualism, for example, between the Soviet Union and France, or between Canada and Iran. Also, in any of these countries, the belief in the availability of these freedoms and entitlements is different from what actually may be available. Reflecting their colonial, revolutionary, and immigrant past, persons residing in the United States have historically been preoccupied with themes connected with freedom, anti-authoritarianism, and commitment to the defense of individual rights and values (Meadows 1973). This commitment has gradually led to extension of more equal opportunity for ethnic minorities and women, and increased legal protection for deviant populations – those defined as eccentrics, criminals, and the mentally ill. The subject of the rights of the individual versus the rights of society continues to be a focus for the destiny of constitutionality, which simultaneously *reflects and effects* culture change. Extending explicit individual rights to minors diminishes the authority of adult parents; enhancing the individual prerogatives for marital partners fosters destabilization of some marriages. Balances between individual and collective rights partly reflect the high significance placed on individual destiny. The emphasis on "self-actualization" – both in popular psychological literature and in the self-expressions of some Americans – testifies to an increased regard for personal enhancement and fulfillment.

The emphasis on individualism has direct and indirect effects on both the presentation of self (in public ways) and the experience of self (in private awareness). These effects are easiest to document in North America since the cultural forms supporting individualism are so manifest; also some evidence for these factors regarding self are available from cross-cultural research (Barnlund 1975). Using several different scales involving verbal disclosure, touching behavior, and interpersonal distance, Barnlund found the American group significantly higher in both content of disclosure and number and variety of confidantes. His subjects also demonstrated a higher amount of both affectionate and incidental touching, and in general reflected less interpersonal distance. Johnson and Marsella (1978) also showed differences persisting in a third-generation sample of Japanese-Americans in contrast to third-generation descendants of European ancestry. Concerns about status, male dominance, female subordination, and deference were related by the authors to paralinguistic status markers inherent in the Japanese language, even though *none* of the subject population spoke Japanese. Differences in speech norms between Japanese and Americans are conspicuous and address issues of both presentation of self and perception of self. Proper use of Japanese demands close attention to status markers (*keigo*) which acknowledge differences in age and station of life. Male and female use of the Japanese language is quite different compared to relatively subtle differences in the American use of the English language (Kramer 1974).

Stereotypically, Americans emerge as open, egalitarian, assertive, relatively unself-conscious, and not as attentive to nonverbal or contextual cues in the public presentation of self. In contrast, the Japanese demonstrate a fine sense of differentiation between the self as a social participant and the self as a personal, internal consciousness, and are more aware of a "dualistic" orientation to the world (see DeVos, this volume). Social participation is guided by explicit norms which require a high awareness of the other person's social self and the contextual features of the encounter. Compared to the United States, there is a narrower range of appropriateness in speech, nonverbal behavior, and permissible actions, particularly as governed by cues relating to status.

Takeo Doi (1973b) has discussed some psychological concomitants of the Japanese awareness of self, using the form of a "twofold layer of consciousness, "*omote* and *ura*. *Omote* (roughly meaning "front") refers to the perception of self as a social object in relationship to other selves. *Ura* (roughly meaning "back") subsumes the private world of inner self – shared with very few persons and, even then, primarily by way of implication and inference. Developmentally, the higher degree of awareness of social self in Japan is connected to socialization procedures in Japan (less verbalization, less physical space) which promote a sensitivity for observing social-interactional cues originating from others (Caudill and Schooler 1973; Pavenstadt 1965).

Minami (1971), in a discussion of the Japanese self, also describes the studied hyperbole of *denial of self* present in the interaction of the Japanese self with other selves, particularly in asymmetric social encounters. Although this is misunderstood and caricatured by westerners, it is expressive of the fundamental norm of *enryo*, which is an institutionalized, and ceremonialized, form of *denial of self-importance* (Kitano 1969; Doi 1973a; Johnson and Johnson 1975). Such a norm is antithetical to the permissible demonstration of mild degrees of narcissism and exhibitionism accepted in some western communities; accordingly this partly accounts for a difference in presentation of self between Americans and Japanese (Barnlund 1975). Overt displays of egoism and accentuation of individualism in Japan are interpreted as being aggressive and are permitted only under specific situations, e.g. during unusual stresses, or as a result of unbearable provocation.

In the west – most clearly in the United States – the sense of heightened individualism affects the balance of family relationships and obligations. Children are socialized simultaneously to be obedient, to submit to rules which protect the rights of others, *and* to develop a progressive independence. Operationally, independence means being able gradually to assume responsibility for their own actions, to be able to abbreviate their demands on others, and to exercise (internal) control over their actions. Independence is acquired through a "push-pull" training which fosters self-expression and self-reliance but punishes excessive manifestations of aggression or stubbornness. Throughout this training the desirability of "becoming independent" is explicitly raised. Contrastingly, in Japan, the prerogative for some forms of life-long (infantile) dependency upon selected others is normatively supported. Discussed as *amae* in a series of publications by Takeo Doi (1955, 1973a), the acknowledgment of interdependencies in family, work, and friendship relations is highly conscious and integral to successful social navigation in Japanese life.

In the United States, the rhetorical belief in independence acts to conceal the complex interdependencies in family and social relationships. Children, adolescents, and young adults who objectively are *not* independent of their families (financially and instrumentally), feel the need to act as if (and to believe) they are, and to disregard transparently dependent aspects of their relationship to parents, teachers, employers, and other superiors. Much of this independence is "psychological" and has the effect of inflating a sense of individualism. This subscription to an inflated view of individualism is condensed in the popular contemporary phrase of "doing your own thing." This expression is revealing in two ways: first, in its blatant assertion of the *right* to personal enhancement, and second, in the belief that an activity can be "one's *own* thing" as opposed to "things" that are done by thousands or millions of other people.

Western self as materialistic and rationalistic

The importance of the analytic-deductive mode has been addressed in a previous section. Since the Enlightenment, the western accentuation of a rational, scientific approach to reality has tended to define spiritual and "immaterial" phenomena as potentially superstitious and dangerous. Preternatural explanations have yielded to a progressive demystifying of the physical environment, through the outstanding accomplishments of research and technological development both in the east and west. In the west, however, the acceptance of the mechanical and logical characteristics of a world of objects *also* constitutes a "belief system." The *psychological* experience of this "belief" in science, in complicated technology and materialism may not be so different to "superstitious" interpretations of reality. For example, the explanation that lightning is caused by an electrical discharge between the ground and certain cloud formations is considerably more accurate than previous beliefs that storms represented the anger of the gods. However the fact that both educated and uneducated persons in the west regard lightning as an electrical rather than supernatural force obscures the fact that ordinary persons do not really "know" what electricity is, except in a vague sense. Also the spectrum of emotional reactions to lightning probably is not much different (as psychological events) whether one endorses explanations through the temperaments of gods or the random actions of electrical charges in clouds.

In any society, belief systems are stratified and composed of a hierarchy of interrelated, causal-explanatory models. Depending on their application these various models may be exclusive or complementary, alternate or incompatible in their application to specific events or within particular contexts. (For example, a particular person's death will be discussed or "explained" differently to the family members by the attending physician, the mortician, and the family minister – all invoking appropriate but varying belief systems concerning mortality.) The contrast between western and eastern belief systems lies not in the pluralistic or stratified system of belief, but in the tendency of materialistic and rationalistic explanations to predominate in the west. A second contrast is that such ascendancy leads to the application of modes of understanding the *material* world to realms of experience and reality that are not easily "materialized" (that is, not readily related to physical structure, particulate existence, or easy quantification). A third tendency of the domination of materialistic and rationalistic beliefs is to discredit formulations not using analytic-deductive modes, and to drive magical and superstitious explanations "underground."

For example, in advanced industrial societies, explanations of the causes of disease favor complex pathophysiological models accounting for etiology, vectors of transmission, processes of tissue damage, mobilization of organismic response and recovery

– including social and psychological factors that may influence this chain of events. The practical value of the ascendence of this scientific form of explanation is not questioned in providing an orientation to the diagnosis, prevention, and cure of illness. The problem rather lies in the fact that such emphasis on the *most authenticated* explanations ignores and suppresses the ubiquitous presence of other ways in which average human beings explain their illnesses or seek relief and cure. In eastern societies (e.g. China, Japan, and India) folk explanations and treatments are highly viable alongside conventional technical procedures (Lock 1976). Such folk beliefs and treatments also abound in western industrial societies – and are not merely confined to ethnic communities (Johnson 1984). However, such practices are categorically discriminated from the ascendent procedures of technical, scientific medicine. In stating this, the author is not arguing for a higher authentication for folk medicine over scientific medicine. The point is that the high investment in rational-empirical approaches to a material reality affect both the presentation of self and the experience of self in western industrial societies, through suppressing and defining other approaches – in a derogatory way – as irrational and insubstantial. This emphasis may unintentionally place a hypercritical standard in judging ordinary experience. Behavior which cannot readily be rationally deduced or explained may be peremptorily considered irrational or eccentric. For example, an individual's explanation and interpretation of some physical symptoms may be exaggerated or inaccurate. Coming down with a severe "cold" may induce a momentary dread of more serious infection or fears of developing a major complication. Fleeting thoughts about such unlikely sequellae run the risk of being defined as "irrational" or "neurotic" – either by oneself or by medical practitioners. This is not to suggest that individuals may not, under certain circumstances, generate reactions to symptoms that are productively understood as *hypochondriacal*. The point is that anything that veers too far away from the actuarial probabilities observed in the empirical world may be defined as "irrational" (Daly 1970)

The overall effect may be to produce a way of thinking that

concentrates attention onto material objects and applies rational-istic models of explanation to immaterial "things." The pre-ference for such explanations may contribute to a loss of the sense of the mystical, and a tendency to consider pathological that which is not "rational" or "logical."

The implication of this for contemporary western religions is that magic and mystery yielded to more rationalistic canons. Ceremonies and practices may deemphasize magical aspects (e.g. "transsubstantiation") and favor allegorical and humanistic interpretations of dogma. In contrast, the major eastern religions appear to have preserved more of a sense of awe and mystery along with a perception of the self as part of a larger social and physical universe. Compared to Buddhist and Hindu practices, the western religious orientation appears separated from the real world. Except in Islamic communities, religious ceremonies are constricted and delimited in both place and time. Religious ways of thinking and practices are not immanent and, unlike medieval times, do not convey a perspective that individual selves are part of a large congregation of persons, residing on a small planet within a nearly unfathomable universe. Instead, the cosmology of western industrial societies is prominently secular. The rhythm of life is related to commercial, manufacturing, and recreational schedules. Consciousness of time is connected to the continuity of working, going to and from work, and the instrumental and recreational pastimes "stolen" between work and family routines. In technologically sophisticated countries – in the east as well as the west – such secular or materialistic concerns displace religious consciousness through elimination of both the opportunity and the incentive for reflection and contemplation.

Secular preoccupations are not, however, a western mono-poly. Such changes are evident in both Chinese and Japanese societies, partly reflecting political and religious reformations in the late 1940s, and a rapid increase in industrial and commercial productivity. In the opposite direction, there has been an increased interest in religion within western countries manifes-ted by church attendance and participation in denominationally sponsored social activities. This interest includes the introduction of many natavistic, charismatic elements as well as the transplantation of some eastern techniques of trance, meditation, and contemplation (see Bharati Chapter 6).

Conclusion

In outline, the history of the western concept of self can be depicted as progressing through three stages. The first of these (pre-Christian times until 1850) was characterized by philosophic, theological, and literary descriptions of the self (using the concepts of soul and mind) stressing the individual nature of subjective consciousness, the ontological separateness of both persons and things, and the tendency to locate responsibility for action in the individual. The second stage (1850–1940) saw the refinement of the self as a concept in psychology at the turn of the century (as in W. James) and the elaboration of the social self as a symbolic-interactional construction in the early 1900s (as in G. H. Mead). The third stage (1940 to the present) has taken a number of directions which are still in a process of development. First, aspects of the concept have been examined in highly operationalized ways within social psychology and sociology (as summarized by Wylie 1974, 1979; and Rosenberg 1979). Second, it has been incorporated as a holistic frame of reference within humanistic psychology and attached to a variety of semiformal, clinical, and philosophic positions – unrigorously associated with existentialism and phenomenology. Third, there has been a convergence in some conceptualizations of the self among a number of disciplines which are pursuing studies of the manifestations of self using new premises, methodologies, and interpretations. Although such work is current and contemporary, it is based on a revival of insights formulated at the turn of the century from the areas of *psychology* (James), *phenomenology* (Husserl), *symbolical interaction* (G. H. Mead), *pragmatic philosophy* (C. S. Peirce), *linguistics* (Saussure), and *psychoanalysis* (Freud).

Despite some common intellectual lineages, contemporary theorists from these fields deal distinctively with the concept of self, reflecting attempts to construct models of the self from systems of explanation within their parent disciplines. While acknowledging pertinent differences in terminology and theory, it is our purpose here to to expose some common trends. It may be helpful to make a short list of disciplines and theorists by way of illustration. Such a list would include *theology* (H. Richard Niebuhr), *psychology* (Walter Mischel, D'Andrade, Pervin and Lewis), *sociology* (Berger and Luckman, Schutz, Douglas, Goffman), *anthropology* (Schweder, La Vine, Singer) and *psychoanalysis* (Kohut, Kornberg).

Although important differences exist among these theorists and disciplines, some commonalities will be listed here as ingredients basic to an expanded conceptualization of self.

(a) There is evidence of a consensus among theorists *that the self is a social construction which is symbolically and signally created* between and among social beings. Self is not, therefore, regarded as a structural entity composed of factors and traits which "add up" to a total person.

(b) Also, although there are variations in description and emphasis, researchers from most of these disciplines see the self as a *phenomenological object which can be productively studied through a series of evanescent actions*. Self, then, is simultaneously a multidimensional entity: instantial *and* diachronic.

(c) Again, ignoring variations, most of these theories of self are *situational and capable of study in naturalistic settings*. Such theories are sensitive to variables that occur in the "specious present" and accept the multivariant consequences of including contextual dimensions in which the action is taking place.

(d) Within many of these conceptual systems, *the self is no longer regarded as a unitary phenomenon* − that is, as an encapsulated, individual variable Instead, the self is accepted as an *interpersonal*, i.e. as an *intersubjective*, unit − even in terms of the self's interaction with its own self. The unit of study, therefore, becomes *interaction* or *transaction* between and among selves.

(e) Since the self is *intersubjective and is seen in the phenomen-*

ological contexts of actual encounters, its manifestations take the form of *communication* and are empirically present in the gestural, semantic, and contextual features of encounters occurring within or between one or more selves. (Recall that introspection and some other intrapsychic activities are regarded as *communications with self.*)

(f) While the self is primarily a social (i.e. *non*-corporeal) concept, it is *intimately connected to bodily experience both ontogenetically and through "here and now" awareness.*

(g) The self is simultaneously *seen as phenomenal and non-phenomenal* (Wylie 1979). That is to say that the self is both overtly communicative and *phenomenal* – involved in "real" encounters – and *nonphenomenal*, in being subject to purposive directions by unconscious and only indirectly observable forces which influence behavior.

(h) Since the self is regarded as manifest, and is observable through communication, important features of the self are logically related to analytic modes which "explain" communication. The use of linguistic and paralinguistic analysis may therefore be expected to illuminate an understanding of self. As such, self acquires substance according to *semantic* (definitional, etymological), *syntactic* (grammatical and logical), and *pragmatic* (extralinguistic and gestural) meanings present in communication.

As an example of this, Singer (1980) has elaborated an exposition of a basis for self theory, synthesizing from C. S. Peirce's theory of signs. As discussed by Singer, Peirce reduced the analysis of sign-function (in language) to the triadic relation of *sign, object,* and *interpretant.* Basically, Peirce (and Singer) suggest that the social self (i.e. self-as-object to other selves) can be viewed like any other consensual symbol, and hence treated as a sign. In a complex argument, Singer extends this to include the nominative *self-as-subject,* which can similarly be analyzed in terms of a two-person model of the "utterer" (of signs) and the "interpreter" (of signs). The details of his synthesis elude condensed explanation here, but are well worth the effort to understand. This synthesis is cited here as a particularly ambitious attempt to reconceptualize self.

By way of conclusion in this present chapter, several other comments seem in order. First, it appears that the concept of self has recently been resubstantiated as a vehicle capable of providing a comprehensive understanding of human behavior, both ideally and cross-culturally. In its extensiveness, the concept may help reduce the gap between epistemological theory building and the complex phenomenal events which are "explained" by the theories. Also, the concept would seem promising in facilitating understanding between those disciplines which study behavior, more so than concepts related to "personality" or "role." Additionally, the concept of self can lend itself to include interpretant variables regarding subjectivity involved in cross-cultural expositions of self.

As a final reflection on recent evolutions in self-theory, the issue of *cause* again deserves mention. Previously, work in various disciplines has been conducted with the hope of discovering factors which can be identified as necessary, sufficient, and predictable "causes" of human behavior. Changes in the theory of self which move toward additional units of study, undertaken in naturalistic settings and focused on situational frames and contexts, tend to diffuse the notion of cause among more variables and conditions. Dealing with complex units of study, multidimensional matrices of information, and more relativistic interpretation of findings, makes the pursuit of distinctive or "final" causes less plausible. Some of the early criticisms levelled at Erving Goffman's microsociological work come to mind. These sometimes took the colloquial form of "Where's the theory?" or "What does all this mean?". These questions may not simply have expressed methodological criticism, but also the exasperation felt on finding that the "causes" of face-to-face behavior often are prosaic and trivial. Perhaps it is the case that the realization of this triviality implicates another western preoccupation: namely, our resistance to acknowledging the specious and prosaic qualities of much of contemporaneous interaction. In our quest to discover truth, we would rather find "entities," essences, and principles to furnish greater security through the objectification of reality, and to find comfort in the discovery of "final causes." Clearly, the renewed interest in the concept of self does not readily promise such security. Also, wherever we may be at the present time in the evolution toward more authentic theories of self (and toward a more coherent understanding of our own selves), we are currently at an exciting but not comfortable point.

In concluding, Benjamin Nelson's (1965) reflections on this dilemma still seem timely:

> "The future of self is extremely obscure in the present historical interim. Depending on their political and philosophical commitments, groups and individuals are describing the self as culture's foremost achievement, mind's vilest metaphysical illusion or society's most noxious disease.
>
> It is still too early to tell how well the Western sense of self will fare in the galactic era ahead. There are powerful forces working at cross purposes in this regard. Whatever the outcome, spiritual directors and systems of direction will continue to play strategic roles in defining stressful situations and aiding men to cope with them. Original nature is too fitful in expression and incoherent in aim to serve Everyman as a trusty guide. So long as each of us is required to be symbolically endorsed by others; so long as all aspire to taste vindication in however vague a sense, we search for our own meaning in a design not of our own devising."
>
> (Nelson 1965: 186)

References

Allport, G. (1943) The Ego in Contemporary Psychology. *Psychological Review* 49: 71.

Ausubel, D. (1955) Relations between Shame and Guilt in the Socialization Process. *Psychological Review* 62: 5, 378–90.

Barnlund, D. (1975) *Public and Private Self in Japan and the United States.* Tokyo: Simul Press.

Becker, E. (1962) *The Birth and Death of Meaning.* New York: The Free Press.

——— (1967) *Beyond Alienation.* New York: George Braziller.

_____ (1973) *The Denial of Death*. New York: The Free Press.

Benedict, R. (1937) Continuities and Discontinuities in Cultural Conditioning. *Psychiatry* 1:161–67.

Bensman, J. and Vidich, A. J. (1971) *The New American Society*. Chicago: Quadrangle Books.

Berger, P. and Luckmann, T. (1966) *The Social Construction of Reality*. Garden City, NY: Doubleday.

Berne, E. (1967) *Transactional Analysis in Psychotherapy*. New York: Grove Press.

Bilmes, J. and Boggs, S. T. (1979) Language and Communication: The Foundation of Culture. In A. J. Marsella, R. C. Tharp, and T. J. Ciborsky (eds) *Perspectives on Cross-Cultural Psychology*. New York: Academic Press.

Boring, E. G. (1950) *A History of Experimental Psychology*, second edn. New York: Appleton-Century-Crofts.

Burton, A. (ed.) (1974) *Operational Theories of Personality*. New York: Brunner/Mazel.

Caudill, W. and Plath, D. W. (1966) Who Sleeps by Whom? *Psychiatry* 29: 344–66.

Caudill, W. and Schooler, C. (1973) Child Behavior and Child Rearing in Japan and the U.S. *Journal of Nervous and Mental Disease* 157: 323–38.

Coles, R. (1981) To Break the Shell of Self. *The New Republic*, January 17.

Daly, R. W. (1970) The Specters of Technicism *Psychiatry* 33:417–432.

De Tocqueville, A. (1965) *Democracy in America*. New York: Mentor. First published in 1835.

DeVos, G. (1960) The Relation of Guilt toward Parents to Achievement and Arranged Marriage among the Japanese. *Psychiatry* 23: 287–301.

Doi, T. (1955) Some Aspects of Japanese Psychiatry. *American Journal of Psychiatry* 112: 691–95.

_____ (1973a) *The Anatomy of Dependence*. Tokyo: Kodansha International.

_____ (1973b) *Omote* and *Ura*: Concepts Derived from the Japanese Two-Fold Structure of Consciousness. *Journal of Nervous and Mental Disorders* 157: 258–61.

English, H. B. and English, A. C. (1958) *A Comprehensive Dictionary of Psychological and Psychoanalytical Terms*. New York: Longhorns, Green.

Feuer, L. (1963) What Is Alienation? The Career of a Concept. In M. Stein and A. Vidich (eds) *Sociology on Trial*. Englewood Cliffs, NJ: Prentice-Hall.

134   Culture and Self

Fisher, S. and Cleveland, S. E. (1958) *Body Image and Personality*. Princeton, NJ: Van Nostrand.
Freud, A. (1946) *The Ego and Mechanisms of Defense*. New York: International Universities Press. First published in 1936.
Freud, S. (1949) *Moses and Monotheism*. New York: Alfred A. Knopf.
—— (1961) *The Ego and the Id*. London: Hogarth Press. First published in 1923.
Fromm, E. (1955) *The Sane Society*. Greenwich CT: Fawcett Publications.
Gelfant, B. H. (1973) The Imagery of Estrangement Alienation in Modern American Fiction. In F. A. Johnson (ed.) *Alienation: Concept, Term and Meanings*. New York: Seminar Press.
Goffman, E. (1959) *The Presentation of Self in Everyday Life*. Garden City, NY: Doubleday.
—— (1967) *Interaction Ritual*. Garden City, NY: Doubleday.
—— (1974) *Frame Analysis*. New York: Harper & Row.
Gregory-Smith, D. (1979) Science and Technology in East Asia. *Philosophy East and West* 29: 221–36.
Grinker, R. R., Sr. (ed.) (1956) *Toward a Unified Theory of Human Behavior*. New York: Basic Books.
Hall, C. S. and Lindzey, G. (1957) *Theories of Personality*, New York: Wiley.
Harre, R. (1977) The Self in Monodrama. In Theodore Mischel (ed.) *The Self*. Oxford: Basil Blackwell.
Hartmann, H. (1958) *Ego Psychology and the Problem of Adaptation*. New York: International Universities Press. First published in 1939.
Heap, J. L. and Roth, A. (1973) On Phenomenological Sociology. *American Sociological Review* 38: 354–67.
Henry, J. (1963) *Culture against Man*. New York: Vintage Books.
Hillman, J. (1971) Psychology: Monotheistic or Polytheistic. *Spring* 15: 193–208.
Hoffman, M. (1960) Psychiatry, Nature and Science. *American Journal of Psychiatry* 117: 205–10.
Inada, K. K. (1979) Problematics of the Buddhist Nature of Self. *Philosophy East and West* 29: 141–58.
Jacobson, E. (1964) *The Self and the Object World*. New York: International Universities Press.
James, W. (1950) *The Principles of Psychology*. New York: Dover Publications. First published in 1898.
Johnson, C. L., and Johnson, F. A. (1975) Interaction Rules and Ethnicity. *Social Forces* 54: 452–66.

Johnson, F. A. (ed.) (1973) *Alienation: Concept, Term and Meanings*. New York and London: Seminar Press.

—— (1984) Anthropology and Psychiatry. In H. H. Goldman (ed.) *Review of General Psychiatry*. New York: Lange Medical Publications.

Johnson, F. A. and Marsella, A. J. (1978) Differential Attitudes toward Verbal Behavior in Students of Japanese and European Ancestry. *Genetic Psychology Monographs* 97: 43–76.

Kernberg, O. (1976) *Object Relations Theory and Clinical Psychoanalysis*. New York: Jason Aronson.

Kitano, H. (1969) *Japanese Americans: The Evolution of a Subculture*. Englewood Cliffs, NJ: Prentice-Hall.

Kliever, L. D. (1977) *H. Richard Niebuhr*. Waco, TX: World Books.

Kohut, H. (1971) *The Analysis of Self*. New York: International Universities Press.

—— (1977) *The Restoration of Self*. New York: International Universities Press.

Kramer, C. (1974) Women's Speech: Separate but Unequal? *Quarterly Journal of Speech* 60: 12–24.

Lasch, C. (1979) *The Culture of Narcissism*. New York: Warner Books.

Lewis, H. B. (1971) *Shame and Guilt in Neurosis*. New York: International Universities Press.

Lewis, M. (1978) Situational Analysis and the Study of Behavioral Development. In L. A. Pervin and M. Lewis (eds) *Perspectives in Interactional Psychology*. New York and London: Plenum Press.

Lock, M. M. (1976) *Oriental Medicine in Urban Japan*. Unpublished Ph.D. dissertation, University of California.

Lonner, W. J. (1979) Issues in Cross-Cultural Psychology. In A. J. Marsella, R. A. Tharp and T. J. Ciborowski (eds) *Perspectives on Cross-Cultural Psychology*. New York: Academic Press.

Marsella, A. J., Tharp, R. A., and Ciborowski, T. J. (eds) (1979) *Perspectives on Cross-Cultural Psychology*. New York: Academic Press.

Marx, M. H. (1963) *Theories in Contemporary Psychology*. New York: Macmillan.

Mead, G. H. (1913) The Social Self. *The Journal of Philosophy, Psychology and Scientific Methods* 10 (January–December).

—— (1922) A Behavioristic Account of the Significant Symbol. *The Journal of Philosophy* 19 (January–December).

Meadows, P. (1973) *American Culture: Themes and Images*. Presentation, School of Medicine, Upstate Medical Center, Syracuse.

Meissner, W. W. (1978) Theories of Personality. In A. M. Nicoli (ed.) *The Harvard Guide to Modern Psychiatry.* Cambridge, Mass.: Harvard University Press.

Miller, D. (1974) *The New Polytheism.* New York: Harper & Row.

_____ (1981) Personal communication.

Miller, R. A. (1967) *The Japanese Language.* Chicago: University of Chicago Press.

Minami, H. (1971) *Psychology of the Japanese People.* Toronto: University of Toronto Press.

Mischel, T. (ed.) (1977) *The Self.* Oxford: Basil Blackwell.

Mischel, W. (1968) *Personality and Assessment.* New York: Wiley.

Murphy, G. (1947) *Personality.* New York: Harper & Row.

Murphy, G. and Murphy, L. B. (eds) (1969) *Western Psychology, from the Greeks to William James.* New York: Basic Books.

Nakamura, H. (1964) *Ways of Thinking of Eastern People.* Honolulu: East-West Center Press.

Nelson, B. (1965) Self-Images and Systems of Spiritual Direction in the History of European Civilization. In S. Z. Klausner (ed.) *The Quest for Self-Control.* New York: The Free Press.

Niebuhr, H. (1970) *Radical Monotheism and Western Culture.* New York: Harper & Row.

Nietzsche, F. (1974) *The Gay Science.* Trans. Walter Kaufmann. New York: Random House.

Nozick, R. (1981) *Philosophical Explanations.* Cambridge, Mass.: Harvard University Press.

Pavenstadt, E. (1965) Observations in Five Japanese Homes. *Journal of the American Academy of Child Psychology* 4: 413–25.

Peirce, C. S. (1934) In C. Hartshorne and P. Weiss (eds) *Collected papers of Charles Sanders Peirce,* vol. V. Cambridge, Mass.: Harvard University Press.

_____ (1958) In P. P. Wiener (ed.) *Values in a Universe of Change.* New York: Doubleday.

Pervin, L. A. (1979) Theoretical Approaches to the Analysis of Individual-Environment Interaction. In L. A. Pervin and M. Lewis (eds) *Perspectives in Interactional Psychology.* New York and London: Plenum Press.

Pervin, L. A. and Lewis, M. (1979) *Perspectives in Interactional Psychology.* New York and London: Plenum Press.

Piaget, J. (1952) *The Origins of Intelligence in Children.* New York: International Universities Press.

Piers, G. and Singer, M. (1953) *Shame and Guilt*. Springfield, Ill.: Charles C. Thomas.

Pike, R. (1966) *Language in Relation to a United Theory of the Structure of Human Behavior*. The Hague: Mouton Press.

Porkert, M. (1974) *The Theoretical Foundations of Chinese Medicine*. Boston: Massachusetts Institute of Technology Press.

Potter, V. G. (1967) *Charles S. Peirce, on Norms and Ideals*. Boston: University of Massachusetts Press.

Rapaport, A. (1953) *Operational Philosophy*. New York: Harper & Row.

Reich, W. (1949) *Character Analysis*. New York: Farrar, Strauss & Giroux.

Reisman, D., Denny, B., and Glazer, N. (1950). *The Lonely Crowd*. Princeton, NJ: Yale University Press.

Rinsley, D. B. (1962) A Contribution to the Theory of Ego and Self. *The Psychiatric Quarterly* 28: 1–25.

Rosenberg, M. (1979) *Conceiving the Self*. New York: Basic Books.

Ryle, G. (1949) *The Concept of Mind*. London: Hutchinson.

Sahakian, W. S. (1975) *History and Systems of Psychology*. New York: Schenkman Publishing Company and Wiley.

Saussure, F. De (1959). *Course in General Linguistics*. First published in 1915. Edited by C. Bally and A. Sechehage with A. Riedlinger. Trans. Wade Baskin. New York: The Philosophical Library.

Schilder, P. (1935) *The Image and Appearance of the Human Body*. London: Trench, Trubner & Co.

Schweder, R. A. (1980) Rethinking Culture and Personality Theory, Part III. *Ethos* 8: 60–94.

Singer, M. (1980) Signs of the Self: An Exploration in Semiotic Anthropology. *American Anthropologist* 82: 485–507.

Slater, P. (1970). *The Pursuit of Loneliness*. Boston: Beacon Press.

Snugg, D. and Combs, A. W. (1949) *Individual Behavior*. New York: Harper & Row

Spiegel, J. (1971) *Transactions*. Edited by John Papajohn. New York: Science Rouse.

Sullivan, H. S. (1937) Psychiatry: Introduction to the Study of Interpersonal Relations. *Psychiatry* 1: 121–34.

_____ (1956) *Clinical Studies in Psychiatry*. New York: W. W. Norton.

Szalay, L. and Maday, B. (1978) Verbal Associations in the Analysis of Subjective Culture. *Current Anthropology* 14: 33–50.

Taviss, I. (1969) Changes in the Form of Alienation. *American Sociological Review* 34: 46–57.

Tiryakian, E. (1965) Existential Phenomenology and Sociology. *American Sociological Review* 30: 674–88.

Toulmin, S. E. (1977) Self Knowledge and Knowledge of the Self. In T. Mischel (ed.) *The Self*. Oxford: Basil Blackwell.

Webster's Unabridged Dictionary (1966) New York: Simon & Schuster.

Wepman, J. M. and Heine, R. W. (1963) *Concepts of Personality*. Chicago: Aldine.

Werner, H. (1940) *Comparative Psychology of Mental Development*. New York: Harper & Row.

_____ (1948) *Comparative Psychology of Mental Development*. Chicago: Follett.

Wright, A. (1964) Foreword. In H. Nakamura, *Ways of Thinking of Eastern People*. Honolulu: East-West Center Press.

Wylie, R. C. (1961) *The Self-Concept: A Critical Survey of Pertinent Research Literature*. Lincoln: University of Nebraska Press.

_____ (1974) *The Self-Concept*, revised edn, vol. I. Lincoln: University of Nebraska Press.

_____ (1979) *The Self-Concept*, revised edn, vol. II. Lincoln: University of Nebraska Press.

Wyss, D. (1966) *Depth Psychology*. New York: W. W. Norton.

PART III

Asian Perspectives on Self

5

Dimensions of the Self in Japanese Culture

George DeVos

Rather than a more conventional approach by way either of personality structure, on the one hand, or by way of social role theory on the other, I shall examine the self in social interaction on several general theoretical levels. I have been using these levels either implicitly or explicitly to understand specific Japanese tensions between the self and the social role.

The first dimension is an "etic" one derivative of Durkheimian social analysis found in sociology – one that concerns itself with *social conformity and cohesion* versus deviancy or anomie. These phenomena are measured by various behavioral indices, which are indirect suggestions of social attitudes held as part of a consistent sense of self.

The second dimension is a more directly "emic" one focusing on Japanese perceptions of their own psychological motivations; their experiences of the *self in social interaction*. These concerns I have obtained by tests and interviews to be categorized in my own "etic" interpersonal framework. Analytically, I separate instrumental concerns into achievement versus alienation; mastery versus incompetence; responsibility or guilt versus irresponsibility; control or autonomy versus dominance or rebellion; positive cooperation or competition versus antisocial expediencies. The expressive concerns are social harmony versus discord or violence; affiliation versus isolation or separation; nurturance versus deprivation; appreciation versus shame or degradation; pleasure or satisfaction versus suffering or ennui. These elementary interpersonal concerns are blended into molecular patterns that give a specific flavor in the experience of being Japanese.

Another consideration is an examination of *status* experienced subjectively. It is in effect a consideration of the relative priorities of social attention either: (a) to the self introspectively as an internal object of concern or, (b) to vertical relationships of different strata of status, or (c) to horizontal relationships with those on the same social level.

On another level of analysis, in some of my writings, I have also considered some aspects of personality structure, within an "etic" psychoanalytic framework involving unconscious motivational patterns. I shall again briefly refer to some of the conclusions that help me understand what underlies certain conscious motivations and avoidances in Japanese conscious thought and behavior.

The "culture and personality" approaches of others researchers interpretet Japanese behavior in terms of both structural and interpersonal relationships. Some of these interpretations include the same interpersonal concerns in interaction as those presented in my framework. For example, T. Doi (1971) and W. Caudill (1962) have explored the continuance of nurturance on the part of dominant status and dependency on the part of subordinate status throughout the life cycle. They stress the difficulty of achieving an inner sense of self, *jibun*, or the exercise of personal autonomy in interpersonal relationships. Japanese remain expressively interdependent and instrumentally hierarchical. The expressive and instrumental are well blended in vertical patterns of relationship. Pursuing this topic, I have become increasingly aware of the structuring of a sense of potential guilt in the Japanese as it has been reflected in their deep sense of social responsibility which is still defined implicitly, if not explicitly, in modified Confucianist terms (1973). These features of the Japanese self made me critical of a "shame" emphasis in understanding Japanese social behavior. What also became increasingly apparent in exploring the interaction patterns of Japanese families in Caudill's subsequent intensive work (Caudill and Weinstein 1969) with early mother-child relations and in my own research with juvenile delinquents in Japan

(DeVos 1980a; DeVos and Wagatsuma 1972) is not only the continuing nurturant-control-dependency relationship between mother and son, but the potential for guilt with respect to possible deviant behavior.

It has been my contention that hierarchical relationships as well as achievement behavior have to be reexamined within their own psycho-cultural context in Japan. The bias of foreign observers sometimes creates ethnocentric distortions concerning how and in what contexts there is an internalization of social expectations in Japanese culture, a topic to which I shall return in greater detail.

Conformity and cohesion in Japanese society

In indirectly assessing attitudes about social cohesion or conformity in contemporary Japanese society, we can approach the Japanese with reference to several social indices used in Europe and the United States by social scientists. Various forms of mental illness, alcoholism, crime, delinquency, divorce, desertion, suicide, and homicide have different national rates, and within national statistics, different rates depending on social class position.

Mental illness in Japan has been difficult to assess statistically. Most psychiatrists believe mental hospital statistics measuring the appearance of mental illness in Japan can be very misleading with respect to the proportionate number of psychotic reactions in the population. They believe it to be not significantly different from that found generally for Europe and the United States.

Perhaps one learns less about the cultural patterning of the "self" in psychotic states since these may be at least partially determined by physiological determinants. However, cultural patterns are very apparent in what are termed "neurotic" conditions. Caudill (1959) and Reynolds (1980), for example, looked closely at *shinkeishitsu*, a specially Japanese interpretation of neurotic internal malaise which is sometimes treated by culturally indigenous healing methods. There are suggestions that it may be a relatively frequent "Japanese" malaise. As such, experiencing *shinkeishitsu* may be indicative of a severe middle-class type of social pressure on a Japanese, related to role expectations being in conflict with other features of the self. As discussed by Hollingshead and Redlich (1958) and others, neurosis in the United States seems to be more characteristically the result of the stricter self-constraints of middle-class social life than are the types of social malaise experienced in lower-class individuals and families. Similarly, Japanese in their middle-class status orientation become severely conflictual when they have inner blocks which interfere with the actualization of role behavior.

There is debate in Japan about the frequency of what can be considered alcoholism. Some psychologists describe alcohol abuse as frequent – especially in lower-class families. Indeed, we found evidence of alcohol problems disturbing some members of the lower-class families we were studying in Arakawa Ward. What was notable, however, was that the individual who drank heavily also tended to maintain role expectations involving regular work habits. What seemed to be an excessive use of alcohol disrupted the ability to maintain employment. Therefore, from an occupational standpoint, alcoholic disruption seems to be considerably less than that found in the United States. A sense of occupational responsibility is part of the Japanese self. Despite excessive use of alcohol an individual feels compelled to maintain his work standards.

Although there are some few cases of heroin addiction and the abuse of pharmaceutical drugs in an addictive manner in Japan, the stricter social control exercised over the import, manufacture, and distribution of drugs has been highly successful in limiting the number influenced. The heavy use of tranquilizers, however, again suggests a high degree of internal social strain felt in the population generally.

Crime statistics are well kept in Japan. In recent years criminal acts by those over twenty years of age have stayed remarkably low in comparison with other industrial societies. They certainly attest to a relative lack of social disaffection and to conformist concepts of the self, on all social levels including the Japanese working class. These statistics on crime are related to the continuing low rate of unemployment reported for Japan generally since the early 1960s.

There has been a shift in delinquency statistics toward an earlier appearance of delinquent behavior in fourteen- and fifteen-year-olds. There may be less conformist attitudes appearing in the younger generation – a loosening of the sense of parental authority. Nevertheless the overall rates among juveniles under twenty remain far below those reported for other industrialized countries.

While the crime rates are quite high for the Japanese minorities – the Burakumin (DeVos and Wagatsuma 1966) and the Koreans (Lee and DeVos 1981) – the relatively small proportion of minority groups, approximately 3 per cent, does not raise the overall crime rate for the total Japanese population to any considerable extent. (Since we are concentrating on the self in the majority of Japanese, I shall not further discuss here the complexity of identity problems and symptoms of social malaise in either of these minority groups.)

The divorce rate in Japan has been rising in recent years but again, compared with various European countries, there is seemingly less breakdown in family continuity and less sexual experimentation. The Japanese domestic situation remains, by and large, impressionalistically at least, more cohesive. Married couples remain self-consciously responsible and committed to the maintenance of family roles.

The lineage system now has less force on the Japanese sense of self than it has had in the past but the nuclear family unit is maintained with the continuing emphasis on role differences between men and women.

All in all, Japanese cities compared with their American counterparts continue to show networks of interrelationships through individuals and families joining various voluntary organizations (reported in Wagatsuma and DeVos 1983). The Japanese *danchi*, or apartment house complex, also evidences informal associations of women that help establish some form of social ties within what could otherwise become a relatively impersonal environment (Kiefer 1968).

I would generalize that most social evidence points toward the greater continuing influence of informal social control and social cohesion within the Japanese groups than is found within their western counterparts. These indices are not the purpose of our discussion; they are used merely to illustrate that we presume that the subjective experience of social life found among Japanese emphasizes group cohesion within the interaction patterns of men in their male occupational role, on the one hand, and of women in their role as mother and housewife on the other.

The man's pattern is manifest in business organizations as reported by Abegglan (1958), Rohlen (1974), and others; and the woman's pattern is manifest in the continuing operation of voluntary organizations which are the continuing daily experience of the housewife as she inhabits her social role (Wagatsuma and DeVos 1983). These patterns of interaction therefore provide strong evidence of the role dimension in the behavioral actualization of the social self among Japanese. The analyses of Lebra (1976) and Befu (1971) both attest, from slightly different perspectives, to centripetal rather than centrifugal forces in Japanese interaction patterns.

One other index of social participation, which may indicate difficulty in particular families, is to be found in the manner in which given Japanese join any new religious movements. The widespread presence of such movements, both in urban and rural Japan, may attest to the functional replacement of village participation in a household lineage system. Urban nuclear families often participate together in the social activities fostered by a cult. Involvement in one of these new sects demands more continuous participation than does simple adherence to a traditional Buddhist or Shinto sect, which demands formal participation only in transitional ceremonies related to birth, marriage, and death.

In sum, we can learn directly from these external sociologically oriented indices of cohesion or social participation something about continuity or change in social organization. Most of these indices attest to a continuity of social cohesion and control in an urbanized and modernized Japanese society. They also indirectly reflect the effect of social pressures to conform on the experiential self. Let us turn now to a more direct examination of the subjective experiences that must somehow be related to the self in the Japanese cultural context.

The actualization of the social self

Childhood experiences

In some respects the novelist is a more reliable informant of the experience of Japanese culture than is the social scientist looking at society from the outside. I shall not try to enter the very difficult topic of the progressive development of self-consciousness at various stages prior to adulthood and of its differences from or similarities to that of children in other cultures. This, of course, is a worthy topic, but one that due to its difficulty has been given relatively little attention in cross-cultural psychology. Most comprehensive studies of psychology, with the notable exception of Piaget's emic methods used cross-culturally, have been basically etic ones in which psychological test results or other manifestations of psychological competence are compared among school children. In effect, many anthropological approaches to subadult Japanese remain etic in that they refer to psychological structures rather than to some measure of actual experiences normative for Japanese.

There are, however, some recent collaborative efforts between Japanese and American psychologists to compare child-rearing, interpersonal behavior in the family, school performance, and social attitudes in youth that give us some indicators of the development of a Japanese self (Azuma, Hakuta, and Stevenson 1984). Kojima (1984) traces for us how, in the premodern Tokugawa period, the Japanese developed their own theories about the nature of child development and the methods of child-rearing that were considered most suitable. Inherent in traditional Japanese thought about child-rearing was the view that human nature is basically good, a tenet of Confucianism that dates back to the scholar Mencius writing in the third century BC. It was therefore readily possible for the Japanese to move self-consciously toward a systematic view of formal education to aid in the restructuring of their society at the onset of the modern period that followed the Meiji Restoration of 1868.

Historically, indigenous Japanese concepts of learning have always emphasized the need for exemplary behavior on the part of mentors. The child was seen to learn from the behavior of others, especially of parents and then, later, of the professional mentor. One taught others through one's own exemplary behavior. A child cannot be expected to behave with restraint or discipline when these are not practiced by parental models. One does not elicit proper behavior through commanding or controlling the learner's behavior but through having the learner acquire an inner comprehension which leads to proper self-regulation.

Keoki Kashiwagi (1967), on reviewing some studies of self-concept, confirmed the fact that there is a tendency for young Japanese to present publicly a more negative self-evaluation than has been reported for American youth. These negative self-evaluations spill over into problems of social phobias and other psychopathological concerns in some Japanese. Ogawa, in his report of depression in Japan (1981), reports on the relatively large number of depressive patients with self-punitive tendencies in their self-evaluation. Kashiwagi postulates that these findings are related to the high cultural value placed on the expression of modesty and also to the strong pressure for social conformity felt by Japanese living within their own system. Studies have agreed that the Japanese tend to regard internal factors as more causally significant than external ones in cases of failure, while they attribute external causes rather than their own efforts to cases of success.

Kashiwagi's studies report gender differences in both concepts of self and social role. These studies point to the fact that there is a larger discrepancy in adolescent women between their idealized roles and their self-assessments. Compared with Americans, both sexes in Japan put more emphasis on self-reflection and self-criticism.

The comparisons by Hess and Azuma of disciplinary modes in the United States and Japan can be seen as a comparison of training in sensitivity to intentional causality (Azuma, Hess, and Kashiwagi 1981; Hess *et al.* 1980). Many of the complex problems in psychosocial development are related to the experience of "intentional causality." If one reads Piaget's early works, based on Swiss subjects of the 1930s, one sees in the various descriptions of pre-causal thought that Piaget illustrates how children's false explanations often involve such intentionality, that is, that other powerful beings have attitudes which must be placated.

The development of subjectivity

The subjective experience of any culture starts as early as the incipient formation of given ego mechanisms that come to constitute the developing personality. The very intensive work of Caudill and his colleagues, for example, well establishes how the Japanese maternal relationship remains distinct from its American counterpart. Caudill and Doi (1963) discuss the manner in which expressive dependent needs are fostered in the intensive mother-child pattern. These needs color intimate social relationships for many Japanese throughout their life cycle. They continue to color the subsequent relationships established outside the primary family. I have elsewhere (DeVos 1980a) attempted to discuss the fact that many Japanese develop what is termed a "field independent" cognitive style despite the strong evidence of conforming behavior in school and elsewhere, and a refinement of interpersonal concerns with acute sensitivity to what others are thinking.

The comparison between Japanese and American classroom processes reveals differences in procedure and consequences. In an American science class, for example, there are prescriptive, directive assignments and the teacher elicits divergent ideas and proposals and does not try to lead to a conclusion. In the equivalent Japanese class, the situation is almost reversed. The class starts with a discussion of the children's various views. They are invited to defend or modify their positions and more than half of the class time is taken up by discussions of alternative positions. Discussions start with the presentation of the children's ideas and beliefs and then, by means of subtle leading questions, the teacher gradually focuses upon the major issues involved in understanding the subject. So the Japanese classroom comes to a convergence of understanding concerning a scientific experiment – the children coming to some form of consensus of experience in the classroom situation. The Americans, on the other hand, start with a prescriptive assignment, and then end up with divergence; learning continues to emphasize independent thought about what has been observed.

As an attempted "etic" observer of both American and Japanese "emic" perceptions, I would say that the trait of being self-critical about what one is doing is more apparent among Japanese than among Americans (e.g. Shikauchi 1978). It seems that the Japanese are more willing to be self-critical about their system or, at least, to countenance the criticism of outsiders. Americans are more apt to be defensive and more easily overtly to contend that their system is the best.

This is not to say that underneath the modesty of some Japanese one finds another layer of deeply assumed attitudes of superiority, especially with respect to discrimination against minorities – a trait shared with some Americans I have studied at some length (DeVos and Wagatsuma 1966; Lee and DeVos 1981). But certainly these features do not interfere with their continual self-criticism of accomplishment and of inadequacies in the self with reference to internalized standards.

As also suggested in the Hess-Azuma studies of early disciplinary techniques (Hess *et al.* 1980; Azuma, Hess, and Kashiwagi 1981), one must differentiate between the socialization of status position and patterns of decision-making. Parental status is not simply a matter of a person in an authority position exercising his or her will over that of a child; rather parenthood is a mentorship that teaches causality in behavior and the consequences of action. Through example, including the demonstration of deference toward others, the parent leads the child to conform to social expectations without the constant tendency to assert autonomy or the need to symbolize independence. Rather the social constraint directs the child toward learning to endure as a means of ultimately realizing one's goals and objectives.

American males consider receptivity to "mentorship" dangerous and the appearance of passivity and dependence shameful. For the Japanese there is no comparable discomfort.

The Japanese mother sensitizes her children to the interpersonal consequences of action. An American mother makes behavior appear as the result of a prevailing will. The Japanese mother supports but de-emphasizes the authority role; she neutralizes the interpersonal confrontational possibilities of constraint, whereas a contention of wills often becomes a focus of the American mother's battle with her child over proper behavior.

In the study of Azuma and his associates there is definite correlational significance between efficiency of communication, maternal expectations for achievement, and the mother's disciplinary strategy. The mother's teaching style and expressions of appreciation and praise, and the emotional climate created in the mother-child teaching efforts are singular for the Japanese context and feeling because they constrain the child's own behavior. Given these sensitivities in the Japanese and the cultural emphasis on social dependency, one nevertheless finds that the Japanese internalize their experiences in such a way that a potential for guilt acts as an internal constraint on any tendencies toward behavioral deviation. Within Japanese society constraint does not depend solely on external dominance and control. Japanese norms on psychological tests, for example, show the Japanese to be relatively high on certain measures of what has been termed "field independence" in the theoretical discussions developed by Witkin and his associates in their psychological research related to school performance (DeVos 1980a). (I shall return to this topic in the context of a general discussion of the internalization of norms in the Japanese.)

One must start examining the very complex interrelated patterning of social concerns related to the social self with the first dependent experiences of mother and child. The intensity of care given to children in Japanese culture is a well-documented culture pattern – the first indication of a general pattern of role dedication reinforced socially. The mother's close maternal care is, for many women, essential to her own sense of self-validation. Ideally speaking, a Japanese mother can become selfless in her dedication to her child and in her absorption in her child's life. Of course, the ideal pattern is seldom realized in its extreme, but the shared cultural expectations in this regard produce a need in the Japanese to believe in and feel gratitude toward an all-giving mother, as they look back on their own childhood experience. As I have discussed previously (DeVos 1973) when considering vulnerability to suicide, there are instances in which this ideal form of maternal care is not experienced by the individual. Nevertheless, there is often a distortion of memory, in many instances toward seeing the mother as an all-giving, all-caring person. The capacity to distort in this direction is influenced by sharing general Japanese patterns of thought about the mother which are exemplified in literature and in film. When this pattern does not work and the person cannot believe that it does, he does not have a recourse to the displaced idealized pattern provided in Christianity by the Holy Family. Indeed, in many instances a deep religious sense remains fixed on idealizing the actual family rather than transcending it and finding expression in idealized deities that provide love, care, or other emotional needs felt to be lacking (Dahl 1975). Some Japanese, of course, can have recourse to concepts of mercy or benevolence in Buddhism or in Kannon, a deity exemplifying mercy; but more generally speaking, one does not find Japanese culture providing a ready recourse to such deities. Some quasi-religious sense of fulfillment is found in idealizing the maternal relationship as it is realized in the family. This sense of gratification to be found in the closeness of the mother is also found in cultural represent-ations of physical pleasures. The Japanese sense of self is "syntonic" with minor expressive pleasures and sensory gratif-ications. Caudill and Doi (1963) and Caudill and Weinstein (1969) point up how the Japanese bath, for example, is one form of direct expressive pleasure and sensory gratification that is elaborated beyond what is customary in the west. The mother's subjective self experiences a central pleasure in the nursing relationship. The sensory experiences of the breast when nurs-ing is a type of self-experience which is often denied in western women. The Japanese mother has no sense of potential harm resulting from indulging the infant nor does she feel uneasy about the sexual meaning of the breast. These attitudes are related to the fact that the mother has the idea that progressive expectations placed on the child will come in good time when the child is ready to bear their burden.

The Japanese child's feelings about his own body are perhaps less ambivalent than those socialization has induced among certain western groups in the past. One's body is a source of minor accepted pleasure to be realized throughout life. However, this body loved narcissistically as a source of pleasure can also become a potential source of displeasure should one's aggressive impulses threaten one's self-control. Caudill and Doi both emphasize how there is a radical repression of aggressive feelings and negative attitudes within the immediate primary family relationships. The mother's "role playing" of the father as head of the family leaves little room for direct criticism of the "self" of the father. It is the role of the father to which she relates that the mother emphasizes, rather than the actual father as a fallible individual whose self may not attain the necessary social ideals (DeVos 1978). The contrary is often apparent in some American social groups where the "self" of the father or the "self" of the mother is what the relationship is about, rather than the role that is being played in relation to the infant or child. This is an experience that a child has − he does not see room for criticism since no criticism can be expressed directly or openly in family relationships. Later he comes to have his own opinions about other family members but characteristically he still does not voice them openly as this would be a breach of expected behavior.

There is a continually intense relationship around the child's progress throughout his period of formal education. Expectations about success as a student are progressively applied. The mother, however, very often participates in the child's work so intensely that the teachers cannot differentiate between a mother's contribution to homework and what is original to the child. Vogel (1965) first documented this type of mother-child interaction in his intensive study of Japanese families. Japanese culture emphasizes the motivational immaturity of the young infant and the fact that this infant "self" cannot be held responsible. Traditional westerners' sometimes stringent child-rearing practices were found to be based on an implicit concept that bad behavior must be, from early on, discouraged, and independence and responsibility encouraged. The infant "self" was perceived as "willful." The "role expectations" of a Japanese infant, on the other hand, were more relaxed, and the oral-contact relationship with the mother is indulged – not being considered damaging in any way to the later social character of the child.

The timing, therefore, of the mode of discipline experienced by the Japanese child can be radically different from that of his western counterpart. This does not mean that the experience of internalization is less exacting for a Japanese child when it occurs, but internalization of norms do not tend to be based on fear of potential punishment for deviancy as has been emphasized in western disciplinary practices.

What I have commented upon several times as the prevailing pattern of discipline exercised by the Japanese is the mother's capacity to use a sensitivity to suffering as a disciplinary mode. This pattern is found later on in other forms exercised by both men and women in Japanese social relationships. Japanese are, of course, quite capable of expressing aggression externally when there is license to do so. More characteristically, however, within the social group there is a tendency for subordinates to internalize aggression and not to express it openly against others. The Japanese, in some cases, give dramatic evidence of autoplastic aggressive forms of suicide where it is the self, in a sense, that is attacked rather than an external social object. My case material revealed what can be considered masochistic propensities in the internalization of aggression in the Japanese, especially in women, when performing their expected roles. This masochism, consciously experienced, sometimes appears as part of a self-sacrificing dedicated adherence to one's expected role. Present privation is seen as related to future success. Theodor Reik (1941), in his book *Masochism and Modern Man*, describes a syndrome he terms "moral masochism" which is directly applicable to some Japanese attitudes in given role situations, for instance that of the mother or of the apprentice taking on a given occupational training for future success. The supreme virtue of endurance through adversity pervades the Japanese sense of self (Wagatsuma and DeVos 1983). Endurance is seen as a virtue which tempers and develops the individual. The experience of pain in the present moving one toward the realization of future goals appears in the mother's maternal dedication as experienced by her child. Mothers tend to "suffer" their children rather than to forbid or inhibit their behavior by using verbal chastisement or even physical punishment. The child, while this form of discipline is going on, learns gradually the vulnerability of the loved one and that control of an offender is exercised not by doing anything to the offender but by self-control. The offender becomes frightened by his awesome capacity to injure the person he loves. Deviant behavior can inflict injury which is irreversible upon the very person on whom one has learned to depend so deeply. One's own behavior can lead to the illness or injury of another by damaging the beloved's sense of self and role.

In a positive sense, the mother expresses the capacity for self-exhaustion on behalf of her child but in so doing creates an awesome sense in the child that aggressive behavior is destructive. As a child is learning the awesomeness of his own capacity to destroy by deviant behavior, he is also learning that he can make others feel bad by dedicating himself to an inordinate degree. If one expresses suffering, another will react with guilt.

We must also observe that early on in the traditional culture there was a very evident split between the role expectations of male and female children and especially in the role expectations directed toward an eldest son as compared with other siblings. The eldest son was the most indulged of the children. As a child he could vent his feelings toward others and in some senses could continue to vent feelings against subordinates until, perhaps, he also learned to take a maternal or paternal attitude. But it is interesting to note that even though this venting of feelings has been possible there is very little evidence of much physical aggression on the part of men toward their children, and indeed there is not that much evidence that many men exercise the right to strike or physically abuse their wives, although one can cite noteworthy cases where men could have been so self-indulgent if they chose. The man in his family *was* somehow constrained, although there was no moral or cultural role constraint against the easy expression of dominant male aggression over others. The reason for this constraint is perhaps that many men internalize the maternal role more than has generally been thought. Robert Bellah very perceptively once cited the fact that curiously the emperor as the imperial father exercises and expresses what could be conceived of as maternal behavior toward his subjects. I would posit that there is more internalization of the maternal capacity for sacrifice than is sometimes acknowledged in the examination of Japanese men's behavior. An important aspect of the pattern of internalized aggression and masochism has been, in the past, a split in the direction of sexual expression. The wife, whether she wanted sexual gratification or not from her husband, tended to become in many instances desexualized, with an increasing emphasis on nurturant aspects of her role exercised toward her husband as well as toward her children. The young girl growing up, in her view of herself, became a little elder sister and would, in a sense, take a maternal attitude toward her father. I remember seeing a television advertisement for Suntori liquor in which a little six-year-old is bringing her tired daddy his shot of whisky to ease him from his hard day at the office.

The wife in the Japanese family tended to remain a central source of bodily comforts and affectional attachment. The husband's aggressive sexuality could be more freely and loosely expressed toward entertainers with no deep emotional involvement. The danger to the family occurred if the dependent attachment was transferred outside the family. This would cause serious complications within the family and a consequent sense of guilt in a man. In the old culture a Confucian emphasis on family lineage tended to reinforce the nurturant aspects of interpersonal relationships and to deemphasize the companionate or conjugal relationship which is conceived of as more reciprocal. The Japanese woman tends to be resigned to a more non-reciprocal nurturant relationship with a dependent husband than her American counterpart. She is less liable than her American or European counterpart to expect affiliation and intimacy as an essential part of the marriage relationship (cf. Blood 1967). She also expects to continue the non-reciprocity of a nurturant mother with a dependent child.

What one also hears said is that the level of expectation of pleasure may be autoerotic or sensual on the part of the woman, so that she finds in some cases substitutes for direct heterosexual gratification when it is not forthcoming from her husband. These are attitudes that are very hard to document since they demand systematic search into rather intimate levels of experience, but in some instances one notes that Japanese women experience satisfaction with the traditional relationship and in other instances one hears that women bear resentment and had hoped that their husbands would be more sexually active and considerate.

I have discussed extensively elsewhere (DeVos 1975) the expressive continuity of dominant – subordinate dependency relationships in Japanese occupational structures. One can do this by trying to indicate the subjective experience of Japanese workers and management within what Hsu (1975) describes as the *iemoto* relationship of the master of a craft and his subordinates, or what Nakane (1970) has termed the "frame" society. Nakane's description of Japanese society distinguishes between two types of belonging – "attribute" and "frame" groups. Attribute groups include both those groups entered by ascription through birth and those entered by acquiring an occupational specialization. In the first category are groups that take the form of clans or kinship lineages. In the second category are groups which the individual enters because of class position or some given occupational definition such as plumber or carpenter. In contrast to such "attribute" groups is the second major type which Nakane considers typically Japanese, that of "frame" organizations. Nakane sees a "frame" organization as a form of social belonging that occurs when the commitment to a particular company or organization is stronger than one's direct commitment to any given occupational specialization that one is performing within the organization. She points out how the Japanese like to sense themselves as working together toward common objectives and that this common purpose satisfies the inner sense of social purpose for the member. In this respect, the self is realized in role behavior not simply related to individual performance of a particular specialization; the sense of identity is located in a priority of loyalty to an organization rather than in one's sense of individual contribution. Therefore a sense of integrity is gained by furthering the total aims of the group rather than by realizing oneself individually or in having others acknowledge one's relative competence. In a small organization loyalty will be to one "master" or "company president." Within larger complex organizations one finds sub-patterns of loyalty to those in mentoring roles. Hsu (1975) cogently describes these extra-familial structures as they function throughout various occupations both traditional and modern.

From an expressive standpoint, a Japanese type of organizational allegiance depends heavily on the various patterns of mentorship and dominance and subordination found within the organization. The hierarchical pattern is implicitly an age-grading one of older/dominant – younger/subordinate. It is the pattern of interpersonal relationship that satisfies a heavy expressive need because this pattern of dominance and subordination is modeled at least to some degree on the idea of parentage derived from the primary family. The paternalism of the older person must be seen as having a truly expressive dimension. If we contrast the attitudes of the Japanese worker, for example, with those of the French worker, we see the extremes. The French are conscious of a lack of affective involvement of superiors with inferiors whereas the Japanese subordinate, whether he receives it or not, tends to expect some expression of mentoring and social concern from some immediate superior. The Japanese, in effect, idealize an expressive form of paternalism. To understand this, we have to see that it is indeed the fantasy of some Japanese who progress through the ranks of a company that to realize their ambition of becoming a company president would entail being able to bestow upon subordinates some gratification of a dependency by taking care of them. Such a fantasy is not to be found among Frenchmen who are attempting to rise in a business or professional hierarchy.

Such fantasies help make the subordinate position more

endurable. There is implicit in the Japanese mentality a sense of age progression which may or may not be realized as part of one's occupational career. One maintains, to some degree at least, the mentality of occupational stages including that of apprenticeship. One receives a low salary in the early stages of a career and puts up with the negative features of low status. One maintains a belief that one is going to progress with age much as one gains mastery in an occupation with continued experience.

The western image of "paternalism" is one that connotes simply an instrumental exploitative use of a helpless or dependent labor force with whom there is no real sense of personal involvement or belonging. The Japanese, in contrast, tend toward strong belief in political and social myths about the collectivity of their nation, company group, or family. The boss *iemoto* or *oyabun* is supposed to have parent-like feelings. Indeed the social expectations of his role often cause him to display overt behavior suggesting such feelings whether they are present in him or not. There are indeed positive fantasies of being protected directed toward superiors. In some instances these expectations reinforce an internalized sense of responsibility on their part. This interplay of expectations resembles the expectations of increased responsibility directed toward the eldest son in the traditional family. He is to internalize the sense of responsibility for others under his authority. Responsibility for taking care of personal matters would be considered intrusive by subordinates were they to be exercised in the west. For example, business executives, foremen, or even higher executives in Japan will sometimes act as go-betweens in assuring a proper marriage for one of their subordinates. This is seen as a part of a parent-like responsibility and indeed a type of nurturant concern with the subordinate. In sum, one finds even on a deep psychodynamic level an age-status network binding individuals into relationships with one another.

In the traditional Japanese system there were no "rights" on the part of the subordinate. The only recourse for subordinates in the past, since they had no contractual relationships, was to hope to induce kindness and benevolence in their superiors. These feelings were induced by invoking potential feelings of nurturance and appreciation from them. This capacity to induce kindness and benevolence in superiors in a manipulative manner is called *amaeru* in Japanese. It has been very cogently discussed at length by Takeo Doi (1971).

The image of the samurai bureaucrat in the premodern culture was that of a man supposedly dedicated to his job of overseeing and helping regulate a domain. What we see most often presented today are the military aspects of samurai, not the bureaucratic actuality which existed during periods of political tranquility (Craig and Shively 1970). Their rule was severe but was also supposedly concerned with the well-being of subordinates within their own class. The psychology of Japanese suicide remains heavily embued with the idea of people using themselves sacrificially to induce ameliorative behavior on the part of superiors, and superiors in turn using their self-sacrifice to induce proper behavior on the part of subordinates. This manipulation of the self autoplastically to induce expected behavior in others is one of the characteristics of Japanese society that helps to explain, if not the overall incidence of suicide in Japan, at least some of the peculiarities of individual cases that one finds periodically even today. The Japanese concern to develop a sense of responsibility in each new generation, out of the nurturant relationship, is then informed by the idea that one's dedicated behavior can be influential whether one is a subordinate or a superior. This sense of responsibility is part of the Japanese concept of social role. One becomes sensitive to the possible hurt one can inflict on the feelings of others; at the same time one can force actions from others by the sacrifice of oneself to one's role because one presumes the other to be conditioned in a manner similar to oneself.

Contrarily, deviant behavior is viewed as a direct assault or attack on the group or family and can be used vengefully when one feels that one has not properly received what is due; hence the idea that individuals can become "warped" in childhood if they are deprived. This term of "being warped" is used to describe delinquents. The Japanese rightfully see that delinquents tend to be resentful first of others in their primary family.

This potential for resentment is part of the self-consciousness of parents. Their proper parental role is to give nurturance to children so that they will become conforming adults.

Such social attitudes seeing compliance to authority, *sunao*, as based on indulgent care during childhood are more current and characteristic in Japan than in other countries. In turn, there is a need to believe in proper authority; although many people have developed a certain disdain for politicians and the like, one does not meet the level of suspicion or hostility toward public figures such as the police that one finds in western countries. There is still a moral ascendancy attributed by subordinates to their superiors. The amount of public respect for administrators is somewhat higher than found in contemporary western states, and whatever the negative feelings engendered, authority is not as readily perceived to be so dishonest as to be totally distrusted. An attitude of respect is more feasible for the Japanese emotionally. It becomes part of an implicit expectation that gratification will be awarded for compliant behavior. In the west a sense that moral obedience gains God's reward of love and nurturance is seldom extended to civil authorities; in Japan it is more readily directed toward the civil authority.

The continuance, even to a lessening degree, of such emotional interaction in a hierarchical social structure is highly repellent to western social theorists. And, of course, to modern rationally committed Japanese theorists as well. They often choose to ignore its operational force in present-day Japanese society or tend to see it as a left-over of feudal thought that somehow has persisted into the present. They implicitly choose the western model of a contract society as the ideal basis for social rational instrumental behavior and they ignore, if not abhor, the continuing force of expressive needs that permeate occupational as well as familial hierarchical structures in Japanese social organization.

Cooperation, competition – harmony, discord

I have been discussing so far how the basic early nurturant relationship pervades other forms of expressive and instrumental interrelationships in Japanese culture. Other forms of interpersonal attitudes result from the structuring of early dependency and its transmutation into later social forms. What one notices in attempting to contrast the Japanese social self with that of westerners is that there is less positing of individualism as a goal. Part of this relative downplay of individualism is related to less emphasis on affiliative needs in guiding behavior. One searches less for intimacy and affiliation on a reciprocal level, that is to say, without status differentiation. Nurturance behavior by its very nature is non-reciprocal. There is a donor and a donee, even though, as I have indicated, there can be instrumental manipulation of these relationships in that the donee also is exercising certain modes of inducing behavior in the donor.

It has often been remarked that horizontal relationships of equals are downplayed in the traditional Japanese culture. This still holds true for a downplay of expressive relationships of a companionate nature in marriage. One must point out, however, that outside the family there has been more instrumentally directed cooperative behavior within voluntary organizations than is generally recognized by outsiders. A great deal of social cohesion and social control is exercised through constrained participation in a wide variety of organizations dedicated to community betterment. How the individual feels about participating is beside the point – one is impelled to meet the social expectations of others as one subordinates self to social role. For example, the PTA in Japan has a much larger proportionate membership of parents than its American counterpart. Men are constrained to join voluntary merchant and artisan organizations (Wagatsuma and DeVos 1983). In the now disappearing rural pattern, men had to participate in local organizations to further collective interests. Women now attend neighborhood organizations in the city. Previously, women's village organizations, as Beardsley, Hall, and Ward (1959) pointed out in their intensive study of Niike, were able to exert influence on collective decisions made in traditional village life. In brief, horizontal social cooperation among those of equal status was not lacking in traditional Japan, although forms of social hierarchy have drawn greater attention and more persistent study. This participation is evidence of how self is continually subordinated to social role.

In our study of delinquency in Arakawa Ward in Tokyo, Wagatsuma and I were impressed with the number of colleagial voluntary organizations which touched on community betterment, including those directly concerned with delinquency control or prevention (Wagatsuma and DeVos 1983). While there are numerous circumstances where people usually relate to one another without some implicit status differential, in Japanese heterosexual relationships this occurs only to a limited degree. One now sees a great deal of social consciousness in a desire for greater equality between the sexes. In the past, an affiliative intimate relationship between the sexes was not developed due to a cultural emphasis on a hierarchical concept of family "harmony" as the ultimate expressive experience also. The wife would characteristically find her greatest closeness to her husband when she was functioning in a nurturing, "maternal" role rather than in a direct heterosexual one emphasizing companionship or shared passion.

In their patterns of friendship, the Japanese tend to have a relaxed intimacy only with individuals of the same age group. This often occurs between school-grade peers. Some such formally derived patterns of friendship can be developed within the context of larger organizations. Rohlen (1974) discusses in detail, for example, how members of the same bank go out together in groups, which is also typical of workers in other companies. It is very difficult, however, for Japanese to develop friendships that are not related either to shared educational experiences or to later experiences within a particular company or organization. This occupational group nexus reinforces the fact that the self is seldom experienced outside the social-occupational context. Conversely, Japanese are implicitly afraid of rejection by their group. They are quick to feel isolation without their presence. But the nature of these relations is not one of intimacy. And within-group processes on an equal level remain subordinate to other group considerations to a considerable degree.

The classic tragedies in Japan were about individuals who formed personal or passionate liaisons that went counter to their social roles. Almost invariably such intimate relationships caused tragedy. This implicit realization of the dangers of following personal proclivities still remains a conscious concern of the Japanese destined to remain within the confines of a tightly organized Japanese social system.

Much of what I have been discussing could have been approached from the standpoint of the influence of Confucian ideology on the family and on consequent social interaction patterns. The principal overarching concept of society imbued with Confucianist teaching is that of harmony. The great disruptor of society within Confucianism is confrontation, leading to conflict and social disorganization. This perception of social relationships is based on an ideal of ordered human feelings. That is, peaceful relationships – the expressive satisfaction of peaceful relationships – occur only when people maintain themselves properly within expected social roles. When this type of social order is maintained there is happiness for all. This, of course, is an idealization of society much as is any other form. What is very apparent, however, is that it is still an implicit ordering principle within the Japanese perception of self. The role dedication that I was describing as ideal for traditional women was part of *Onna Daigaku*, the Confucian "great learning for women." Although such formal exposition of role behavior has long since disappeared from the direct consciousness of social life, it nevertheless remains as a directed emotional undercurrent which helps to explain Japanese feelings about marital life.

The Japanese find ultimate satisfaction in "belonging." This sense of belonging can shift from one that is realized through a quasi-religious reverence for the family as an enduring corporate entity to more secularized ideas of the establishment of groups or occupational relationships through which one can realize, as the Japanese term it, *shiawase* – comfort, contentment, and happiness defined in very material terms. In the past the sense of expressive contentment within the household was to be obtained by following Confucian ideals of harmony and order. For the Japanese, the *ie* was a framework for clearly divided roles. Members derived personal satisfaction from working cooperatively. Nurturant and dependent needs could be realized within this framework. This realization did not necessarily occur primarily in the husband and wife relationship. The sharing of one's intimate self in companionship and communion was not considered a goal of marriage. It was not an institutionalized expectation of the marriage bond and indeed at times such sharing was considered detrimental to proper role behavior in marriage. The Japanese sense of belonging traditionally did not derive from any sense of direct mutual understanding but was related to a diffuseness in the sense of one's self in which any painful awareness of an existential separateness could be avoided by holding to a sense of one's self as a family member. Such a loss of boundaries has been found satisfying to many members of religious bodies. A sense of group identity gives one strength to go beyond one's own personal defects or limitations in the interdependence that occurs. For some of its adherents, Christianity in the west satisfies such a basic social need instead of merely offering a dogma.

The Japanese emphasis on role behavior rather than on intimate personal communication is well illustrated by differences found among the families of our Arakawa Ward study. Our normal controls and sample families with delinquent children differ significantly in the manner in which harmony was maintained and discord avoided (DeVos and Wagatsuma 1972). There is no difference in the role behavior of the fathers of these families with respect to achievement and competence. Many in both groups are obvious economic, vocational, and personal failures, but the mothers of non-delinquents expressed far less direct criticism and disdain of their husbands' shortcomings. In the six hours of interview time we held with each mother more than three-quarters of the mothers of problem children expressed a direct and unequivocal dissatisfaction with and sometimes even contempt for their husbands. Many of them describe in graphic terms the type of discord and disharmony that characterize their marital life. Although the mothers of non-delinquent children also criticized their husbands they did so less frequently and less intensively and only very indirectly, and seldom in the presence of their children.

In both groups we also found women whose basic personality propensities were not at all in accord with the demands of their social sex roles. Many of these women felt themselves to be more dominant and aggressive and even more impulsive than their acceptable role behavior warranted. We felt that the psychologically available techniques for role maintenance, especially dedication to self-controlled behavior within the woman's role, made the critical difference between the mothers of delinquents and non-delinquents. On a psychodynamic level, the integrative mechanisms available to mothers of the normal controls were somewhat better than those of the mothers of delinquents. Thus, the mothers of non-delinquents, whatever their propensities, had better psychological means at their disposal to maintain self-control and through the maintenance of this self-control to maintain the necessary harmony considered ideal in the family relationship – whatever the actual inadequacies of their consort. In the Confucianist concept, the Japanese father was never to be treated in any way that was disrespectful of his role or position. Whatever the woman's unrealized need for mutual affection or even dependency, she was required to treat the husband as the symbol of authority and succession in the family.

The Confucianist ethic and its particular moral aspects help us understand why there is such concern about direct instrumental confrontation as a means of solving problems in Japanese society. To contend openly is to disturb the harmony of the group which must be maintained at all costs. It has less to do with the idea that subordinates should not initiate behavior, for, in fact, subordinates may initiate suggestions and activities sometimes more readily than is the case in highly instrumentally organized social hierarchies in the west. The reason for permitting subordinate initiative so readily is that there is a presumption of ultimate loyalty on the part of everyone in the group. Group process depends upon this implicit assumption of permanent membership and ultimate loyalty. One cannot distrust the individual motives of members of one's group and function effectively. Any display of direct antagonism or personal competition is considered disruptive to the underlying harmony of the group. One can only arrive at decisions in the Japanese group through consensus; there is no minority position. This applies even to the primary family. I have had numerous anecdotes told me about family decisions with regard to occupational choice. In some instances, the total family membership was at least formally consulted in order to determine whether or not a family member should take a particular job. This family consensus remains basic to "legitimate" marriage arrangements. The harmony of the family was a prior consideration and took precedence over concepts of personal affiliation in marriage arrangements.

Because one sees no evidence today of dogma about Confucianism in Japan, it is often erroneously assumed that Confucianism is dead or that it has had no continuing effect on the structuring of affective relationships. The point to be made about harmony, as an expressive concern, is that it underlies instrumental cooperation within any group. Beneath this instrumental level of cooperative enterprise one still finds a Japanese sense of self in social role that is first experienced as a family member, and then later re-experienced when entering an occupation. One again seeks to find personal satisfaction in being in some form of social harmony with others − both in the hierarchical relationships that occur in the group and in horizontal relationships with those that are in the same age cohort. It must be stressed that vertical relationships remain as important in a company as relationships of a horizontal nature which provide companionship. In seeking to understand Japanese expressive satisfaction one must attend both to continuing nurturance on the one hand and harmony on the other and see how often these take precedence over the actualization of intimacy in relationships that are to any extent exclusive of social role considerations.

The introjective displacements of aggression

In most of their social relations, Japanese are expert at maintaining a Confucianist harmony and peacefulness, on the surface at least. They suppress any obvious forms of intra-group discord, let alone violence. However, if we were to limit our examination of Japanese culture to normative patterns and overt social role behavior, we would fail to understand how disruptive or destructive impulses are also displaced and emotional interests expressed through culturally patterned forms. One must look beneath the level of self-awareness at the unconscious psychological mechanisms channeling aggression into relatively non-destructive social routes.

I have already suggested that one such adjustive function is the transmutation of certain forms of aggression into what may be termed moral masochism. In my past research I have looked at this pattern of introjection of hostility with reference both to the internalization of guilt and to concern over mastery and self-control. The fact that the Japanese become highly internalized individuals is manifest also in the fact that in cognitive development one finds evidence of what are termed "field independent" (Witkin 1978) forms of problem-solving. I have discussed elsewhere (DeVos 1980a, 1981) the fact that the Japanese do not fit the generalization that a sensitivity to social approval and cooperative attitudes is more characteristic of a "field dependent" cognitive pattern, while "field independent" individuals tend toward competitive interaction patterns and individualistic social goals. This relationship between cognitive patterns and forms of social sensitivity is a complex one – suffice it to say here, Japanese socialization patterns emphasize a type of internalization that influences cognitive development. In a good number of individuals one finds evidence of self-regulated perceptual independence in cognition coexisting with a need to behave outwardly in a socially sensitive manner.

The Japanese are an anomalous culture. They manifest highly internalized social standards, and at the same time exercise forms of self-control that make them seem to be totally conforming to their social group and its interests. The intrapsychic tensions engendered over belonging take several forms. I have discussed these at length in the context of Japanese suicide (DeVos 1973: chapter XVII). I discussed, for example, the relation between internally directed aggression and the special conditions and forms taken by Japanese anomic or altruistic suicide. Some suicides are related to what I term "role narcissism" and other forms of suicide are related to the maintenance of harmony within the social group. In anomic Japanese suicide one sees how aggressive feelings aroused by loss of status due to the mistakes of others as well as of the self can readily result in a suicidal act. One also sees in the patterning of illness in Japan how some individuals can introject hostility by using their own bodies as an ambivalent object. Also, as mentioned earlier, particular forms of neurosis prevalent among Japanese also evidence an internal debilitation due to inexpressible hostility (DeVos 1980b).

Projective use of the "outsider" in Japanese culture

The Japanese think that the maintenance of a harmonious group in Japan depends on not bringing in disruptive outsiders; moreover, in-group harmony and high standards may be maintained by out-group disparagement and contempt. This causes a basic problem in extending Japanese organizational principles outside Japan. What is notably lacking in Japan in the transmutation of aggression in comparison with certain other cultures are patterns of projection expressed through institutionalized concern over witchcraft and sorcery. While the supernatural is not used projectively, Japanese can at times deflect both direct aggression (in the form of violence) and indirect aggression (in the form of disparagement) on outsiders perceived as vulnerable due to their lower status or their perceived racial inferiority.

Therefore, while there is severe internalization and the repression of aggression toward anyone considered part of legitimate society, the Japanese culture does allow for the systematic scapegoating of "outcasts" including their caste-like minorities of Burakumin and Koreans. These minorities are seen as committing the disavowed and the unacceptable as well as lacking in manifest accomplishment due to inferior heredity. The past displays of self-righteous arrogance committed during wartime foreign occupations, as well as the continuing inability to assimilate those of supposed or actual different cultural backgrounds, both attest to the outward projection of internal tensions receiving no outlet through ordinary social channels.

Culturally, the Japanese have been taught that they are of unique origin. Under conditions of militarism this sense of group uniqueness created extreme difficulties in relating to outsiders perceived as inferiors. Today one still sees evidence of these difficulties in the inability to assimilate outsiders into Japan or even to deal easily with outsiders in the economic marketplace. This cultural attitude helps us to understand why it is difficult to expand in-group organizations beyond a totally Japanese membership. Korean Japanese cannot find easy acceptance in a Japanese organization. Japanese organizations are based on the implicit idea that group members are somewhat merged in their collectivity. They share the same goals and have similar implicit interpersonal affective patterns which allow them to work together in harmony without any form of individualistic or "alien" notions which would break up the basic melded harmony of the group. But even more than that, they envisage that merging of the self is only possible with others of the same heredity. There remains a deep current of racist feeling, if not racist thought, in many Japanese (Lee and DeVos 1981). This racism allows for a ready displacement of unresolved concerns with high standards – leading to worry about an incapacity to actualize accomplishment or an expressive insecurity about self-worth – onto outsiders perceived to be more incompetent or unworthy than the Japanese in their accomplishments.

Motives for achievement in Japan

For years, I have questioned the generalizations of Ruth Benedict (1946) which suggested that the Japanese were, in effect, behaviorally more motivated by shame than by guilt. This is an issue which still remains controversial. I have contended that the actual structuring of guilt in the personality of many Japanese tends to be hidden from western observation since there has been a lack of empathic understanding of what it means to be part of a Japanese family system. Western observers tend to look for guilt, conscious or unconscious, as it is symbolically expressed with reference to a possible transgression by the individualized self of limits imposed by a generalized ideology, or a religious system circumscribing individual sexual and aggressive impulses.

I argue more broadly that potential for guilt is related to the internalization of norms involving a sense of the potentially destructive effect of failure or deviant behavior on one's parents. There is also the danger of expressing "destructive" behavior through other independent behavior that goes counter to role expectations. Such feelings are not easily appreciable by outsiders. *Ongaeshi*, when directly translated into English as the return of parental favors or obligations to parents, does not convey to the western observer the emotional nuances it has for a Japanese. Even though it is indeed a terrible transgression not to honor parental obligations, *tsumi*, translated as "sin," is never used to describe the feeling of guilt a Japanese can experience as a consequence. Nevertheless, looked at from the level of emic experience, failures to perform properly are indeed symbolically "destructive" to someone whom one loves and on whom one depends. Conversely, for many Japanese, sexual behavior is guilt-producing only when it actually disrupts the family and is therefore "destructive" to others one loves. Therefore I have contended that the subjective experience of "destructiveness" of many Japanese should they fail to meet expectations is part of a moral system involving a potential for guilt built around family duties and obligations. Japanese social behavior in its long-range consequences is constrained by this internal realization of guilt over failure more than by considerations of "face" or "shame." This is not to deny that there is also continual sensitivity about not stimulating outside attitudes that might bring damage to family or group honor. If through poor performance outsiders can disparage one's nation or family one has been guilty of bringing disgrace. Hence one must atone by taking the blame and removing oneself as unworthy. It is the destructive consequences of one's behavior that cause guilt and the release of aggression toward the self. One cannot easily project failure onto outward circumstances; often only one's own body is available.

Hence it is my contention that emphasis on honor or shame sanctions in an honor-oriented society, whether Sicilian or Japanese, does not preclude the presence of severe guilt resulting from the unconscious destructive or aggressive meaning of social transgression or failure to perform well.

Strong feelings of anxiety related to conformity are evident in the Japanese, but severe guilt becomes more apparent when the underlying motivation contributing to manifest behavior is intensely analyzed. Shame is a more conscious phenomenon among the Japanese, more easily verbalized, and hence more readily perceived by outsiders as influencing behavior. But a potential to guilt often seems to be a stronger basic long-range determinant of career behavior whether as a man in an occupational role or a woman as wife and mother. What has been the basis of the contrary argument concerning self-consciousness about shame in the Japanese? Seen historically, the Japanese have often been pictured as having developed extreme susceptibility to group pressures toward conformity as a result of several hundred years of tightly-knit feudal organization. This strong group conformity is often viewed as associated with a lack of the personal qualities that foster individualistic endeavor. In this context, the achievement of the Japanese in modernization has often been considered to be a group manifestation of achievement rather than something that has occurred as a collective response of highly internalized individuals. Achievement, for example in Americans, has been discussed by Riesman, Denney, and Glazer (1950) as shifting from inner-directed motivation to other-directed concerns with conformity and outer group situations. Perceived in this framework, the Japanese traditionally are considered to have been other-directed and what the outsider considers "sensitivity to face" and attention to protocol suggests that this continual susceptibility to social pressure traced psychoanalytically may presumably be derived from underlying fears of abandonment. Personality patterns integrated around such motivation, if culturally prevalent, could lead a society to be dominated by a fear of failure and a need for recognition and success. Social evaluations are used as a sanction rather than more self-contained codes instilled and enforced in early life by parental punishment, as has been considered the method practiced in the west.

The child-rearing patterns in Japan indeed manifest early permissiveness in regard to weaning and bowel training and many observers have indicated there is also a very notable lack of physical punishment. There is also evident ridicule by peers and rejection of imperfect or slipshod performance by mentors. There is considered to be a strong relationship between early permissiveness and susceptibility to external sanctions. One can see that this line of reasoning would lead to the conclusion that the Japanese could easily be classified as shame-oriented and that their concern over success and failure could be explicable in these terms. However, this formula does not hold up well when reapplied to an understanding of individual Japanese either in Japan or in the United States. Clinical cases consistently give evidence of depressive reactions and an inability to express hostile and resentful feelings toward parents. Feelings of guilt are engendered and these feelings must be seen as related to an inability to express aggression outwardly, leading to intrapunitive reactions.

It must be noted that statements concerning a self worried about potential worthlessness may also result from the repression of aggressive feelings and the turning back of these negative attitudes on the self. This turning in of negative attitudes is not due to physical punishment but to the sense that one's aggressive behavior toward loved ones makes for a worthless individual. So that what some would consider "shame" actually can be an expression of depressive propensities toward negative attitudes about the self. These attitudes do not depend on external witnesses nor on the external considerations of others, but are forms of self-assessment that are inflicted by the individual on himself. In the self ideal which is developed in the Japanese and becomes part of the internalized super-ego, strivings toward success, day-by-day hard work, and purposeful activities that lead to long-range goals continue to be related to guilt feelings easily aroused in respect of parental obligations. Transgression in the form of laziness or other nonproductive behavior is felt by many Japanese to injure their parents who have been self-sacrificing for them and thus this nonconforming behavior leads to feelings of guilt. There are psychological analogs between this Japanese sense of family responsibility to parents and what we find in the west in what has been described by some as the Protestant work ethic. Bellah

(1957), in his incisive volume, *Tokugawa Religion*, perceives and illustrates in detail a definite relationship between ethical ideals in the Tokugawa period and the rapid industrialization of Japan. He points up the obvious parallels in Tokugawa Japan to the precapitalistic ethical orientation found evident in Protestant Europe according to the analysis of Max Weber.

These issues have taken us beyond a direct discussion of the experiential self into forms of structural analysis of personality. Nevertheless, even on the level of the self, concern in some Japanese with obligation and responsibility is experienced subjectively and sometimes termed *giri*, *gimu*, or *on*. Although semantically translated differently, these concerns can indeed be an expression of feelings that are functionally related to guilt rather than to a potential for shame. Most of the evidence that I have forwarded from my psychological test analyses in Japan point toward the presence of guilt. What I have not perhaps sufficiently stressed is that this material at the same time gives much less evidence than might be expected, in terms of projective fantasy, of feelings of being observed by others as a social deterrent. In effect, much psychological evidence points at least as much toward internalized concerns as toward some preoccupation with the external views of the society as they influence the individual.

I would think that the evidence related to the presence of a sense of potential guilt as part of the self of many Japanese is related to my discussion of the evidence of a field independent style of perception in cognitive development as more character-istic of Japanese than a field dependent one (DeVos 1981). One can cite an evident relationship in Anglo-American children between "field independent" cognitive patterns and a self focused on more open competitiveness and less concern with hurting the feelings of others (Kagan 1974; Madsen and Shapiro 1973). One cannot therefore generalize that this relationship of an individualistic self and field independence will also hold true in a culture in which there is continual social scrutiny of the effect of one's behavior on the group. Indeed, Witkin's last formulations (Witkin 1978) stress a necessity to distinguish outer social sensitivity related to the feelings of others from structural considerations of personality. In the Japanese we have evidence of field independence (DeVos 1980a, 1981) but also a culture pattern that stresses a continuing self-conscious sensitivity over how one's own behavior will cause reactions in others. It is necessary therefore to analyze how behavior of an "independent" or "selfish" nature is somehow associated with a propensity to sense guilt in Japanese socialization. While cognitive patterns depend on an independent view of outer reality, constraints on manifest behavior are shaped by a sensitized awareness of their consequences for family as well as self. But one must not therefore infer that there is always a direct structural linkage in personality between continuance of field dependence and social sensitivity. Indeed, a concern with the feelings of others is independent of cognitive variants in personality. This is quite apparent if we examine Japanese socialization.

Japanese are highly internalized individuals, and seen psychodynamically their pattern of internalization has to be related to other processes involved both in resolving early identifications as well as in assuming later adult social roles. In the child's experience, the more difficult it is to try to live up to the ideal role behavior expected of him or her the more likely he or she is to develop ambivalence toward the source of the ideal. This ideal need not directly emphasize prohibited behavior as is the case when punishment is the mode of training. When shame and guilt have undergone a process of internalization during the course of an individual's development, both become operative. This occurs despite the relative absence of external threats of punishment in the Japanese and the more overt concern with the opinions of others concerning expected behavior. In an internalized Japanese, behavior is always judged by a super-ego ready to deem one worthless should one fail. Self-evaluation occurs without the presence of others. A simple dichotomy relating internalized shame only to an ego ideal and internalized guilt only to an automatically operative punitive super-ego is one to be seriously questioned. The formation of an internalized ego ideal in its earlier forms is more related in the Japanese to the social expectations and values of parents. The motivations that move a developing young adult toward a realization of these expectations can and do involve considerable guilt among Japanese whether it be in making an occupational choice or a marriage choice as related to family expectations (DeVos 1973). In brief, shame and guilt are both potent forces for socialization in Japanese culture. Both emerge in the presence of failures to meet the demands of ego ideals instilled early in youth by parental expectations and values. I do not accept the belief that shame is associated with failures to meet the ego ideal and guilt is associated with failures to a punitive super-ego. This notion, popular in many circles of anthropology and psychiatry, does not reflect the fact that shame and guilt are both internalized conditions despite the relative absence of external threats and the extensive concerns for others' opinions. This matter takes us perhaps a little too far into structural analysis from that of the experiential self but one cannot avoid a very necessary consideration of the presence of guilt as related to shame in the Japanese if one is to understand Japanese social behavior.

Concern with adequacy in instrumental behavior versus concern with will

Another theme which merits more than a brief mention in the Japanese experience of the self as related to the internalization of achievement motives is the recurrent concern with adequacy or competence in Japanese self-evaluation in contrast to the concern I have obtained from some western examples.

Japanese, on constructing fantasies concerning achievement motivation, tend to stress problems of personal adequacy as a principal concern. In response to similar stimuli American children and adults are more concerned with the willingness of the individual to take on a socially induced task rather than any worry about their capacity to do so. I have often argued that it is easier for an American to see achievement as a question of individual desire and autonomous will rather than to recognize possible underlying worries about whether one is sufficiently capable or talented. The Japanese, in contrast, more generally do not like to consider problems of volition which would be deemed self-centered and selfish in nature. Questions of self-interest would bring the individual into conflict with his social group. It is much easier psychologically to worry about the individual's capacity to achieve. The virtue of endurance, as well as being a Japanese concept of willpower, is reflected in the belief that, if the individual works hard and persists, he can overcome his limitations. The outside circumstances, such as poverty or discrimination, cannot be blamed for individual failure; the body – perhaps. One can be handicapped by illness but even handicaps can be overcome if the determination to succeed – the commitment to a goal – is sufficiently strong. There is an implacable optimism in many Japanese. The goal of mastery is not to be obtained quickly – or by magical means – or through luck.

I would contend that these instrumental goal-directed attitudes tempered by worry over personal adequacy are not related to worry about an observing world. They are a mark of rigorous, demanding self-evaluation. Questions of worthiness do not arise in relation to a demanding, severe, and potentially punishing patriarchial deity. They arise in relation to a demanding society. They arise in evaluating oneself against idealized social figures who have met the challenge of this society – the parents or the *sensei* who have gone before. To paraphrase Lafcadio Hearn, the western tyranny is the one over the many, the Japanese tyranny is the many over the one.

Conclusions and discussion

In this chapter I have reversed somewhat the priority of the order of consideration of interpersonal patterns from some of my previous writings on achievement motivation. In the present instance, I have emphasized more strongly the expressive aspects of Japanese concerns rather than commencing my discussion with the instrumental patterns which have been the primary concern in my writings on Japanese role behavior. The essence of instrumental behavior is that it is goal-oriented – that it has objectives to be realized regardless of the affective components found in the necessary behavior. What I have again emphasized is how the Japanese sense of duty and obligation is very central to understanding instrumental motivations. This sense of responsibility, I have contended, is highly internalized. Social constraints so very evident in external patterns of social control in Japanese society are also internalized, albeit with some costs in terms of personal tension for most Japanese; and additional costs, in terms of suppression of personal needs, for Japanese women. Behavior, if not thought, remains in harmony with the external reinforcements of social control in Japanese society. Japanese socialization tends to legitimize authority rather than raise issues about autonomy. There is a positive assessment of subordinate compliance rather than the characteristic ambivalence about being or remaining subordinate found prevailing in American society, for example. The American concept of the social self, at least for males, goes to great lengths to emphasize the ideal of development toward autonomy and the liberation of the self from external authority as part of social growth. The Japanese concept of instrumental behavior de-emphasizes autonomy as an acceptable mode of instrumental interaction with others. Rather, the within-group emphasis is on cooperative behavior and the necessary social subordination of oneself, on the surface at least, into a harmonious mode of instrumental realization with others of one's own group, very often under a symbolically perceived boss, *iemoto*, or company president. Such cooperative behavior in turn can be put in a highly competitive frame of reference with respect to others outside the group. The ritually reinforced sense of social belonging within an organization takes precedence over any forms of individual realization of goals. Competitive inclinations cannot be released toward others close by, but are expressed through regulated competition as part of a group. The Japanese sense of accomplishment can be realized in group success. The analogy that comes immediately to mind is that Japanese groups are like football teams or other forms of team sports in which one can successfully compete only if one subordinates oneself to the group. Single stars who overemphasize their individual prowess may be disruptive to group spirit and, at least overtly, they must contain themselves within the group purpose in order to continue to function as part of the group. Conversely, unethical behavior is sometimes tolerated toward the outside since there is no feeling of necessary identification with one's competitors; and it is in some forms of unethical behavior that one can perceive most clearly the Japanese lack of identification with others that are not part of their own group. And as mentioned already, it is very difficult to bring outsiders in as part of one's cooperative team since the underlying expressive considerations may be considered lacking. One cannot therefore separate out Japanese cooperative behavior as a form of strictly instrumental juxtaposition of individual needs. There is in the cooperative behavior itself a continual expression of a sense of belonging. The rituals exercised in Japanese companies in the morning might seem slightly ridiculous to the western observer. The idea that people do gymnastics together or sing company songs can be seen by more instrumentally oriented outside observers as perhaps a waste of time and unnecessary to the proper functioning of a commercial or industrial organization. To the Japanese, however, such behavior symbolizes the collectivity and the sense of belonging, which are positively experienced, as well as focusing on the instrumental purposes of the organization.

The Japanese sense of self is directed toward immediate social purposes, not toward a process of separating out and keeping the self somehow distinct, somehow truly individual, as remains the western ideal.

A final caveat: the above description and analysis is one suggesting a normative orientation. As a country of over one hundred million inhabitants, it is the utmost presumption to suggest that this normative orientation represents the inner experience of most Japanese. Many are aware of this pattern and manipulate it cynically. Others submit to expectations, resigned to the insurmountable difference between the ideal and the real in the behavior of others. Yet others are aware that they are caught by a necessity to orient their behavior in conformity with this pattern, whatever their personal experience to the contrary, including their primary family experiences which may be far from the ideal of nurturance and legitimately functioning authority. Indeed Harumi Befu (personal communication) has

taken the rather provocative theoretical stance that the group
orientation has been overemphasized at the expense of the
continuing evidence of patterns of individual integrity in the
face of group conformity. There are individual heroes in
Japanese history and in Japanese fantasy, as witness the popularity of lone heroes in the samurai epics or in stories of Yakuya
villainy. I would agree with the point that there is a sense of the
heroic and the tragic in Japanese culture, but the sense of
tragedy in this respect far outweighs any fantasy of a potential
triumph of the individual.

There are, indeed, many introspective Japanese who are
acutely aware of the difference between the social person – or
the mask they wear protectively – and the inner being guarded
from exposure to others. Some authors have been able to convey
in their thinly disguised autobiographical experiences this difference between *tatemae* – the outward presentation of the social
self – and the painfully hidden *honne* of inclinations and
proclivities (Dazai 1958; Mishima 1970). But what is most often
depicted in this material is that one continues to behave, self-
protectively, in socially expected ways – whatever the hidden
aspects of the self (Wagatsuma and DeVos 1978).

For some, the idealization of the family is part of a quasi-
religious security system based on illusory rather than real past
experiences in childhood. Indeed in clinical cases one finds
forms of alienation related to early maternal deprivation (DeVos
1973: chapters XVII and XVIII).

There is, however, relatively little recourse to universalist
religious beliefs to assuage or to compensate for needed
benevolence or loving concern. A personally related deity is
unavailable. Instead, the illusion of having these needs filled is
reaffirmed by some Japanese who manage to distort their past
family experiences so as to feel gratitude directed toward their
parents and mentors (Dahl 1975; DeVos 1980b). Some forms of
Japanese therapy "readapt" the individual, permitting him or
hcr to perform in the expected manner by releasing feelings of
gratitude socially whether there have been objective reasons
to do so in the past or not.

I started my paper with a brief look at indices of social anomie or deviancy and have ended with a too brief mention of the secret selves of many Japanese. The fact that, relatively speaking, Japan functions today as a successful society attests to the centripetal force of shared illusions as well as the external reinforcement of social sanctions; and conversely, it attests to the centrifugal weakness of unshared secrets or personal fantasies.

References

Abegglen, J. G. (1958) *The Japanese Factory: Aspects of Its Social Organization.* Glencoe, Ill.: Free Press.

Azuma, H., Hakuta, K., and Stevenson, H. (1984) *Child Development in Japan and the United States.* San Francisco: Freeman.

Azuma, H., Hess, R. D., and Kashiwagi, K. (1981) *Mother's Attitudes and Actions and the Intellectual (Mental) Development of Children.* Tokyo: Tokyo University Press.

Beardsley, R., Hall, J. W., and Ward, R. E. (1959) *Village Japan.* Chicago: University of Chicago Press.

Befu, H. (1971) *Japan: An Anthropological Introduction.* San Francisco: Chandler.

Bellah, R. (1957) *Tokugawa Religion.* Glencoe, Ill.: Free Press.

Benedict, R. (1946) *The Chrysanthemum and the Sword: Patterns of Japanese Culture.* Boston: Houghton-Mifflin.

Bennett, J. W. and Ishino, I. (1963) *Paternalism in the Japanese Factory.* Minneapolis: University of Minnesota Press.

Blood, R. O., Jr. (1967) *Love Marriage and Arranged Marriage.* Glencoe, Ill.: Free Press.

Caudill, W. (1959) Similarities and Differences in Psychiatric Illness and Its Treatment in the United States and Japan. *Seishin Eisei (Mental Hygiene)* 61–2: 15–26.

_____ (1962) Patterns of Emotion in Modern Japan. In R. J. Smith and R. K. Beardsley (eds) *Japanese Culture.* New York: Wenner-Gren Foundation for Anthropological Research.

_____ (1976) Social Change and Cultural Continuity in Modern Japan. In G. A. DeVos (ed.) *Responses to Change.* New York: Van Nostrand.

Caudill, W. and DeVos, G. (1956) Achievement, Culture and Personality: The Case of the Japanese Americans. *American Anthropologist* 58(6): 1102–126.

Caudill, W. and Doi, T. L. (1963) Interrelationships of Psychiatry, Culture and Emotion in Japan. Reprinted with permission by the

U.D. Department of Health and Welfare from Iago Galdston (ed.) *Man's Image in Medicine and Anthropology*. New York: International Universities Press.

Caudill, W. and Weinstein, H. (1969) Maternal Care and Infant Behavior in Japan and America. *Psychiatry* 32: 12–43.

Craig, A. M. and Shively, D. H. (eds) (1970) *Personality in Japanese History*. Berkeley: University of California Press.

Dahl, W. (1975) *Religious Conversion and Mental Health in Two Japanese American Groups*. Unpublished Ph.D. dissertation, Department of Anthropology, University of California, Berkeley.

Dazai, O. (1958) *Ningen Shikkatu (No Longer Human)*. Trans. D. Keene. New York: New Directions.

DeVos, G. A. (1973) *Socialization for Achievement: Essays on the Cultural Psychology of the Japanese*. Berkeley: University of California Press.

—— (1974) Cross-Cultural Studies in Mental Disorder: An Anthropological Perspective. In G. Caplan (ed.) *American Handbook of Psychiatry*, vol. 3. New York: Basic Books.

—— (1975) Apprenticeship and Paternalism: Psychocultural Continuities Underlying Japanese Social Organization. In E. Vogel (ed.) *Modern Japanese Organization and Decision Making*. Berkeley: University of California Press.

—— (1976) The Interrelationship of Social and Psychological Structures in Transcultural Psychiatry. In W. P. Lebra (ed.) *Culture-Bound Syndromes, Ethnopsychiatry and Alternate Therapies*. Honolulu: University of Hawaii Press.

—— (1978) Selective Permeability and Reference Group Sanctioning: Psychocultural Continuities in Role Degradation. In M. Yinger (ed.) *Major Social Issues: A Multi-Community view*. Glencoe, Ill.: Free Press.

—— (1980a) Ethnic Adaptation and Minority Status. In W. Lonner (ed.) *Journal of Cross-Cultural Psychology* 11(1): 101–24.

—— (1980b) Afterword. In D. K. Reynolds, *The Quiet Therapies: Japanese Pathways to Personal Growth*. Honolulu: University of Hawaii Press.

—— (1981) Adaptive Strategies in American Minorities. In E. E. Jones and S. J. Korchin (eds) *Ethnicity and Mental Health*. New York: Holt, Rinehart & Winston.

DeVos, G. A. and Wagatsuma, H. (1966) *Japan's Invisible Race: Caste in Culture and Personality*. Berkeley: University of California Press.

—— (1972) Family Life and Delinquency: Some Perspectives from

Japanese Research. In W. P. Lebra (ed.) *Transcultural Research in Mental Health*. Honolulu: University of Hawaii Press.

Doi, T. L. (1971) *Amae No Kozo (The Anatomy of Dependency)*. Tokyo: Kobunsho.

Dore, R. P. (1973) *British Factory, Japanese Factory: The Origins of National Diversity in Industrial Relations*. Berkeley: University of California Press.

Hearn, L. (1904) *Japan: An Attempt at Interpretation*. New York: Macmillan.

Hess, R. D., Kashiwagi, K., Azuma, H., Price, G. G., and Dickson, W. P. (1980) Maternal Expectations for Mastery of Developmental Tasks in Japan and the United States. *International Journal of Psychology* 15: 261–76.

Hollingshead, A. and Redlich, R. C. (1958) *Social Class and Mental Illness: A Community Study*. New York: Wiley.

Hsu, F. L. K. (1975) *Iemoto: The Heart of Japan*. New York: Halstead Press.

Kagan, S. (1974) Field Independence and Conformity of Rural Mexican and Urban Anglo-American Children. *Child Development* 45: 765–71.

Kashiwagi, K. (1967) The Cognitive Development of Sex-Role in Female Adolescence. *Japanese Journal of Educational Psychology* 15: 193–202.

Kiefer, C. W. (1968) *Personality and Social Change in a Japanese Danchi*. Unpublished Ph.d. dissertation, Department of Anthropology, University of California, Berkeley.

Lebra, T. S. (1976) *Japanese Patterns of Behavior*. Honolulu: University of Hawaii Press.

Lee, C. and DeVos, G. (eds) (1981) *Koreans in Japan: Ethnic Continuity and Minority Problems*. Berkeley: University of California Press.

Madsen, M. and Shapiro, A. (1973) Cooperative and Competitive Behavior of Urban Afro-American, Anglo-American and Mexican Village Children. *Developmental Psychology* 8: 16–20.

Mishima, Y. (1970) *Confessions of a Mask*. Tokyo: Tuttle.

Miyake, N. and Azuma, H. (1978) Maternal Communication Style and Its Effect on Child Cognitive Task. *Japanese Journal of Educational Psychology* 27: 75–84 (In Japanese).

Nakane, C. (1970) *Japanese Society*. London: Weidenfeld and Nicolson.

Ogawa, K. (1981) A Study of Negative Self-Awareness in Interpersonal Relationships. Tokyo: Shobo Shoten.

Reik, T. (1941) *Masochism in Modern Man*. Trans. M. H. Beigel and G. M. Kurth. New York: Grove Press.

Reynolds, D. (1980) *The Quiet Therapies: Japanese Pathways to Personal*

Growth. Honolulu: University of Hawaii Press.

Riesman, D., Denney, R., and Glazer, N. (1950) *The Lonely Crowd: A Study of the Changing American Culture*. New Haven, Conn.: Yale University Press.

Rohlen, T. P. (1974) *For Harmony and Strength: Japanese White-Collar Organization in Anthropological Perspective*. Berkeley: University of California Press.

Shikauchi, K. (1978) Effects of Self-Esteem on Attribution of Success and Failure. *The Japanese Journal of Educational Psychology* 18(1): 35–46.

Vogel, E. F. (1965) *Japan's New Middle Class: The Salary Man and His Family in a Tokyo Suburb*. Berkeley: University of California Press.

Wagatsuma, H. and DeVos, G. (1978) A Koan of Sincerity: Osama Dazai. *Hartford Studies in Literature* 10(1,2,3): 156–81.

_____ (1983) *The Heritage of Endurance*. Berkeley: University of California Press.

Witkin, H. A. (1969) Social Influences in the Development of Cognitive Style. In D. A. Goslin (ed.) *Handbook of Socialization Theory and Research*. New York: Rand McNally.

_____ (1978) *Cognitive Styles in Personal and Cultural Adaptation*, vol. XI in the Heinz Werner Lecture Series. Worcester, Mass.: Clark University Press.

Witkin, H. A. and Berry, J. W. (1975) Psychological Differentiation in Cross-Cultural Perspective. *Journal of Cross-Cultural Psychology* 6: 4–87.

6

The Self in Hindu Thought and Action

Agehananda Bharati

Introduction

Hindu India has been traditionally concerned with the "self" as an ontological entity. It has articulated its concepts of the "self" as a perennial theme of its philosophies, far more intensively and extensively than any of the other societies studied in this symposium. The purpose of this contribution is to set the complex, not always consistent doctrinal presentation of the Hindu self into a triple perspective: first, to analyze its internal (i.e. emic) semiotic, that is, the "text" of Hindu views of the self; second, to trace the effects – or the lack thereof – of these views on Hindu individual and social action; and third, to put these two into a comparative (i.e. etic) framework, so as to incorporate them into the ken of the symposium – in other words, to make them amenable to cross-cultural scanning. This task is both tall and wide. If "self" were to be analyzed in Hindu emic terms, that alone would imply a perusal of the primary and secondary texts on Indian philosophy and metaphysics, since the self in all Hindu systems of thought is a much more central, if not *the* central, theme of Hindu thinking, and certainly more so than it is in western secular thought and in the Judaeo-Christian-Muslim traditions. But this is not an exercise in retrospective indology. Of the several uses of "self" in this essay, the Hindu metaphysical notion is only one. The task is wide, because I must try to bridge the cognitive and the conative spheres of being and acting Hindu. This, let me submit, has not been done. The orectic sphere of Hinduism is, of course, the core of the anthropology of India; in this literature, the self, both emically and etically conceived, does not play an important role, since anthropology is concerned with societies rather than with individuals. Also, indology and anthropology have not really come to grips with each other's problems and approaches, and they are not really at ease in each other's company. But I regard this project as one which is both indological and anthropological – it does not straddle an uncomfortable fence.

Critical versus traditional analyses

This effort involves a continuous putative dialog between the informed traditional Hindu scholar, to whom I will refer as the pandit(s) throughout the essay, and the modern, analytic scholar or scientist, both Indian and western. While the pandit is more or less of one piece in disciplinary terms, his partner in this dialog is not – to wit this conference, encompassing psychologists, anthropologists, sociologists, etc., who are much more different from each other in disciplinary terms than are pandits of whatever Indian traditional discipline. I will refer to the modern, western-trained analytical partners as "scientists" and will keep the dialog between pandits and scientists alive throughout this essay.[1]

To the modernized urban Hindu who enters a dialog either with a pandit or a scientist, the term "self" is almost always tantamount to the notions of Advaita Vedānta – or rather, to the modern Hindu's highly abridged and often bowdlerized understanding of the Advaita Vedānta doctrine. Therefore, when it comes to talking about the self, the otherwise non- or even anti-traditional Hindu urban person's views are in line with those of the pandit, the most highly traditional Hindu (of whom he may be in general suspicious), and not with those of the scientist (whom he admires). The *advaita* (literally "without a second," i.e. monistic) doctrine is ancient and is first exhibited without compromise in the canonical Upaniṣads, about 700 BC on a very cautious estimate. However, the doctrine was more solidly articulated and most firmly established by Śamkarācārya, an eighth century AD brahmin monk and founder of the Daśanāmi Order of Sannyāsins, the most prestigious religious order in Hindu India. His importance to Hinduism is equal – and this has been pointed out many times – to that of Thomas Aquinas to medieval Europe and to scholarly Christianity. New modern Hindus tend to get upset when I say (which I do) that the doctrine of *advaita*-monism is intellectually quite simple; they insist that *advaita*-monism is so profound that it is hard to comprehend. This is simply not the case.[2] Since the self (Sanskrit *ātman*) is pivotal to the doctrine, the staggering number of commentaries and subcommentaries produced on the doctrine during the last twelve centuries gives the impression to modern Hindus that the teachings involved must therefore be complicated. What Śaṃkarācārya assembled from the canonical and other texts, especially from the Upaniṣads, was a monistic core which he wanted to see as their central core, although it is doubtful that the highly heterogeneous writings of those texts bear him out. Be that as it may, the monistic template which he and his followers until our own day share can be stated in a few sentences. There is one and only one being in existence, the absolute (*brahman*, a neutral noun in Sanskrit, which is a confusing homonym with Brahmā, the demiurgic creator of Hindu mythology, but which has nothing to do with him). This *brahman* is without form. The multitude of other beings, souls, selves, gods, demons, beasts, stars, and planets, etc., are erroneous superimpositions on the One, the *brahman*. The task of the wise is to break through this delusion of multiplicity and to realize his *numerical* identity with that One. Somehow, the existence of all these other entities must be explained away or, rather, *meditated* away, since purely bookish learning and philosophical discourse do not accomplish this irreversible negation of multiplicity. The way in which this explaining away is done is indeed complex and it forms the bulk of all the monistic compendia constituting the enormous *advaita* literature of Hinduism. Still, the basic idea is quite simple as an idea. It would be quite silly to state, from a modern philosophical viewpoint, that the idea is either true or false. *Pace* Popper, it is neither verifiable nor falsifiable – it is one religious, metaphysical doctrine among the many that India has produced, and it is only modern Hindus' claim that the teaching is *scientific* which raises the modern thinker's ire. It is an important doctrine in Hindu India, and I would say it is the most highly prestigious. It has been standard-setting all along and particularly in this century, due to the fact that a bowdlerized version of it diffused to the west and thence back to India through the work of Swami Vivekananda at the beginning of this century. There is a specifically Indian dimension to this, which may have generated the intellectual climate by which Vivekananda and the twentieth-century Hindu sermon after him were informed: great teachers and great teachings tend to congeal into social formations in a more highly definable manner than, say, the acceptance of Christianity or Islam did in other parts of the world. For in India, followers of one teacher and, *mutatis mutandis*, of his doctrine, tend to become castes (*jāti*), i.e. endogamous social units. Now the followers of Śaṃkarācārya and his monistic interpretations of the canonical texts are the South Indian *Smārta*-brahmins, regarded, somewhat grudgingly, as the highest among the high priestly castes of India. Since a good proportion of India's secular leaders (Sir Sarvepalli Radhakrishnan, second President of India and one-time Spaulding Professor of Indian Philosophy at Oxford, was a *Smārta*) and of outstanding public figures – writers, scientists, etc. – belonged to that relatively small group, the past five or so decades' notion prevalent among Indian intellectuals and their western sympathizers, that monism is the crux of Hindu thought and that monistic views about the self are somehow pan-Hindu notions, is centrally important for our study, perhaps analogous to European and French intellectual notions after the Second World War (no longer at the time of writing, though) that French thinking was existentialist thinking.

Hindu traditional (emic) concepts of the self

Let me quote some important entries from an important collection: "the self is actionless," "the self is always attained," it cannot be described as being "like this" or "like that"; it cannot be the object of experience; it consists of bliss; it consists of breath, of food, of knowledge, of mind; it is the controller of all; it is (also) corporeal; it is described as "not not;" it is different from the individual soul in name only; the difference between the embodied self and the highest self is only a metaphor; its differentiation from the self is due to ignorance only, it is God; and about thirty more entries which characterize the absolute, the self, as the one and only existing being (Deutsch and Van Buitenen 1971).

None of the scholastics of the Hindu tradition was concerned with the empirical self in any manner resembling that of psychologists, anthropologists, sociologists, and even poets in the west. All Hindu traditions talk about the self either in order to reject its ontological status (as in Advaita Vedānta just quoted, and in Buddhism), or to assimilate it to a theological and metaphysical construct, which is a Self with a capital "S." When any of the Hindu traditions speak about what might look like the individual, like an empirical self, it is not to analyze but to denigrate it. The term most frequently (and not too felicitously) translated by "soul"[3] in indological treatises in western languages is *jīva*, cognate of course with Latin *viv-*, Russian *-jiv(od)*, "life," consists of lust, anger, avarice, infatuation, egotism, and a whole list of "undesirable" qualities; the *jīva* does not merely "have" those qualities, it *is* them. The self as the basis of such important human achievements as scholarship, artistic skill, technological invention, etc. is totally ignored in the Indian philosophical texts.

One might think that such abstruse thoughts could only have been relevant and exciting to an intellectual or religious elite, creating and perpetuating an ivory-tower syndrome that would not affect Hindu India at large. Commonsense and intelligent intuition might suggest that the non-scholarly Hindu had a down-to-earth notion of something very much like the subject-matter of an "empirical self." Such an intuition, however, would be wrong. Hindu thoughts and perceptions, Hindu values – *all* Hindu values – have been thoroughly informed by these seemingly recondite concepts. I would go even further than that: I claim that Hindu notions of the self were generated and are being perpetuated from that metaphysical-speculative base just like western notions of self were generated and perpetuated by the empirical epistemologies created in ancient Greece on the secular side, as well as by the Judaeo-Christian (plus Islamic) doctrines of the soul as an ontological, self-conscious entity. When these two meet on ecumenical grounds today, on international forums of intelligent discourse, Hindus attempt to assimilate western empirical notions to the Hindu doctrine, but western thinkers do not do the reverse; they do not try to explain Hindu ideas about the self in empirical terms, except for that segment of western thinkers who underwrite a Jungian paradigm or who have converted to Asian modes of thinking. Jung himself can well be seen as a prime convert to eastern modes of thinking about the self.

Viewing Hindu "ideas" of self in thought alone, analyzing the Hindu cognitive map without any attention to the orectic and the affective templates, is no longer difficult, since this has been done and is being done by the host of straight "indologist" textualists as well as by writers on comparative religion. On a cautious estimate, there are some two hundred books and monographs in western and an even larger number in Indian languages, as well as an impressive number in Japanese, which deal exclusively or by thematic incorporation with the cognitive aspects of Hindu notions of the self. S. N. Dasgupta's (1922–55) five volume *History of Indian Philosophy* could be used as a reference work, tracing concepts of self through all Indian systems of thought, brahmanical (Hindu), Buddhist, and Jaina. Of the popular, semi-popular, and apologetic type, there is an ever increasing amount of literature in western and Indian languages dealing with the self and drifting off into eastern wisdom chatter; this genre includes the writings of all the assorted itinerant swamis in India and the west, all of which can be read as exhortations and explanations about the self.

The Hindu self in action – a tentative statement

When it comes to combining the cognitive, conative, and the affective dimensions of the self, however, matters are grim. To my knowledge, there is at this time no book-size monograph on the Hindu notion of self as it affects action. A number of articles dealing with action as *Hindu* action are found in Gandhian and other ideologized publications. The entire field of Gandhian thought deals with a refurbished, active self. Nothing of it is analytic.

I found Francis L. K. Hsu's (1963) treatment of Hindu and Indian assessments of human action very helpful indeed. G. M. C. Carstair's (1958) classic is next in line, followed by sundry references, central and peripheral, in a large number of articles in anthropological and sociological journals. Still, the Hindu views of self in action have not been singled out as a central issue, and I hope that this effort will be a beginning, at least in anthropological terms, for research on conation in Hindu India, research focusing on emic and etic perceptions of the self in action.

Hsu's ingenious diagram "Man, Society, and Culture" (see Chapter 2 in this volume) comes in handy at this point, since it provides a cross-culturally fertile matrix, eminently so for the Indian situation. Here, we have to assign an additional level, i.e. level 8, and mark the center as a point in the geometrical sense of the term, i.e. as a location without extension. This would be the *aṇu*, "atomic," definition of the *ātman*, the absolute, elaborated as *aṇu* in many scholastic Hindu traditions. Hsu's levels 7 and 6 (his Freudian "unconscious" and "pre-conscious") roughly correspond to the Hindu *jīva*: level 3 (the unexpressible conscious) corresponds exactly to the construct of *māyā*, seen both as individual and cosmic delusion, and described as *anirvacanīya* which means *exactly* "unexpressible." Levels 4 and 3 (the Chinese *jen*, i.e. expressible conscious and intimate society and culture) could probably be equated with *saṃsāra*, i.e the individual and social realm of conscious interaction. Levels 1 and 0, however, would merge into one entity in the Indian vision, i.e. *prapañca*, literally "all manifested things."

We have seen that the empirical self, the entity which denotes the individual acting in the world and which is intended when the Hindu speaker uses terms which translate as "I" or "the mind" or "the heart" (as in the Hindi *main cāhtā, jī cāhtā, man cāhtā,* "I wish . . . ," "the heart wishes . . . ," "the mind wishes

..." which are used interchangeably in common parlance), is interiorized as hierarchically lower than the "self" of the religious tradition.But – and this will be crucial in this paper – it is this lower self which the alien has shown to India, which has conquered India by its impact, and which has made Indians to emulate it, hateful though such a suggestion may be to Hindus. Western man is seen as the master of the empirical self and as the mentor in consummate worldly success. This is why the west is envied, mistrusted, and coveted all at the same time – western college education, the English language, travel abroad, and anti-western sentiments pronounced as part of India's official culture today are some of the manifestations of these contrastive perceptions. As a sequel of the western man's mastery of the empirical self and thereby of the empirical world, he is seen as poor in spirit, not realizing or not wanting to realize, hence basically incapable of grasping the meaning of his true, non-empirical self.

Hindus feel that the true self can – and should – be realized, and the empirical self sublated, and this process is seen as the consummation of human efforts, so that having accomplished it confers the most powerful charisma, i.e. that of the sadhu, the holy man.

Whether or not we take a Whorf-Sapirian stance, there is no doubt that linguistic models emit powerful impetuses to conation in India. M. Biardeau, illustrious successor to the illustrious Louis Renou's chair for indology at the Sorbonne, is most certainly a textualist by training and temperament, yet she wrote an important essay dealing with the plausible correlation between Indian (i.e. Sanskrit) terms and Indian lifestyles. Biardeau (1965) points out that philological (read indological) tools have reached their limit with regard to the analysis of purely cognitive notions about the self in India. On first blush, terms connoting the self (*ātman, ahaṃkāra, jīva*) might seem to imply subtle nuances of little importance to any behavioral analysis. For even the pandit virtuosi who ponder about categories and sub-categories generated by Sanskrit terms which could all be rendered "the self" never claim that Hindu ways of acting in society and acting in the world are somehow coordinated with these terms. Nor does the pandit who revels in minute disqui-sitions about *ahaṃkāra* ("ego-marker"), *jīva* (soul, individual), and close to a dozen other terms comprising the semantic field of selfhood, exhibit significantly more complex patterns of behavior than the ordinary Hindu who knows and uses only one or two of the available terms denoting his ego or self. He also knows that human actions and decisions are prompted by karmic forces which are linked to a metaphysical notion of the self, even though he does not usually feel compelled to look for the doctrinal specifics.

Biardeau argues that *ahaṃkāra* is the key junction in the progressive manifestation of the world out of the undifferenti-ated chaos. In the classical Sāṃkhya system, *ahaṃkāra* is the second of the cosmic principles which evolve from *pradhāna*, the primordial matter; it comes after *buddhi* (intellect, the cognitive apparatus) and before *manas* (cognate with Latin *mens*, the "mental organ" in that important school of Indian thought) (Biardeau 1965:62).

It is very important to realize that all Hindu notions of the mind, the ego, the entire psychological apparatus are *material* conceptions in philosophical terms; not of course in psychosoma-tic terms nor in terms of occidental mind-brain parlance, which is nonexistent in indigenous Indian thought. From the canonical manifestations of mind (*buddhi*, "intellect") via *manas*, "the thinking organ," conative energizer, to the body of flesh, all these are conceived of as matter, albeit of different degrees of subtlety and density – the body is the crudest, thickest of these material entities, *buddhi* the subtlest. These are visualized as layers superposed on one another, literally called "sheaths" (*kośa*) in Hindu philosophical thinking. In the canonical Upaniṣads, the self is successively defined as the gross body, then the senses, the mind, intellection, and finally the *ātman* which equals *brahman*, the ubiquitous absolute which has no form and no matter. The underlying notion seems to be that short of full, intuitive identification with the non-material *brahman*, we – i.e. our bodies, senses, and minds – are material selves. And it is in the Upaniṣads that we have the first parabolic statement of successive identifications of the self from the gross to the subtle to the non-material, together with its conative ramifications. In the *Chāndogya Upaniṣad*,[4] which is one of the two oldest and most revered canonical texts of Hinduism, the story, in a highly abridged form, goes somewhat like this: Indra the god and Virocana the demon went to a famous sage to be instructed by him as to who or what was the real self, as to who or what was the absolute, the unchangeable, the immovable, which people are supposed to worship or be aware of. The sage gave them his instruction all at once, telling them it was they themselves who were all that. The demon, being just a demon, thought, that's fine with me; he went back to his abode, and continued to eat well, drink well, make love well, dress well, and do generally pleasant things, since he understood the sage's "it is you" to mean "it is your body" (which, of course, is what ordinary people everywhere understand when someone points at them saying "you"). Indra however, being a god, wasn't so sure. He too went to his celestial palace and had fun, but soon noticed that he, i.e. his body, was all but unchangeable – that it shrank when he ate less, swelled up when he gorged himself, and so on. Back he went to the sage and asked for clarification. But to no one's great surprise, the sage repeated his instruction "It is you." This time Indra thought maybe the sage meant his visual, audial, tactile, olfactory, and gustatory senses, as when someone says "you hear" or "you touch" or "you smell" or "you taste"; but these too changed at all times and didn't resemble what he had heard about the immutable absolute, the *brahman*. Back he went again, only to get the same answer. Eventually, after several such returns, he realized what it was that the sage's instructions referred to: it was that nucleus underlying all those layers of thought-matter, sense-matter, and body-matter, and that "self" was indeed formless, immutable, absolute.

The cognitive assumptions here are quite evident. The conative assumptions are implied, and can be read off the detailed story. The person who identifies with his body is a demon – he lives the life of a hedonist at best, of a lecher or a drunk at worst; the person who thinks he is his senses leads the life of an esthete at best, and of a psychopath at worst; while the person who thinks his intellect is the self, or that he is the intellect, leads the life of a thinker, scholar, or scientist at best and of a paranoid-schizophrenic at worst. All these are, of course, somewhat modernistic and somewhat facetious interpolations, but they work in the field, since I have suggested these very extensions to a number of Hindu pandits who had not previously been exposed to this kind of highly occidental argument. They all checked out and were found appropriate interpretations of the text. It is my suggestion that Hindu cognitions and conations, by and large, follow these sequential identifications first enunciated in that magnificent text. I remember a very large gathering of people – not a religious gathering by any means – in a major city in Northern India, where everybody talks to everybody and invites others to listen and share; it is called a *melā*, literally a fair, but it often looks as though the trade and business aspects are an excuse for talking world-views. An old brahmin asked me what I was doing at that time, and I told him I was translating a philosophical treatise from Sanskrit into English. The name of the text was *Bhāmatī*, and his eyes lit up; he beckoned the bystanders to come close, and he said: "This man here is translating an important book. It says a man's house has just caught fire and burnt down; the man runs out and shouts, 'I have caught fire, I am burnt out.' What nonsense."

On another occasion, a truck-driver called out to a pedestrian to get off the road, pointing at the latter's feet, implying he would roll over them if he didn't. But the man shouted back, "Are you calling me? If you are, point at my heart, not at my feet – I am not my feet." Observed statements of this sort indicate a cognitive-conative pattern which, although informed by doctrinal notions at one time, is quite unique to the Indian situation and has definitional properties. Cognitive-conative boundaries can be seen as part of the ethnic boundaries between peoples and cultures. Ramakrishna Paramahamsa, the famous Bengali saint of the late nineteenth century, explained to his disciples, *"hrtayam* [i.e. Sanskrit 'the heart'] [is] this [here, i.e. me];" he restated ancient doctrinal knowledge, first pronounced in the canonical Upaniṣads, that the absolute *brahman* is fully contained in the "space within the heart" (*daharākāśa*, Chāndogya Upaniṣad III, 12/7–9). But the pedestrian in Old Delhi and the truck-driver knew neither about the Upaniṣad nor about Ramakrishna's latter-day popularization. Hindus will point out that all human beings point to their hearts when they point to themselves, rather than to their toes or their head. Neatly spoken, we might here have an emic statement which also happens to be etically true, like the medieval monk's statement that the indulgences do not so much lead the soul out of hell as they fill the coffers of the church. When Ramakrishna was asked about the meaning of *mantra*,[5] he gave his own etymology, *"man-tor,"* i.e. "the mind is [now] yours" which in Bengali sounds vaguely homonymous with *mantra*. Of course, this is sheer fancy, linguistically speaking, but that is quite beside the point: the saint's words, the canonical text, and completely untutored modern Hindus share a cognitive-conative map: they assign different types of actions and passions differentially to different layers of selfhood. These assignations by and large follow the scriptural sequences: gross actions belong to the gross mind, the body-mind; subtler actions, feelings, and thought connected with the affective realm belong to the sensuous mind; while esoteric intuitions belong to pure cognition, to the most central, the space in the heart, identified with the absolute. At the time of this writing, anthropologists suggest that the Indian self is not an individual, but a "dividual," and this makes sense; but more about this later.

Hindu perceptions of the active (empirical) self: a necessary linguistic excursus

All the "great dicta" (*mahāvākyam*) of the Upaniṣads establish the numerical identity between the individual and the cosmic self. The truth seeker thus discovers his true, permanent self, quite different from the self he produced and preferred within society. Biardeau is not a native speaker of English, hence when she says about the absolute self "which becomes for him the one thing desirable" (1965: 81) this confuses the issue. It is not that the self is to be desired, but that it is and always has been the one and only true self; and there is no connection between "x exists" and "x is desired," at least not in philosophical parlance.

An East German indologist, unfortunately unknown in the west since his work is not being published at this time, put his finger on it when he speculated on the linguistic coercion which Sanskrit and its successor languages hold on the Indian mind. In more general terms, this is again a Whorf-Sapirian stance, and it was elaborated by Hajime Nakamura (1964) in direct application to Indian thought. Johannes Mehlig, in a presentation to the Philosophical Faculty of the University of Budapest in May 1979, said, and I translate: "[by decree of the Sanskrit nominal formation of the verb *sat*, 'to be,' into *sat*, 'being,' as an ontological entity] empirical concepts [*empirische Vorstellungsformen*] are transformed into metaphysical categories of thought and conversely, empirical concepts are causally explained by metaphysical categories of thought." This is either something different from the Whorf-Sapirian mode, or else it is a highly sophisticated application of that thesis. Let me add, however, that Mehlig had never heard about Whorf or Sapir – I asked him about it. Mehlig, whose presentation will see the light some day, I hope, shows the origin of this uniquely Indian leap as rooted in the Ṛgveda, the oldest Indo-European text. The modern Hindu self-concept can be traced without much padding to that notion. Modern Hindus, and especially brahmins who are learned by ascription if not by acquisition, seem to apply this ancient equation "to be = being" in thought and action. India's prime minister was a brahmin, and the grassroots vote went to her even after her apparent demise, engineered, so one might assume, by the alienated minority – journalists, lawyers, and politicians whose political model is an import into India, i.e. western democracy. She insisted she was a socialist. E. M. S. Nambudripath is the leader of the most articulate segment of India's communist party. He is not only a brahmin, but a Nambudri brahmin, a linear descendant of Śaṃkarācārya's patriclan as he proudly insists (anthropologically, there is little reason to doubt that this is true, since the Nambudri brahmins are a small community and since about sixty linear generations have elapsed between Śaṃkarācārya and Nambudripath).

India's politicians are active people; they do things and occasionally they get things done. To the ignorant western

political scientist or political philosopher, it seems incredible
that communists, socialists, Hindu fascists, and the whole gamut
of politico-ideological opinion can be represented by people who
are also Hindus – not only nominally so, but more or less *engagé*
Hindus. Mrs Gandhi visited holy men and had been photograph-
ed with them a number of times. The late Subhas Chandra Bose,
arch-charismatic of India's struggle for freedom, sympathized
with the Bolsheviks, then collaborated with the Nazis and the
Japanese in the Second World War – yet India sees him as a sort
of an avatar; as a young man, he was about to join a monastic
order, whose abbot dissuaded him from doing so. Everyone
knows about Mahatma Gandhi who was a political and a
religious figure rolled into one in a manner never witnessed
before or after. To western audiences, a communist is not usually
seen as a feasible Christian, if he takes either ideology seriously.
In India, however, there is no felt cognitive dissonance. The Self
is the *sat*, the one and only existing being; it is the *paramārtha*,
the absolute; everything else about a person is *vyavahāra*,
ephemeral, conventional, relative. Marxian, Maoist, Fabian,
fascist – all these are *vyavahāra* superimposed upon the true self
which is in no way touched by or susceptible to these modifications. Such is a pervasive Indian interpretation of persons,
actions, and ideas, and it is so axiomatic that no one really talks
about it unless pressed to do so. The notion that any set of ideas
or actions is acceptable since it is derivative, secondary, and
alien to the true self, is quite unimpeachable since it is warranted
by texts which have the same epistemological status as direct
perception or valid inference: the word of the *śruti*, the canonical
texts, i.e. the Vedas and Upaniṣads, have the same power of
proof as perception and syllogistic inference.

A Belgian Jesuit missionary who had spent the better part of
his life proselytizing Hindus and keeping them to the faith,
complained to me: "When you commiserate with Hindus, about
their poverty and the general lack of positive events in their
lives, they tell me, don't bother, God is eternal! How can I
contradict? But why on earth is God's eternity marshalled when
misery and poverty are pointed out?" What this man did not
realize was that modern Hindu parlance, in English or in an

Indian vernacular, *assumes* familiarity with the monistic axiom, and thus the implied ellipsis, "God is eternal, you are really God, hence these tribulations are not really yours." Another time, I met Mother Theresa — close to two dozen years before she received the Nobel Prize. I suggested she might like the fact that Hindus love to talk about religion and listen to religious talk, and that they honor all saints and prophets. But this was not how she felt. "When I ask them to love and worship Jesus Christ," she mused, "they say, oh yes Mother, we love Jesus, we love Krishna, we love Buddha, we love Muḥammad . . ." And that, of course, is not what Mother Theresa and the Societas Jesu had or have in mind.

Like all articulate votaries of religion Hindus quote scripture; and like most, I assume, they quote certain passages more than others. Or, if the passage is too long, they quote its purport. Thus, the *Puruṣa Sūkta* of the Yajurveda is well known to millions of articulate Hindus, and Mr Gandhi quoted it in spite of the fact that, on a first reading, it seems to go against his teaching that a man is what he does, and that he is not what he is born into. Both the *Puruṣa Sūkta* and the much better known *Bhagavadgītā* state matters rather clearly: the brahmins emerged from the head of the supreme being (as anthropomorphically meditated upon), the *kṣattrīyas* or warrior-lords came from his arms, the merchant castes from his thighs, and the laborers from his feet. One would expect that politicized modern Hindus should take exception to this institutionalization of inequality by canonical decree. Not so. Swami Vivekananda, who claimed to be a socialist, don't ask me why, said about the *Puruṣa Sūkta*, "But let us not forget that the whole man (*puruṣ*) and the whole society rests on the feet." Such a mood is echoed by high-caste urban Hindus today. Rather than rejecting the text outright as the Buddha had done twenty-five centuries ago, a modernistic, political meaning is imputed to the text. The *Bhagavadgītā* makes no bones about it: "Never must one give up the work for which one is born [literally the 'cognate vocation,' *sahajam karma*], even if it is inferior" (XVIII, 48). It then continues in the same vein, that it is better to do one's own inborn work well than trying to do another one's (inborn) work. Again, this text was

Mahatma Gandhi's favorite, and he quoted it abundantly, though not those passages dealing with duties by birth rather than by achievement. All this is grist to our mills: the scripture has it all, the scripture establishes and condenses the true self and delineates the relative, ephemeral, illusory, hence radically un-true self. I think the most important, though unconscious motivation for modern Hindus' retaining the scripture rather than rejecting it as modern values are imported and introjected lies precisely in the immense comfort the Hindu tradition provides in giving canonical sanction to the irrefragable ontological dichotomy between the *paramārtha* (absolute) and the *vyavahāra* (relative) universes of discourse and of being. Once you abandon this psychological sinecure, you have to fend for yourself, so to speak, and you are accountable for contradictory ideas and actions.

External interpretations – wise and otherwise

Hardly any writing since Katherine Mayo's *Mother India* (1927) has annoyed Hindu intellectuals more than Edward Shils's (1961) small monograph about them. Not too many Indians outside the academic community which has access to university libraries have read the book, but somehow the word has gotten around. When he wrote toward the end of the volume:

> "If the Indian intellectual can come into a situation in which he perceives and accepts real tasks, when he will draw on whatever resources are within himself and his cultures, traditional and modern, to solve them, then the synthesis, so much yearned for, will come forth. It will come forth . . . from ardent exertions to solve real scientific problems, to discover something true and important through scholarship, to write poems and novels about what one sees with one's own imagination, and to apply one's knowledge and skills to the handling of tasks for which one is responsible with a responsibility one accepts and affirms."

(Shils 1961:119)

Shils failed to declare his axioms: "real" for him, means "real in the empirical sense as conceived by the majority of western thinkers," as does his "one should exert" where "one" means the empirical self of the scientist, or the Judaeo-Christian individual conceived as fully existent in the ontological sense. I think Hindu ennui at this opusculum and at the spirit of arrogance which is perceived to underlie it is due to Shils's basic exhortation. For Shils recommends squarely that the metaphysical self of the Hindu be scrapped *stante pede* and with due dispatch to be replaced by the empirical and ... or Judaeo-Christian individual self so long interiorized by western man.

R. S. Khare is an outstanding Indian anthropologist who teaches at the University of Virginia. He has published seminal work on high-caste Hindu groups in northern India as well as about the ritualistic and ideological dimensions of food in Hindu society. In his book on the Kanyakubja brahmins of northern India (Khare 1976), he quotes a retired chief justice belonging to that community, who muses about the fact that "a modernist becomes a traditionalist in his old age." He gradually gives up some physical comforts, and generally acts and talks in a manner which seems less mundane and more spiritual. Khare then concludes the quote: "Most of all, he may retract his 'self' from the external world as a turtle does under its shell." Now I don't know if the quotation marks around "self" are the judge's or Khare's. I suspect the latter, since this is a quotation from spoken reflections, and there are no quotation marks in speech outside Victor Borge's humorous attempts. I think there is a reason for the quotation marks as here applied: the book is meant for anthropologists, and it is written by an Indian anthropologist who talks about his own society. But since anthropologists must write etic prose for other anthropologists, "self" must be put in parenthesis to indicate, it seems to me, that the judge's use is part of the emic flow. The turtle withdrawing into its shell is an almost unmodified quotation from the *Bhagavadgītā*, and the simile is well used, and overused, by pious Hindus. Whether the judge spoke to Khare in Hindi or English makes little difference here. The rendition being in English, "self" again must be parenthesized so as to avoid the temptation germane to a non-Hindu reader however informed, that this is the same as the empirical self of the non-Hindu which would not require any quotation marks. On the other hand, Khare, like many Indian social and other scientists, feels awkward about the indologists' imputation of Hindu classical thought to modern, urban, secular Hindus.

Hajime Nakamura is a professional philosopher, a practising Buddhist, and by incorporation rather than by main focus, an indologist. He is profoundly concerned with Indian notions of the self; as a Buddhist, he must reject any construction of "self" as erroneous. As an indologist, he is probably more sympathetic toward the *advaita* model of *ātman-brahman* monism, particularly since most specialists agree that northern Buddhism's key concept of the void (*śūnyatā*) is thematically closer to the advaitic Self than it is to any other Indian philosophical construct – the identification of *śūnyatā* with *brahman*, however, has been mercifully abandoned by serious scholars. Nakamura's textual enthusiasm outweighs his contextual application. His extensive treatment of the Hindu notion of self, both empirical and metaphysical, as an absolute conceived in monistic union must raise sociological and anthropological eyebrows. His *Ways of Thinking* (Nakamura 1964) is a truly monumental work. His generalizations and reflections about Hindu behavior are Procrustean and overly simplistic. He really talks about ideal rather than actual behavior. He shares the western orientalists' tendency to identify a quasi-emic "ought" with the Hindu cognitive-conative totality. I say "quasi-emic," because Hindus who reflect on the self either as an empirical entity or as the absolute, and to their mutual relation from total distance (as in the radical dualistic schools) to total identity (as in *advaita* thinking) – do not do so the way Nakamura does. For as would be expected, Hindus reflect on their self via a series of cognitive compromises with the foreigner – western or Asian – which he does not have to make and doesn't know how to make unless he also happens to be a field-anthropologist working in Hindu India. Ironically, modern urban Hindus are likely to take Shils's rather than Nakamura's side in this conceptual juxtaposition: it is not so much that the Hindu intellectual is alienated from his grassroots or that he turns grudgingly occidental in his intellectualism and that he therefore feels unhappy doing Hindu things at home. Rather, the model is a Faustian one, *pace* Goethe, *"zwei Seelen wohnen, ach, in meiner Brust;"* he feels that the eternal *ātman* in him is being enticingly infringed upon and invaded by the empirical self. "This Self, i.e. *ātman*," writes Nakamura, "is regarded as identical with the Absolute, the ultimate Ego, and both are equally called *ātman*" (Nakamura 1964). Throughout the whole book, he attempts to deduce actual behavior, actual value orientations, actual conations from religious doctrines – Hindu ... Buddhist for India, and Buddhist of various forms for Tibet, China, and Japan. All this is very fascinating, but it does not quite work, because the philosophical stipulative "ought" and the sociological-anthropological "is" don't wash, unless we also analyze Hindu apologetic patterns and modern Hindu ways of squaring the absolute "ought" with the "is" of day-to-day actions. I attempted to do this in an earlier publication (Bharati 1970a), but this presentation offers a more highly focused and improved package. It must also be pointed out that Nakamura's Buddhist position, though drastically opposed to the Hindu notions of "Self" in Hindu–Buddhist doctrinal parlance – and this opposition has been codified and elaborated for close to two millennia – though the Buddhist core-doctrine of "no-self" (*anatta* in Pali) and the Hindu core-doctrine of "Self" (*ātman*) are mutually exclusive and polarized, *both of them together* radically contrast with *any* of the western perceptions of the self, from the Judaeo-Christian to the general systems and cybernetics-informed notions of self. H. V. Guenther (1964) and J. Macy (1978) see some linkage between Buddhist conceptions of non-self and general systems theories but their presentations do not even begin to ease the extreme polarization between Indian autochthonous (Hindu and Buddhist) and western notions of the self.

Some blurring and some fuzziness, however, has to be admitted: some of this century's western schools of thinking, largely psychological and comparative religionist, have indeed tried either to weaken or to remove that contrast. I am talking of course about writers who have consciously incorporated Indian modes of thinking in their work. The entire set of Jungian psychologists, all the continuing presentations and publications emerging from the Ascona group in Switzerland, the Chicago school of the history of religions, Mircea Eliade, Charles Long, Kitagawa, and an assortment of therapists along the west coast of the United States, but by no means only there, psychiatrists of the anti-psychiatric establishment persuasion (R.D. Laing in Britain, and of course such renegades from academic psychology as Timothy Leary and R. Alpert *alias* Baba Ram Das) – have no doubt achieved a diminution of the polarity, even though their acknowledgment by the main-line professions involved has been less than enthusiastic. Then there is of course the enormous bulk of ever-increasing pseudo-Asian cultism in America which was humorously lambasted by a Hindu woman writer (Mehta 1980) – I am not talking about them at all, as this symposium is not concerned, I would assume, with the lunatic fringe.

Hindu concepts of self and Buddhist concepts of self and non-self, thus share family resemblances so strong that they cannot be juxtaposed except by radical contrast to western notions. This means that even though orientalist scholars like Nakamura and virtually all indologists in the west talk expertly about Hindu notions of self, polarizing them with the Buddhist core teaching of non-self, the Hindu scenario which affirms the existence of a self is not therefore closer to the Judaeo-Christian and later scientific-empirical notions of self in the west than it is to the central Buddhist doctrine of non-self. Western notions of self are systemically unrelated to Indian notions, Hindu, Buddhist, and Jaina.

The force of "self" – perceptions in Hindu strategies for living (and dying)

Does this account for differences in Hindu strategies for living and in Hindu action as compared to western ideas of the self in western thought and action? Nakamura and most indologists I know think it does. I don't. Let me elaborate.

If there were such a thing as an average Hindu, matters would be easier. But there is no such animal just as there is no textbook leopard in the jungle – every single actual large cat has his scratches and bruises and malformations. At best we may say that there are several kinds of average Hindu who entertain discernible cognitive and conative notions of self. What is common to all of them, however, is that we have to deal separately with their cognitive notions of "self" and its orectic corollaries. The indologist and orientalist cannot do that – he lacks the equipment. The anthropologist who knows indology can. I suggested earlier that modern Hindus' actions, especially political actions, are often viewed by the actors as an extension of the *paramārtha* (absolute) – *vyavahāra* (conventional, empirical) dichotomy of brahmin (and Buddhist) thought, where ideas roughly align with the former and action patterns with the latter pole. But while actions can easily be accommodated under the *vyavahāra* rubric, since the *vyavahāra* is multifaceted, unpredictable, anomic, chaotic, the situation is more complex on the cognitive side. I have stated that many if not most of the radical leaders of India are high-caste people, usually brahmins. Louis Dumont, the French sociologist whose understanding of Hindu society and the caste system is unsurpassed and whose *magnum opus* (Dumont 1970) has provided the dominant focus of all caste studies not only on both sides of the Atlantic but also in India during the past decade, has more recently turned to the history of economico-political thought in Europe; and with brilliant results. *From Mandeville to Marx* (Dumont 1977) may seem unrelated to the Indian *Homo Hierarchicus* at first blush, but I must quote Puccini's Cavaradossi singing *recondita armonia di bellezze diverse*. As a byproduct, probably unintended by Dumont, *From Mandeville to Marx* presents a negative printout, as it were, of the brahmin mind who chooses communism and reads Marx, because he finds in the Marxian dialectic a possible modern way of continuing a metaphysical argument which points, both cryptically and strongly, to the inalienable *ātman* in a new peripathetic purity. Alienation and alienated labor are then fascinating, supportive concepts for the learned Hindu who seeks tradition in even extreme modernity. Paraphrasing Marx, Dumont writes, "the worker, thus separated, alienated from his product, is in consequence alienated from his activity as producer and, again, from the manifestation in him of the characteristic of the human genus – namely, the free, conscious action on nature" (Dumont 1977). Without damage to Marx and without abridging the *ātman-brahman* complex, this is readily understood by the born keyholders to the glorious domain of brahmanical thought, to align the self as *ātman* with the social self, or the self of social action, which has become the individual self. The Hindu can now read "the worker" as the human being in general, *all* of whose actions alienate him from his true self. The capitalist confiscates the surplus value produced by the worker, just as desire, passions, the body-mind congeries – in other words *māyā* – alienate the human being from his true self, the *ātman*. I don't believe any communist leader in India has formulated this matter, and few of them have read Dumont. Yet I challenge skeptics: this is the way the Hindu high-caste radical would like to formulate his quest; it is for him no longer a question of traditional versus modern, but of good thought versus inferior thought.

There are certain, somewhat ominous, implications here for articulate Hindus of this day and age. People who quite literally won't kill a fly or a mosquito, strict vegetarians and teetotalers, admire Hitler and make no bones about it. Why? Even if they admit the holocaust (there are many who don't and who think it is all American propaganda) and the atrocities of the Nazi era, the man Hitler is admired. He is admired because, like Subhas Bose, he was a sort of latter-day *rishi* (seer): he espoused the svastika, an ancient and revered Vedic symbol; he was, so Hindu pandits insist, a *brahmacāri* (a chaste bachelor), he did not drink, and he made Sanskrit a mandatory subject in German high schools! The inanity of these notions never seems to strike those pandits who have been persuaded by evidence that none of these things, except the choice of the svastika as a non-Jewish-Christian symbol for the party, is true. He taught the subjugators of India a lesson. He was a man who could kill without killing, *pace* the second canto of the *Bhagavadgītā* 2, 19: "he who thinks of his self as a killer or as one being killed doesn't know what's true." Hitler could do all these things because German scholars had removed the Veda from India and they learned all their scientific and war-making secrets including the atom bomb (no one believes the Americans invented it – the Germans did it on a Vedic recipe) from ancient India. I am not making this up – this pretty much represents a pattern of views widely held by grassroots pandits in India, unalienated by English language knowledge and use. Very few actually propound such views, but there is public support for these notions – the RSS and its founders were Hindu fascists and they wield considerable oppositional power in spite of not being a named party competing for office at this time. Guru Golwelkar, the deceased founder, visited Nazi Germany and molded the training and drill of the RSS quite outspokenly on the model of the Hitler youth.

Pointing to such rather drastic excrescences of self-conation in Hindu India is more than a pedagogical device. The Hindu elite shares such views by and large, and the fact that they are not usually announced publicly is really quite irrelevant. A well-known brahmin political scientist holding a professorship at one of the University of California campuses recently told me that he was an anti-Semite; that he thought there was wisdom in certain aspects of fascism; and that he rejected the liberal views of the eastern establishment which he identified with Jewishness and a latent Jewish conspiracy. Being a learned man, he does refer to Hitler and Mussolini as perverse. In a recent book, this individual, who shall remain nameless, talks about self-actualization, self-consciousness, self-correction, self-definition, self-knowledge, self-mastery, *and* self-transcendence, and he switches between orthodox Indian concepts of self (quoting the *Ātmabodha*, a spurious but important text ascribed to Śaṃkarācārya) and occidental intellectual uses of "self." I do not like the book at all, for many reasons I cannot go into here, but I think it could be seen as a sort of *vademecum* of the high-caste Hindu self in thought and especially in action, by way of prescriptions or recommendations for actions in the world, particularly political action. If you don't know much about the obscurantism of neo-Hindu writing, the book might strike you as an exercise in elegant political philosophizing. It is, however, much more than that – it could not have been written by a non-Hindu political scientist. I recommend it as additional reading after this symposium to anyone who asks me about it.

In recent years, the Dravidian section of India, i.e. the extreme south, has developed a highly politicized trend to move away from the northern, i.e. the Sanskritic, model of human thought and action. A. Bêteille (1971), an Indian anthropologist, reports on the "self-respect" movement, *svayammaryādai*. The choice of a name for that potent movement which affects some thirty million people, mostly Hindu, Tamil anti-brahmin, anti-north Indian purists, have been trying zealously to "purify" the Tamil language of Sanskrit terms. This, however, is not substantially easier than it would be to try and eliminate Latin words from Italian or French. That *svayam* is a Sanskrit loanword in Tamil (so is *maryādai*, Sanskrit "honor"), is highly revealing. *Svayam*, or its abridged form *sva* (cognate of course with Latin *suus-a-um*) is a personal pronoun just like its cognates in all Indo-European languages. It is a personal pronoun, which does not entail a "self" sememe. In classical texts, we find the concept of *svadharma*, loosely and inaccurately rendered "self-norm" by several indologists, which is seen as deciding and legitimizing those actions which are desirable for a person on account of his birth into a caste. But this really relates to "one's proper duty" and there is no reference to any further notion of "self." No speaker of any Indian language will confuse "self" as *sva(yam)* with the metaphysical self (*ātman*). However, the Indian independence movement appropriated the Sanskrit lexeme as *though* it denoted a person, a self, as in *svarāj*, "self-rule," or in the aforementioned RSS (*Rāshtriya-svayaṃ-sevā-saṅgha* "national 'self'-help association"). The *sva(yam)* is a personal pronoun as a lexeme, but a possessive pronoun as a sememe, exactly like the German "*eigen*" – as in Max Stirner's *Der Einzige und sein Eigentum*, which the English translator correctly rendered *The Ego and His Own*, and not, as a putative Hindu translator might have styled it, *The Ego and Its Self*. The Tamil ideologues' choice of *svayammaryādai* for "self-respect," it seems to me, is a probably not too conscious way of modernizing the classical concept of self, which is tantamount to the Sanskritic, northern – self, *while at the same time shifting its meaning from the cognitive to the conative-active pole*. Such a shift, of course, would indeed mean a very radical modernization at least by way of ideological recommendation. This use might move the user away from canonical, deeply internalized notions of the self as part or whole of a spiritual absolute. This theory is supported, I believe, by a neologism which straddles the cognitive-conative fence: in modern north Indian vernaculars, the term for suicide is *ātma-hatyā*, which is literally, and consciously, a translation of the German *Selbstmord*.[6] This neologism suggests *ātman* as the metaphysical self, which cannot be killed; the attempt to do so is deviant, because the suicide *fails* in the attempt, since what he kills is not what he intends to kill. The empirical ego returns in an undesirable form, so he has gained nothing. Now the Indian neologist could just as well have chosen *svayaṃhatyā* for *Selbstmord*. Since the classical *ātman* for "self" remains numinously loaded, an unloaded term (i.e. *sva-*, *svayam*) should have been chosen.

Psychological aspects of Hindu identity and self-representation

"Unilateral dependence and a high degree of mental mutability of all phenomena are two of the most basic elements of any true supernatural orientation" (Hsu 1963). The statement, and Professor Hsu's reflections on Hindu India, are indeed a masterkey to the conative aspect of the self in India. Such "unilateral dependence" is abundantly clear in India because although cognitively the ancestors (*pitris*, more about whom further down) are "dependent" on the oblations and libations of their surviving kinsmen, that dependence remains unilateral. The ancestors are propitiated with a view to preserving or enhancing their favor. Food offered to the gods or to holy men is redistributed and becomes *prasād* (holy and purifying leftovers). The whole idea of *prasād* is that of spiritual and temporal fortification, but the movement of the presentations is unidirectional. The ancestors don't do anything in return, they consume the offered food as marching rations en route to a better existence. True, they do not do any harm to the proper givers — but the apotropaic ritual highlights precisely the unilaterality and unidirectionality of the whole system. For after all, not doing me any harm is not really the same as doing me good.

"The magic of the gods," says Hsu on the same page, "can change air into water, lead into gold, one into many and man into beast; in other words, the mutability of all into one or one into all." As a consequence, I would add, the question of an ontologically firm and epistemologically stable self is a moot question, in Hindu emic terms, whenever the reference is to the orectic, to activities. It is shrinkable and expandable along with the transactions it initiates or perceives, be they ritualistic operations or the business of daily living. It used to rouse my ire when perfectly literate Hindus made statements like "I am a vegetarian and I am a meat-eater." I did not realize at that time the identificatory significance of such a statement, thinking this was meant facetiously or as a *bon mot*. But this is simply not the case; the speaker falls squarely into Hsu's pattern. His self – i.e. the ephemeral self that says and acts "I" – is sometimes that of a non-vegetarian, as when he moves among foreigners or among modern urban Hindus who do not observe any food rules, when he may also be a whisky drinker. When at home with his kinsmen or with traditionalists, he is a vegetarian. This is not to be understood, however, as a statement of time-sequence as though it implied "I am a vegetarian and teetotaler Mondays through Fridays from 9–5, and a non-vegetarian on Saturdays and Sundays." It means that there is no cognitive dissonance in such self-representation: it is not an infringement on the law of the excluded middle. Rather there is no fixed empirical self which cannot ascribe two mutually contradictory positions to itself as agent. Mutually exclusive statements and contradictory actions do not pose a cognitive conflict in their simultaneous and/or correlative occurrence. The self is, *pace* Hsu, mutable. It is a bracket for a class of subselves on the model of the phoneme which is the class of its allophones. Later on in the text, Hsu pinpoints the matter even more succinctly: "Mutability is the idea of *ātma* translated into an approach to interpersonal relations. Extreme mutability will negate the difference between life and death, between one man and many, between men and things, between ego and alter, etc." (Hsu 1963:175). This paraphrases the Upaniṣadic dictum *bahusyāṃ prajayeya*, "may I be many, may I bring forth." Hsu did not seek canonical brahmin support when he wrote the book – but he has it.

When you ask a grassroot Hindu's identity, he will give you his name, the name of his village, and his caste. If he is a south Indian brahmin and a traditionalist, he will introduce himself to you with a Sanskrit formula, which translates: "Of the *gotra* [seer's lineage], of the Ṛgveda [or Sāmaveda, whichever Veda his family belongs to], born in the house of X [his remembered agnatic ancestor], grandson of so and so, son of so and so; I am Mr Srinvasa Iyer." The empirical ego comes last in this formula, and it terminates a line of descent which starts with the sublime, the revealed, the immediate proximations to the absolute. But neither he nor any Hindu will introduce himself in terms of that absolute directly, unless the situation is arcane or ritualistic. The *Śivācārya* – the priest in south Indian Śiva temples – performs certain *mudrās* (gestures) and pronounces certain incantations which establish *Śiva-bhāva*, that is, his identity with Śiva: but nobody refers to him as Śiva outside the ritualistic situation, just as in the less sophisticated sections of the Hindu village population no one calls the shaman, in day-to-day life, by the name of the deity who possesses him during trance. The late Professor Father Wilhelm Koppers, my first anthropological mentor, suggested that these shamanistic identifications are similar to the folks in Oberammergau, Bavaria, which has the famous Passion Plays – and where the man who plays Jesus is called "Jesus" throughout the year. Koppers was wrong, of course, there is no such similarity, mainly because the Bavarian Catholic not only has no metaphysical backup mechanism to establish hidden divinity, but such a claim would be the gravest heresy in the strict dualism of official Christianity.

For the Hindu, interpersonal identity is never the postulated metaphysical identity even when the doctrine is known. Self-representation in empirical action is invariably a representation in social, then secondarily in occupational terms. This of course is important in cross-cultural comparisons: Americans and Europeans will identify themselves primarily and immediately by their profession or skill, or by their immediate action, e.g. "I am fishing"; it would be rather strange if a western person introduced himself as "I am son of so and so . . ." The reversal of the identificatory order between the west and India is important, and it signifies a polarization between the fixed, immutable self of the westerner, and the mutable self of the Hindu. Some might object that the Hindu way of self-introduction does not reflect mutability any more than the western way. But it does; the fact that ego comes last, at the end of a chain of spiritual and personal ancestry, implies that the chain does not end here, and that the self-identifying link, the speaking ego, is not really that important.

What happens in the ritualistic situation as in the case of the Śivācārya mentioned a bit earlier, or in the case of a much larger number of non-specialists, has, however, more than just provisional meaning. Akos Östör reports: "having renounced their social identity, the (Bengali) devotees take on the identity of Śiva himself" (Östör 1980). But what happens occasionally or is made to happen by ritualistic management reflects an extra-ritualistic reality, and this emic fact reinforces what now turns out to be a dual mutability: the self is many selves seriatim, but it is also the supreme self, or Śiva, or any mythological synonym of the absolute.

G. M. Carstairs is a British social anthropologist with a psychological and psychiatric base. He spent his entire childhood in India, and I believe he was a practising psychiatrist in Britain. His Twice Born (1958) not only became a classic for the anthropology of contemporary India, but it was widely read by the adherents of the culture and personality school, or psychological anthropology as some preferred to refer to their craft during the 1950s and early 1960s. Then for close to two decades, culture and personality seemed to dwindle, and anthropology teachers spoke about it with embarrassed whispers, as it were. Then about ten years ago it was revived, and it is now well and thriving, albeit in a much more sophisticated form than during the days The Twice Born was appreciated. For the cultural psychology of India, however, the book did remain a classic and will be regarded as that for a while to come. However, Carstairs is not an indologist, and he does not notice at all that standard English – and standard Indian English to which he had been exposed during a substantial part of his life – is not a sufficient instrument to probe India in depth. Thus when he characterizes persons and castes as "self-centered," this does not make sense – at least not emic sense – in the Indian context. When Ceylonese Buddhists speak English – and Ceylonese English is identical with Indian English – they always stress that the Buddha's main doctrine was that of *selflessness* (*anatta*) and that Buddhism could therefore provide general and specific guidelines for people at large, and the United Nations specifically. But what the English-speaking Ceylonese Buddhist does not know or does not tell, depending on the degree of his sophistication and knowledge of the Pali canon, is that the Buddha's use of "self" had nothing whatever to do with the modern English use of the term as in "selfish," "self-centered," etc., since the Buddhist term is a metaphysical one which denies the ontological reality of any notion of "self," especially the brahmanical notion which he found in those Upaniṣads which had already gained vogue in his day. Contrary to the pious Buddhist's hope, the Buddha's advice would be quite dysfunctional for the United Nations or for that matter for any other nation, since any ascription or reality to selfhood is an egregious error. Now Carstairs knows Hindi fairly well, I assume. In modern Hindi parlance, there is the term *svārth* (*sva-arth*, "for one's own purpose"), and in Urdu *khudgarz* (Persian *khud*, "self," and *-garz*, "being involved with") – both of which are translated as "selfish"; but there is a deep structural difference between the Hindi and Urdu use, albeit synonymous. Hindi, being a Hindu language deriving its vocabulary mainly from Sanskrit, can of course *not* use the Sanskrit term for self (*ātman*) for that composite of recent origin (I do not believe *svārth* was used before European contact); Urdu is predominantly a Muslim language deriving its vocabulary from Arabic via Persian, and there indeed "self" as a metaphysical, ontological entity makes sense. This means that the Muslim understands *khudgarz* exactly the way the English speaker understands "selfish." The longlasting linguistic interpenetration and symbiosis between Hindi and Urdu has resulted in a frequent surface structure synonymization, particularly when an English term is sought. This lengthy introduction to Carstairs's credits and debits is necessary, and I will now quote some salient elicitations from his *Twice-Born*. "Girdhari Lal," he writes,

"was one of the first to impress upon me the connection between this solipsism and the Hindu religious life. 'When she dies,' Girdhari Lal said, pointing at his elderly wife while three of his children listened respectfully, 'I'll become a wandering *sadhu*.' 'But [Carstairs interjected] these sons and daughters, don't they miss you?' 'Why should they miss me? I am on my way to God, that's all.' Dalumal also spoke of becoming a wandering holy man, undeterred by the fact that he had a wife and a young child, and many debts. 'You don't think of anything else at all, you think of God only; you just feel sure that your family will get whatever is fated for them.'"

(Carstairs 1958: 31)

Carstairs (1958) then comments, "The rationalization for this *supremely self-centered* attitude to life is that each carries within him an *ātma*, a spark of God-stuff, and that his highest duty is to tend this *ātma* with such diligence that it swells into a flame, and ultimately merges with the light of the divine soul, the *paramātman*."

I don't know from where Carstairs had gotten his theological information. He is of missionary background, and it may be that whatever Hindu theology got to him in those days was reinterpreted through Christian diction. But the symposiasts and the audience here know by now that the notion of a different *ātman* for each individual is a *contradictio in adjecto*, since the equation *ātman-brahman* is a minimal Hindu theologeme. In religious and secular discourse, Hindus would use *jīva* if they wanted to report such spiritual transactions as a religious quest, or striving toward the divine. Once a Hindu does use *ātman* the implication is that the speaker was well advanced in the quest. Then, the possible diction, "my *ātman* is striving for union with the *brahman*," would be a statement of achievement, not one of quest, since the *ātman-brahman* identity has been fideistically established in the case of such a speaker. It is a fact, and I have been witness to it on many occasions, that holy men (*sādhus*, *sannyāsins*) in India, when asked by their devotees as to whether they had achieved that supreme oneness, answer in the affirmative without any qualms. Among the famous charismatics of the past several decades, this has been part of their self-representation, and it would be totally mistaken to see it as a figure of speech permissible to the advanced soul. It is no such thing, it is meant *verbatim*. Sathya Sāī Baba, who has an estimated ten million followers, declares, "I am God, you don't have to look anywhere else." The late Meher Baba said much the same and used the first person in all his writing when he spoke about divinity.

Carstairs's examples are extremely well chosen, though. His informants' quotations are very typical indeed. Once a Hindu registers fulltime absorption with the true "self," he feels – and society does not rebut or impugn this feeling – that he has no further obligations to society. This explains the baffling acceptance and toleration of holy men, even if they do things that would be thoroughly resented in others; "Guru Maharaj" Bālayogeshvara, the former "boy saint" of Astrodome fame, asked his devotees to give him motorbikes, a Maserati, and TV sets. "Although Guru Maharaj is the perfect master," his managers proclaimed, "he is also a boy and needs all these entertainments." The amazing thing was that his American disciples had by that time been so thoroughly indoctrinated into the Hindu mood that they did not object – and indeed, the TV sets, motorbikes, and 25-inch Zeniths kept coming. A Hindu woman from Trinidad told me, "Sāī Baba IS God, I have seen it." How so? "He materialized holy ashes [*vibhūti*] and precious rings and watches from nowhere." Could these not be stage magic feats? "Of course not, he is God. You and I are God too, but we don't know it." What is happening in this type of discourse belongs to a pattern quite unique to the Indian scene: the metaphysical truth is there and it is known, but the empirical miracle reaffirms the possibility of seeing that truth. This, of course, explains at least in part the – both Indian and western – image of India as the land of miracles. Miracles wrought – or perceived as such – are not just congeries of fabulous stage tricks; they underwrite a pervasive, totally internalized world view.

Since the "self" of the holy man is no longer the empirical self of all others (including of those who feed him), giving him gifts, small, large, and very large, is seen as a ritualistic offering to divinity – and the basis of Hindu ritual is oblation and libation to divinity.

Modernizing the resilient Hindu "self"

As would be expected, critique of these endemic views comes entirely from recent, alienated reform movements, political and religious, movements whose votaries think they are "modern" – the Ārya Samāj ("society of Aryans"), the Brahmo Samāj, to name the most important (see Jones 1976; Kopf 1979), and of course Gandhi's movement and the Indian national movement in general. But all these had been generated, unwittingly and unwillingly, by the British. The type of criticism which both the Ārya and the Brahmo Samāj focus on these pan-Hindu attitudes could have been made, and indeed was made, by Christian missionaries in earlier days. I have discussed this matter in an earlier publication (Bharati 1970a:16). Western models of religious service are largely samaritan models. Modern Hindu movements, including the important monastic Ramakrishna Order founded by Swami Vivekananda, adopt this Judaeo-Christian value orientation, and they have thereby achieved rather impressive gains in the field of agricultural and sociocultural experimentation. Still, they have a long way to go to be grassroots Hindus. During the *kumbhamela*[7] in Allahabad, a monk of the Ramakrishna Mission, who held an MA degree in English from a major Indian university, was about to take his dip in the Ganges along with the monks of the more traditional orders, when a rugged looking, middle-aged monk, who looked younger than the Ramakrishna monk, stopped him, and ordered him to go back and take his dip with the lay people, after the monastic orders were done with their holy bath. When I asked this rugged monk why he objected to the Ramakrishna monk's taking his dip with other monastics, he said, "Those people who pick up the stool of the sick shouldn't be here." That was a somewhat direct statement of the pervasive notion that it is the king (or his surrogates, the state, etc.) who has to feed and cure his people, it is the secular teacher who has to teach people important skills, and it is the holy man whose sole duty is to show the way to unification with the higher self. Social work and medical services are all right in their own domain, but they must not intrude into the circle of total purity as during the auspicious bath in the Ganges at the *kumbhamelā*.

Common to all levels of Hindu sophistication, from villager to pandit, one notion is axiomatically present: that whatever the body is, it is *not* the self. Axiomatic, and very old, this notion has canonical sanction, for example the Indra-Virocana story adumbrated earlier in this presentation. In everyday parlance the body is seen as alien, hostile. It is, as it were in Freudian terms, the paramount "id," juxtaposed with the opposing the sovereign real self, the *ātman-brahman* complex. The senses are the gates to that body, and the mind holds the keys to those gates; hence mind *per se* is dangerous, it must be controlled, since its powers excite the senses which in turn make the body do their behest – especially the sexual, which must be curbed, denied, cast off at its source, if possible. This packet was picked up even by the American converts to Hinduism in the International Society for Krishna Consciousness (ISKCON), *vulgo* the Hare Krishna movement. Whenever one of their leaders observes a *karmi*, that is, an ordinary, non-initiate mortal, do worldly things like flying a plane or polishing her nails, he tends to mutter, "Mind, mind." Although this organization is strictly dualistic (*dvaita*) by way of its spiritual lineage, this axiom remains intact – whatever the body, the senses, the mind, the intellect are, they are not the self. If you take the body to be the self, then you are the demon Virocana, say in the guise of Arnold Schwarzenegger, the famous body-builder; if you take the intellect to be the self then you are a slightly nobler demon, maybe a minor deity (*deva*) in the guise of Bertrand Russell or Noam Chomsky.

The body, that grossest object mistaken for the self (I am talking Hindu emics now) is constantly defiled by blood and excrements, and is unspeakably polluting in the menstrual cycle or in death. The defiled and defiling aspect of the woman's body has also dangerous magical potential – which fact is a joy to ethnologists, to wit Mary Douglas's important work (Douglas 1966). The self, the ātman, is totally pure – another reason why it cannot be the body, which is a "bag of filth." One school of Indian thought, the archaic Jaina philosophy, teaches that defilements like sins and polluting acts actually infiltrate into the substance of the soul and pull it down to the nether regions. Jainism, probably the oldest of the surviving autochthonous schools of India (see Jaini 1979) identifies bodily matter with the principle of pollution.[8]

It is my theory that stereotyping people relieves the members of a society from the odium of empirical self-acceptance – that is, of accepting oneself fully as body and senses and mind and whatever – where the culture of that society denigrates the human body. Hindus stereotype people very much as others do, but I think the tendency is rather more visible than in other societies known to me, proof of which I see in the enraptured acceptance of popular low-brow media, e.g. the Hindi movies, which are, filmically speaking, the bottom of the barrel of movie possibilities (Bharati 1977). In the movies, everybody is either good or bad – a bit like in the old-time westerns in this country – there are no shades and nuances, as indeed there cannot be, where typecasting is the matrix of value judgments. An Indian woman anthropologist observes, talking about young Bengali women, "A man is considered handsome if he has a great element of physical smartness such as cricket players display. While these girls observe the Śibarātri-brata [a religious festival enjoining a fast and contemplation of Śiva, the god of ascetics] they also dream of a husband who will be a combination of Śiva, Krishna, Romeo, and Gregory Peck" (Roy 1975). The enormous popularity of Hindi movies seems directly related to this – all dramatis personae are stereotypes, and movies that show real people – like the ones produced and directed by Satyajit Ray, who recently moved out of India to California in sheer disgust – are failures. I think that stereotyping as the basis of interpersonal assessment goes hand in hand with a weak self-esteem, since the empirical self is then viewed stereotypically, too, there being no actual (i.e. empirical) model for a self which could be seen as the basis of the decision-making process, or as possessing the possibility of personal integrity. The Hindu psycho-physical-sensual ephemeral "self" cannot generate such complex, calibrated, sometimes tender products as radical criticism (including criticism of the entire non-self *ātman-brahman* tradition), or being ethical in spite of having an affair with another woman's husband, or choosing a qualitative rather than a quantitive approach to anthropological fieldwork. The Hindu text, internalized for a hundred generations, assigns a brisk and un-fuzzy list of behaviors to the empirical self – starting from valor, heroism, and passions, and ending with sloth, deceit, utter pollution. The characters in the movies fit these ancient, nononsense categories fully – Woody Allen's or Rainer Werner Fassbinder's or Ingmar Bergman's productions have little appeal even to the most sophisticated Hindus I have known.

The already quoted passage from the *Bhagavadgītā* puts a seal on all this: "do the work for which you are born" legitimizes the caste system, but that is a minor point and unimportant here; it also legitimizes, reflects, and reinforces modal stereotyping in lieu of decision-making based on those autonomous processes of individuation which might result from accepting the empirical self as sovereign and hence infinitely variegated.

One of Roy's basic assumptions is that Bengali women, as they grow toward and past their menopause, tend to switch their loyalty to the guru, the sadhu, the religious teacher. Bengali critics did not like her argument too much, but I think she is right. The empirical self is ill-defined and weak, the social self is devalued by age, heralded by the cessation of the reproductive function, so that older women, especially widows, have to fall back on the untouched, unchanging self – but since they do not have any metaphysical-doctrinal expertise, they attach themselves to the ones who do – the gurus, sadhus, and so on. Since most women have too low a self-esteem to aspire to become saints themselves, the next best thing is to serve a guru who fully represents the elusive absolute – elusive, but the only construct left intact.

The Hindu "dividual" – an anthropological venture

McKim Marriott at Chicago is to the anthropology of India what Talcott Parsons was to sociology – he is the most quoted author, quoted both by Indian and western anthropologists. Recently he has developed a complex model for Indian, especially Hindu behavior, a monistic and transactional model as he calls it (Marriott 1976). His research during the past three decades has focused on food transactions and the definition of status and rank which these transactions at once generate and symbolize. In his seminal analysis he writes:

> "Persons – single actors – are not thought in South Asia to be 'individual,' that is, indivisible, bounded units, as they are in much of western social and psychological theory as well as in common sense. Instead, it appears that persons are generally thought by South Asians to be 'dividual' or divisible. To exist, dividual persons absorb heterogeneous material influences. They must also give out from themselves particles of their own coded substances – essences, residues, or other active influences – that may then reproduce in others something of the nature of the persons in whom they have originated."
>
> (Marriott 1976: 111)

Marriott sees the Indian person – in emic vision that is – as transactional and transformational. Whatever objections some scholars may have regarding Marriott's model,[9] it is highly apposite for my own analysis here presented: the "self," in a monistic world-view, inasmuch as it is not the formless, quality-less, unqualified *brahman*, can *only* be a transactional self, whose code is cognitive and whose transactions are conative. It is therefore material, in philosophical terms – not as grossly material as the body which is a part of that "dividual" self, but material nevertheless.

Ralph Nicholas and Ronald Inden, both at Chicago, too, follow a kindred line when they state that the body is the locus of Bengali notions of kinship (Nicholas and Inden 1977). The key term in Bengali matrimonial transactions is *rasa*, literally "juice," and a woman merges and loses her entire personality into her husband's *substance* at the wedding. This is of course not some sort of disguised romantic kitsch – it is a hard ritualistic situation with no nonsense about it. The same concepts are held by all Dravidian groups in the south. It is not only that the *gotra* (lineage with a mythical seer as apical ancestor) of the bride dissolves in her husband's *gotra*; it is not only that she merges the gods of her family of origin with the family gods of the husband; she actually changes her natal essence for that of her husband's, she merges it with his quite literally – not through sex and childbirth as romantic western readers might be inclined to think, but in a truly material sense. For instance, south Indian women, even – or perhaps especially – high-caste women, eat their food from the plantain leaf from which the husband has just eaten his meal – totally unthinkable for any other two persons in India, related or not, as food touched by human lips directly or indirectly is *ucchiṣṭha*, "polluted," and is quite literally seen as not fit for human consumption.

It makes sense in any context to talk of funerary matters at the end of a synoptic-analytic statement on how people view themselves. As we have seen, the Hindu self-in-the-world is never a firm, homogeneous entity, a substratum as conceived in the Judaeo-Christian traditions. Rather, the Hindu self constantly contracts and expands along with the complex variety of ritualistic transactions of which it is the object. Recently Jonathan Parry (1980) suggested that the brahmin ritualist, seen as the purest of all Hindus by classical Indian sociologists like Dumont, is really (or, should I say, "is sometimes also," to ameliorate Parry's generalization) the absorber of the defilements of his clients, which he ingests with the offerings given by them. Their acceptance and consumption is the funeral priests' lot, but it can cause gruesome illness or death and a tortuous existence in their next incarnation (Parry 1980: 88–111).

Still, Parry and Dumont do not really make mutually exclusive suggestions. Rather, the brahmin's self can be seen as expanded, as in his ritualistic identification with Śiva in the case of the above-mentioned southern Śivācāryas; and also as contracted through defilement, as when the brahmin consumes food offered by lower-caste clients as in the case of the funerary priests in Varanasi. Or, as in the case of the Gayawal priests at Gaya, the central Hindu site for all obsequial rites, he temporarily becomes the buffer between the dead and the survivors; until the proper ritual centering on the presentation of five white balls of rice has been concluded, the deceased is a *preta*, a ghost, then after the conclusion of the ritual he joins the *pitris* (ancestors). The funerary priest who effects these changes in the status of the deceased's soul straddles the fence of being a *preta* and being a *pitri* himself, until the transaction is completed. In Marriott's terms, the sacerdotal substance contains and is affected by the prestational codes of the *śrāddha* (obsequial) ritual. No one can illustrate this as graphically as Parry, when he writes:

> "The specialist himself becomes the *preta* or *pitri* as the case may be. He is worshipped as the deceased, is dressed in his clothes, is made to wear his spectacles or clutch his walking stick, and is fed his favorite foods. If the deceased was a woman, then a female Mahābrahman (funerary priest) should (theoretically) be worshipped and presented with a woman's clothing, cosmetics, and jewelry. At a rite which marks the end of the period of the most intense pollution the chief mourner, and then the other male mourners are tonsured by the barber. But before even the chief mourner, the Mahā-brahman should be shaved as if he – as the *pret* itself – were the one most deeply polluted by the death. Nor is all this merely a matter of the brahman's *impersonating* the deceased. It is also a matter of making him *consubstantial* [both italics are Parry's] with the deceased."
>
> (Parry 1980:93)

Parry, of course, was inspired – as were most anthropologists – by Marcel Mauss's *Gift* (1966), whose words (written half a century before Parry's report) Parry quotes: "Even when abandoned by the giver it still forms part of him . . . one gives away what is in reality part of one's own nature and substance, while to receive something is to receive a part of someone's spiritual essence" (Mauss 1966:9, 10; Parry 1980:105).

A comfort: the possible existence of the Hindu self

We have now come full circle. We began with metaphysics, moved on and through conation with feelers into the sociocultural parameters of views of self. If we see these two preceding parts as thesis and antithesis, we might view a biologist-cum-philosopher's disquisition about the self in its total personal and cosmic perspective as a sort of synthesis. That person is Alex Comfort (of *The Joy of Sex* and *More Joy of Sex* fame — these popular publications have crowded out the reading public's familiarity with his other writings). In an amazing little book (Comfort 1979), Comfort goes *medias in res* by tapping the yogic (and tantric) dimensions of the Hindu self-concept. He writes:

> "Close introspection of the I-experience is one way of induc-ing alarming yogic dissociation and a possible reason for our neglect to examine so general an experience may lie in the threat which insight would pose to the universal conventions underlying human thought and action. With the growth of neurology, neuropharmacology, and computer science it is bound to come, however. It will be interesting to see what the analysis of I-ness does to the I in cultural terms — probably little, in view of its convenience, as the discovery that the earth is round affected mariners but not pedestrians, and mariners only at one remove from 'commonsense' perception. Provided, that is, that our insight into what I-ness is does not widen still further our capacity to tamper with it."
>
> (Comfort 1979:28)

He then quotes salient Hindu scriptures selectively, to show that the oceanic experience sought by the mystic apparently coincides in content, if not in form, with the drier statements of the monistic texts. Whether this is historically true or even conceptually cogent is, for our purpose, not too important. But in the light of these relational possibilities one might construe the Hindu notion of self as one conceived and formalized as *ex post facto mistico*. This is of course what the Hindu traditionalist claims. What makes the rapprochement between Hindu and western intellectuals so difficult in discussing these matters is the unfortunate tendency of modern Hindus to present these doc-trines and these mystical reports as on a par with scientific truth. Comfort is of course brilliantly right when he says a bit further on:

"The aim or knack of yoga is at root non-conceptual or I-less perception. The insight which sees it as a rupture of the veil of illusion seems basically correct: the conventional barrier between self and environment is, in oceanic states, temporarily removed, and the I ceases to be experienced as separate, though it remains active as the experiencer of the unconventional situation."

(Comfort 1979: 36)

Comfort (don't forget he is a biologist by training and taught biology at University College London before he moved to Santa Barbara, California) provides a cue here; he elaborates that the Hindu notions of self and non-self might have some structural correspondence in the neural system which could in principle be verified. He uses Pribram's hologram as a model (Pribram 1977), but I am in no position to build upon that, since this is the domain of biologists and neurologists.

"This is the shamanic experience," Comfort says, "the human susceptibility to altered states of consciousness, ranging from dreams, which we still have, to compelling waking sensations of otherness, and oceanic experiences – the feeling of total oneness between all the surrounding non-Self and the Self of the observer" (Comfort 1979: 70). Not only shamanic, I will add, but also highly elitistic brahmanical – and normative in the creation and persistence of the self-concept of Hindus. What was often seen as either primitive or clinical outside the Indian scene, especially in the pre-crosscultural days of Freud and his successors, is read in the canonical texts of Hinduism as the supreme cognitive and conative achievement. Conative also, because the tradition insists that all the canonical statements about the *ātman-brahman* oneness are meant not only definitionally (*nirṇaya*) but also conatively (*vidhi*) as methodological promptings toward efforts leading to that realization. Indologists know how this works – in the final analysis, the aged, experienced, worldly-wise Hindu regards the proper action as that of *nivṛtti*, withdrawal, turning away – asceticism, in other words.

In a global perspective, the Indian development is quite unique. The oneness and otherness experience, far from being relegated to heresy or insanity as in other literate parts of the world, was canonized as the supreme consummation for the religious virtuoso. Not only that, it became normative in the formulation of selfhood as the main line of Hindu thought and action.

Let us be clear that I meant business, radical business, in stressing the difference between Hindu and western conceptions of the self, regardless of the ire I am going to incur on the side of Indian colleagues. In a recent important anthology, Bredemeier wrote that in addressing questions of power, deviance, justice, selfishness, altruism, stratification, efficiency, monopoly, strategies, tactics, and morality – all conative terms, perhaps terms totally circumscribing conation – the focus has to be on the "nature of rational adaptation by a self-oriented being" (Bredemeier 1978). Could this be the postulated focus of the self-oriented Hindu being as well? Etically yes, emically no. Emically, at least as visualized by the most prestigious Hindu hierophants and their style-setting successors, rational adaptations by the self-oriented being would be quite simple to descry: the only rational decision would be to intuit the self as the only existing being and to reject everything else, including power, deviance, justice, tactics, and so on. The hallmark of the sage, in the words of Śaṃkarācārya, is *nityānitya-vastu-vivekaḥ*, "the discernment between the eternal [i.e. the higher self] and the non-eternal [i.e. the non-self, or ordinary self, everything else on Bredemeier's list]." There is scope for (empirical) self-oriented adaptations; but it belongs to an inferior category of reflections on the self and its actions – inferior, albeit ubiquitous.

Summary and conclusion

The key problems of this presentation were of a semantic kind. Sorting out those Indian terms which have so far been translated by "self" – glibly, naïvely, or with the best of intentions – and taking a hard look at how the Indian terms operate in actual human actions, I pursued this approach by illustrating how the metaphysical self (*ātman*) invades the Hindu empirical self *en route* to modernity, and how this empirical self, hitherto deprecated, rejected, kept under the lid, or else embarrassingly present, is constantly being eroded by the cosmic, metaphysical *ātman*, from the village temple to Delhi International Airport.

The Hindu *ātman* remains radically pervasive, the cynosure of Indian cognition and conation, notwithstanding the complex strategies of dissimulation which characterize India's official self-image today. I selected those elements in Hindu thought and modal behavior which contrast most sharply with western and other notions of "self" investigated in this volume. The focus of contrast guided my choice of illustrations from live situations in India today.

The empirical self, the ego as actor surrounded by other egos, is systematically marginalized in the Indian tradition so as to exalt the "true," i.e. the non-empirical, self, often identified with the cosmic absolute pure and simple. The lack of a sense of historiography, the lack of a sense of humor where humor is defined as the capacity and the desire to generate cultural self-persiflage, are some of the consequences of this template.

Indian expressions of personal identity, and neologisms in the Indian vernaculars which must incorporate hitherto alien notions about selfhood (e.g. *ātmahatyā* for "suicide") pinpoint pangs of passage. Is the arcane self, the *ātman*, to be abridged or slighted in the process of generating and sustaining a new empirical self which yielded the technological and scientific advantage to its erstwhile purveyors, western man? Will the empirical self remain somewhat marginal for a while yet?

A blend of transactional analogy as recently suggested by Marriott and the sort of hermeneutic analysis employed by Parry in his study of funeral rituals proved helpful in rounding off the somewhat jagged outline of the Hindu self: a self that is "dividual" rather than individual, a self that expands and contracts under the aegis of substance and code in ritualistic offerings and in a wide range of social transactions. I emended this by my own in-field observations over many years, for instance of the Śaivite priest who becomes Śiva during a highly structured ritual, in contrast to lower-level shamanistic possession or purely histrionic identification with other persons as in the case of the Bavarian Passion Players.

Finally, following Alex Comfort, I suggested that the Hindu metaphysics of "self" might conceivably indicate some sort of overarching ontologically valid paradigm which would of course also make it truly cross-cultural. Or, to put it radically, it might just be possible that the Hindu self is indeed the philosophically most adequate intuition of selfhood, if only it can be peeled out from beneath the recondite, arcane, obscurantist diction in which it has been encased.

Notes

1 It goes without saying that there is no longer any ethnic or cultural division between pandits and scientists; there are many scientists of high Nobel Prize caliber in India today, and there are many pandits in the west: orthodox rabbis, ministers, and even a good many professors of religious studies at secular university departments. Still, the pandit approach remains polarized with the science approach; it is not a question of personnel, but rather one of methodological predilection.

2 Grist to my mill came from the audience at the end of the panel session in Honolulu. A south Indian woman (probably a *Smārta* brahmin) who was there on an East West Center fellowship, got up and said (almost) verbatim: "How can you say that *advaita* is easy to understand? The mind is not the self, and the mind cannot grasp *ātman*, thousands of scholars have wracked their brains to understand it, but they can't, because it is only their minds that try to understand." What the lady did was to exemplify precisely what you will be reading in the next few paragraphs, and what I said immediately following this, during my presentation in Honolulu: that the Hindu exegesis of the "self" follows a Hindu scholastic, i.e. emic pattern – it is the pandit's statement all along, and it precludes the definition of "self" as an empirical entity. Mrs Jagadīsvarī's (the lady's name) reprimand was a fine piece of ethnographic data supply, the more welcome since it was totally unsolicited, unexpected, spontaneous.

3 "Soul" is an inveterately Judaeo-Christian (*cum* Muslim) term that should really be avoided altogether in indological discourse. There is no Indian word which means "soul" in the Judaeo-Christian-Islamic sense, because the soul is sempiternal, i.e. *created*, in these traditions, whereas it is uncreated, without beginning and without end in all the

autochthonous Indian traditions, not only in Hinduism. If one wishes to insist on the use of either "soul" or "empirical self" in indological parlance, "empirical self" is rather more appropriate, or at least less misleading as a translation of "*jīva*," than "soul." One might conceivably argue that the long lists of vices constituting *jīva* are also attributes used by certain schools of western psychology.

4 Of the several readily available translations of the Upaniṣads the most readable is that of Swami Nikhilananda, q.v. The Indra-Virochana story is quite impressively interpreted here and deserves to be read by those interested in the "self" as a powerful metaphysical structure.

5 By now, *mantra*, along with *guru* and other Indian terms diffused westward during the cultist 1960s, has become part of the hospitable English vocabulary. The *Random House Dictionary* wrongly defines it as a Hindu word or formula to be recited or sung. It is more than that – it is an audial-phatic syllable believed to have mystical powers when properly practised. My own definition is longer, more technical, and more specific: "a quasi-morpheme or series of quasi-morphemes, or a series of mixed genuine and quasi-morphemes arranged in conventional patterns, based on codified esoteric traditions, and passed on from one preceptor to one disciple in the course of a prescribed initiation ritual" (Bharati 1965a:111).

6 I know this on the authority of the late Professor Raghuvira, who told me that Daulat Ram Deo, an engineer who had studied and worked in Germany in the early 1930s and who wrote and published a German translation of the *Satyārtha Prakāśa*, "Light of Truth," by the founder of the Ārya Samāj, Swami Dayānada Sarasvatī, had first introduced *ātma-hatya* for suicide into north Indian literary parlance, consciously translating the German *Selbstmord*.

7 Literally "convention of Aquarius," every sixth and twelfth year (when Jupiter enters Aquarius), millions of Hindus and virtually all Hindu monastics who can make it, convene at Hardvar or Allahabad or Nasik to solidify and regenerate Hinduism in a truly Durkheimian way. The event lasts up to ten days, and the procession and sacred bath of the monks is the festive culmination of the *melā*.

8 It should be noted that although the Jainas today form a very small part of the population of India (less than 2 per cent), there is virtual exchangeability of the lay Hindu and Jaina idiom. Jainas and Hindus of the same caste (usually merchants) intermarry freely and always have.

9 Marriott and the Chicago anthropologist are rejected by such old-

time hardline (although young in age) indologists as P. Gaeffke and W. Halbfass at the University of Pennsylvania. They feel that these speculations are playfully concocted and that they do not have any foundation in the Sanskrit texts. This may be so, but what Marriott and anthropologists observe and report is not texts and norms, but actual contemporary people and the way they digest and modify the traditional norms.

References

Bêteille, A. (1971) *Caste, Class, and Power*. Berkeley Calif.: University of California Press.

Bharati, A. (1965a) *The Tantric Tradition*. London: Rider.

——— (1965b) Hindu Scholars, Germany, and the *Third Reich*. *Quest* (Bombay) 44: 74–7.

———(1970a) The Hindu Renaissance and Its Apologetic Patterns. *Journal of Asian Studies*, 29/2: 267–88.

——— (1970b) The Use of "Superstition" as an Anti-Intellectual Device in Urban Hinduism. *Contributions to Indian Sociology (New Series)* 4: 36–49.

——— (1977) The Anthropology of Hindi Movies. *Illustrated Weekly of India* (January 30 and February 7), 102/3: 24–31, 22–27.

Biardeau, M. (1965) Ahaṃkāra – the Ego-Principle in the Upaniṣads. *Contributions to Indian Sociology (New Series)* 8: 62–71, 81.

Bredemeier, H. (1978) Exchange Theory. In T. Bottomore and R. Nisbet (eds) *A History of Sociological Analysis*. New York: Basic Books: 453.

Carstairs, G. M. (1958) *The Twice Born*. Bloomington, Ind.: University of Indiana Press.

Comfort, A. (1979) *I and That: Notes on the Biology of Religion*. New York: Crown.

Dasgupta, S. N. (1922–55) *History of Indian Philosophy*, vols I–V. Cambridge: Cambridge University Press.

Deutsch, E. and Van Buitenen, I. A. B. (1971) *A Sourcebook of Advaita Vedanta*. Honolulu: University of Hawaii Press: 300–30.

Douglas, M. (1966) *Purity and Danger: An Analysis of Concepts of Pollution and Tabu*. London: Routledge and Kegan Paul.

Dumont, L. (1970) *Homo Hierarchicus*. Chicago: Chicago University Press.

——— (1977) *From Mandeville to Marx: The Genesis and Triumph of Economic Ideology*. Chicago: Chicago University Press: 152.

Guenther, H. (1964) *Tibetan Buddhism Without Mystification*. Leiden: E. J. Brill.

Hsu, F. L. K. (1963) *Clan, Caste and Club*. New York: Van Nostrand: 52.

Iyer, R. (1979) *Parapolitics – Toward the City of Man*. Oxford: Oxford University Press.

Jaini, P. (1979) *The Jaina Path of Purification*. Berkeley, Calif.: University of California Press.

Jones, K. (1976) *Ārya-dharm: Hindu Consciousness in Nineteenth Century Panjab*. Berkeley, Calif.: University of California Press.

Jordens, J. (1979) *Dayananda Sarasvati: His Life and Ideas*. New York: Oxford University Press.

Khare, R. (1976) *The Hindu Hearth and Home*. Durham, NC: Carolina Academic Press.

Kopf, D. (1979) *The Brahmo Samaj and the Shaping of the Modern Indian Mind*. Princeton, NJ: Princeton University Press.

Macy, J. (1978) *Interdependence: Mutual Causality in Early Buddhist Teachings and General Systems Theory*. Unpublished Ph.d. dissertation, Syracuse University.

Marriott, McK. (1976) Hindu Transactions: Diversity Without Dualism. In B. Kapferer (ed.) *Transaction and Meaning. Directions in the Anthropology of Exchange and Symbolic Behavior*. Philadelphia: Institute for the Study of Human Issues.

Mauss, M. (1966) *The Gift: Forms and Functions of Exchange in Archaic Societies*. London: Cohen and West.

Mayo, K. (1927) *Mother India*. New York: Harcourt Brace Jovanovich.

Mehta, G. (1980) *Karma-cola: Marketing the Mystic East*. New York: Simon & Schuster.

Nakamura, H. (1964) *Ways of Thinking of Eastern Peoples*. Honolulu: University of Hawaii Press.

Nicholas, R. and Inden, R. B. (1977) *Kinship in Bengali Culture*. Chicago: University of Chicago Press.

Östör, A. (1980) *The Play of the Gods: Locality, Ideology, Structure and Time in the Festivals of a Bengali Town*. Chicago: Chicago University Press.

Parry, J. (1980) Ghosts, Greed, and Sin: the Occupational Identity of the Benares Funeral Priests. *Man* 15/1.

Pribram, K. (1977) Holonomy and Structure in the Organization of Perception. In J. Nicholas (ed.) *Images, Perception, and Knowledge*. Dordrecht, Netherlands: G. Reidel.

Roy, M. (1972) *Bengali Women*. Chicago: University of Chicago Press.

Shils, E. (1961) *The Intellectual between Tradition and Modernity: the Indian Situation*. The Hague: Mouton Press.

7

Selfhood and Otherness in Confucian Thought

Tu Wei-ming

The purpose of this paper is to present an enquiry into the idea of the self in the Confucian tradition, the Confucian tradition as a mode of thinking and a way of life that still provides a standard of inspiration for people in East Asian societies. In presenting such an enquiry, I am critically aware of the complexity of the historical landscape as background and the complexity of the modern intellectual milieu as a discourse. I am also aware that the elasticity of Confucianism, as it has undergone more than two millennia, inhibits generalizations about its views on perennial issues such as the idea of the self. Notwithstanding the special problems one encounters in articulating a particularly "Confucian" idea of the self, I shall nevertheless try to show that a characteristic Confucian selfhood entails the participation of the other and that the reason for this desirable and necessary symbiosis of selfhood and otherness is the Confucian conception of the self as a dynamic process of spiritual development.

I have elsewhere defined the Confucian quest for sagehood, in the ethico-religious sense, as ultimate self-transformation as a communal act (Tu 1979). This definition involves two inter-related assumptions: (a) the self as a center of relationships and (b) the self as a dynamic process of spiritual development. Since the former has been more fully studied by cultural anthropologists, social psychologists, and political scientists in subjects such as family, socialization, and authority patterns in pre-modern and contemporary China (Pye 1968; Hsu 1970, 1971; Wolf 1974, 1978;Ahern 1981), our attention here will be focused on the Confucian idea of the self as development.

To differentiate the Confucian project from a variety of psychological technologies – transcendental meditation, holistic healing, rebirthing, dynamic living, and the like, currently in vogue throughout north America – which also claim self-development as an underlying assumption, it is helpful to note that, in the Confucian sense, self as development is a lifelong commitment which necessitates a ceaseless process of learning. Furthermore, Confucian learning is not only book-learning, but also ritual practice; it is through the disciplining of the body and mind that the Confucian acquires a taste for life, not as an isolated individual, but as an active participant in the living community – the family, the province, the state, and the world. The idea of "ritualization," which implies a dynamic process of self-cultivation in the spirit of filiality, brotherhood, friendship, discipleship, and loyalty, seems to capture well this basic Confucian intention (Tu 1972; Erikson 1977).

A distinctive feature of Confucian ritualization is an ever-deepening and broadening awareness of the presence of the other in one's self-cultivation. This is perhaps the single most important reason why the Confucian idea of the self as a center of relationships is an open system. It is only through the continuous opening up of the self to others, as the assumptive reason seems to suggest, that the self can maintain its wholesome personal identity. The person who is not sensitive or responsive to others around him is self-centered; self-centeredness easily leads to a closed world, or, in Sung-Ming terminology, to a state of paralysis (Chan 1969:530). Therefore, to encounter the other with an open-minded spirit is not only desirable; it is as vital to the health of the self as is air or water to one's life. The well-known statement in the *Analects*,[1] "Wishing to establish oneself, one establishes others; wishing to enlarge oneself, one enlarges others," enjoins us to help others to establish and enlarge themselves as a corollary of our self-establishment and self-enlargement. Strictly speaking, to involve the other in our self-cultivation is not only altruistic; it is required for our own self-development.

It is commonly assumed that by stressing the importance of social relations, Confucian thought has undermined the autonomy of the individual self. In this view, a Confucian self devoid of human-relatedness has little meaningful content of its own. Since the self in Confucian literature is often understood in terms of dyadic relationships, a Confucian man's self-awareness of being a son, a brother, a husband, or a father dominates his awareness of himself as a self-reliant and independent person. If we pursue this line further, the Confucian man is seen predominantly as a social being whose basic task is to learn the science and art of adjusting to the world (Weber 1951:235). If this is accepted as the reason why the presence of the other is significant in Confucian self-cultivation, Confucian ethics would hardly be differentiable from the common-sense notion that we are inescapably bound in a human community.

That the Confucian tradition has attached great importance to sociality, both in its formative years and in its subsequent developments, is beyond dispute. Surely a defining characteristic of Confucian thought is its concern for social ethics (Balazs 1964). But underscoring the significance of this particular dimension of Confucian thought should not lead to the conclusion that social ethics is all-embracing in the Confucian mode of thinking. In actuality, the evidence seems to show that, in a comprehensive understanding of the Confucian project, the social dimension is, on the one hand, rooted in what may be called a Confucian depth psychology, and on the other, must be extended to a realm of Confucian religiosity in order for its full significance to unfold. In other words, if we choose to employ terms derived from disciplines established in modern secular universities to characterize the Confucian idea of learning to be human, it is vitally important to realize that notions such as social adjustment hardly tell us the whole story. Concepts such as personal integration, self-realization, and ultimate concerns must also be used. It is outside the scope of this paper to pursue further the art and strategy of interpreting Confucianism. Let it suffice to suggest that the Confucian emphasis on sociality is laden with fruitful ambiguities and that if we do not prematurely tie up loose ends, Confucian sociality is laden wth profound psychological and religious implications (Smith 1967).

We now return to our earlier question, what is the significance of the other in the Confucian project of self-cultivation? Since it is no longer satisfactory simply to note that the Confucian approach to ethics is solely sociological, we need to explore another track. To begin, let us examine in some detail the father-son relationship in the context of self-cultivation. The conventional belief is that since "filial piety" is a cardinal value in Confucianism, a salient feature of the father-son relationship is the unquestioned obedience of the son to the authority of the father. For the son to cultivate himself, in this view, he must learn to suppress his own desires, anticipate the wishes of his father, and take his father's commands as sacred edicts. His receptivity to his father is thus the result of his concerted effort to internalize the "super-ego," to the extent that his conscience automatically dictates that he do what his father wishes. Latent aggressiveness toward, not to mention hatred of, his father is totally repressed in belief and attitude as well as suppressed in behavior. Understandably, the Confucian son, overpowered by the authority of the father, evokes images of weakness, indecision, dependency, and conformity.

However, even if we accept this one-sided interpretation of the father-son relationship, the subjugation of the son involves a mobilization of internal resources which implies a complex process of internal adjustment, as well as accommodation and harmonization. For one thing, it is the willing participation of the son, socialized by a long and strenuous education supported by the community and sanctioned by the political leadership, that underlies the whole enterprise. Imagine, in Freudian terms, the complicated mechanism required to transform, indeed purify, the Oedipus complex in the Confucian son. The common impression that the traditional Chinese society, steeped in Confucianism, managed to impose the unquestioned authority of the father on generation after generation of submissive sons is predicated on the false assumption that since the Confucian son had little choice, there was no opportunity for him to exhibit any voluntarism on matters of filial piety. One wonders if the control, even in its most efficacious phase, could really accomplish this without turning the so-called filial sons into hypocrites and psychopaths. Can a society survive, let alone provide any healthy environment for personal growth, if a large portion of its male population is instructed to follow the dictates of gerontocratic dogmatism with no appeal to any transcendent authority?

Furthermore, the son's obedience to his father is not only restricted to the world of the living. For example, in the *Analects*, filial piety is attributed to a son because he chooses to follow his father's will posthumously for three years (1: 11). But even this is only the beginning of a continuous reenactment of a memorial ritual in which the presence of the father, through the art of imagining, is made real throughout the rest of one's life. The *Book of Rites*[2] describes in some detail the psychological state of the filial son in mourning:

"The severest vigil and purification is maintained and practised in the inner self, while a looser vigil is maintained externally. During the days of such vigil, the mourner thinks of the departed, how and where he sat, how he smiled and spoke, what were his aims and views, what he delighted in, and what he desired and enjoyed. By the third day he will perceive the meaning of such exercise. On the day of sacrifice, when he enters the apartment [of the temple], he will seem to see [the deceased] in the place [where his spirit-tablet is]. After he has moved about [to perform his operations], and is leaving by the door, he will be arrested by seeming to hear the sound of his movements, and will sigh as he seems to hear the sound of his sighing."

(Fung 1952: 351–52)

As Fung Yu-lan notes, "to gain communion with the dead through abstraction in this way, hoping that '*peradventure* they could enjoy his offerings,' is nothing more than to give satisfaction to the emotions of 'affectionate longings'" (Fung 1952: 352).

The commitment of the son to the father is therefore a lifelong commitment and a comprehensive one at that. If the father, or at least the image of the father, is forever present, what symbolic act does the son employ to "kill" his father so that he can eventually declare his independence? Normally one would think that when the son begins to care for his aged father, he can then take the comfort of realizing himself as a provider, a giver. However, the ability to support one's father is classified as the lowest among the three degrees of filial piety in the *Book of Rites*, the other two being honoring him and not disgracing him (Chapter 21; Fung 1952: 359). After all, it is not only the father in the flesh that the son must learn to obey and respect. The father's ego ideal must also be realized. It is precisely in this sense that Fung Yu-lan explains:

> "On the spiritual side, filial piety consists, during the lifetime of our parents, in conforming ourselves to their wishes, and giving them not only physical care and nourishment, but also nourishing their wills; while should they fall into error, it consists in reproving them and leading them back to what is right. After the death of our parents, furthermore, one aspect of it consists in offering sacrifices to them and thinking about them, so as to keep their memory fresh in our minds."
>
> (Fung 1952: 359)

This normative view of filial piety seems incompatible with the well-known Confucian proverb: "There are no erroneous parents under heaven." If what the proverb conveys is simply that, in the obedient eyes of the son, the father is incapable of committing mistakes, then its meaning is certainly in conflict with the idea of "reproving him" and even "leading him back to what is right." However, since the Confucians do recognize that it is human to err, a corollary of the Confucian belief in human perfectibility (Munro 1969, 1977), they can certainly accept the plain truth that their fathers do sometimes fall into error. The "erroneous parents" then must be taken to mean wrong parents in the sense that they do not fit our ideals of parenthood. Surely the Confucians recognize that there are unfit parents. Common observation as well as legal judgment helps us to detect that this is not at all unusual. Traditional China must have had a fair share of this kind of human tragedy also. Confucians have not been blind to the blatant reality of unfit parents. However, what is one to do if one's father falls short of being fatherly? It is not at all difficult to condemn unfit fathers, but when and how can I say that my own father is unfit for me? Indeed, what is the significance of committing myself to the value that my father, no matter what he is or does, is always my father?

The Confucian perception on this matter deserves our attention because the "reality principle" applied to the father-son relationship addresses not only the question of the super-ego but also that of the ego ideal in a thought-provoking way. Especially noteworthy, in this connection, is the underlying assumption that a social dyad is not a fixed entity, but a dynamic interaction involving a rich and ever-changing texture of human-relatedness woven by the constant participation of other significant dyadic relationships. Methods of analysis based upon either the theory of conflict resolution or a sort of hydraulic mechanism of damming and releasing only scratch the surface manifestation of the father-son dyad. Usually these methods do not address the embedded meaning structure, let alone the spiritual values that sustain it.

The Confucian approach takes as its point of departure that the father-son relationship is absolutely binding. Unlike the minister in the ruler-minister relationship, whose overriding concern for righteousness may compel him to criticize openly, indeed remove himself from the relationship as public protest, the son ought not to sever his ties to his father under any circumstances. The trite and commonplace observation that one cannot choose one's father is here maintained as a core value. The Confucian proverb that there are no erroneous parents clearly indicates that since we owe our origins to our parents and since our existence itself is inextricably linked to our parental relationships, we must recognize the continuous presence of our parents in every dimension of our lived reality. Our bodies, for instance, are not our own possessions pure and simple; they are sacred gifts from our parents and thus laden with deep ethico-religious significance:

"The body is that which has been transmitted to us by our parents. Dare anyone allow himself to be irreverent in the employment of their legacy? If a man in his own house and privacy be not grave, he is not filial; if in serving his ruler he be not loyal, he is not filial; if in discharging the duties of office he be not serious, he is not filial; if with friends he be not sincere, he is not filial; if on the field of battle he be not brave, he is not filial. If he fail in these five things, the evil [of the disgrace] will reflect on his parents. Dare he but be serious?"

(Fung 1952:360)

Filial piety so broadly conceived as the source of all virtues may be the result of politicized Confucian ethics (Hsü 1968), but the idea of continuing a biological reality because of its spiritual meaning as well as its social and political significance is unmistakably an original Confucian insight.

An important feature of this insight is the recognition that the father's ego ideal, his wishes for himself as well as what he has created as standards of emulation for his family, is an integral part of the legacy that the son receives. The idea of continuity must not be taken literally to mean the continuity of a biological line. An unbroken genealogy for several generations surely calls for celebration, not to mention the happy outcome of establishing and enlarging the family fortune to include numerous talented and prosperous descendants. Yet it is the scholarly achievements, the cultural attainments, and the quality of life of the family that really define a successful Confucian father. Enhancing the father's reputation entails a set of conditions beyond the cherished value of allowing the family line to continue. Mencius is perhaps misinterpreted as having subscribed to the simple view that producing male progeny is the most important duty of the filial son (Mencius 1970:4A:26, 4B:30). In a patriarchal society, the birth of a son may have been conceived as a minimum requirement for continuing a family line, but the transmission of the father's legacy clearly involves a much more complex process of symbolic interaction.

The plight of the legendary Sage-King Shun is a case in point (Mencius 1970:5A:2). Born as the son of a brutish man in the Eastern Barbarian region, Shun, in response to the exemplary teachings of the Sage-King Yao, became a paradigm of filial piety through self-development. He was able to do so against overwhelming odds. For one thing, his father colluded with his stepmother and his half-brother in a series of plots to murder him. Due to divine intervention, or in Confucian terminology, to his extreme sincerity that reached heaven, he escaped each threat of calamity unscathed. Never was his filial love for his undeserving father compromised. For this exceptionally inspiring expression of virtue, not to mention inner strength and personal dignity, he was offered the throne by Yao to rule the Middle Kingdom as an exemplar. For our purpose, it is illuminating to note that in this legend Shun does not appear merely as an obedient son, for had he been unquestioningly submissive to the brutality of his father he would have endangered his life, which in turn would have implicated his father in further unworthiness. It is precisely in this sense that in the *Sayings of the Confucian School*, Confucius instructs the filial son to endure only light physical punishment from an enraged father (*K'ung-tzu Chia-yü* 1968). To run away from a severe beating, the argument goes, is not only to protect the body which has been entrusted to him by his parents but also to respect the fatherliness in his father that may have been temporarily obscured by rage.

The dilemma by which Shun was confronted was, of course, much more difficult to escape. There was hardly any indication that the old brute was a caring person. Shun's strategy, as it were, was to do what his moral sense judged the best possible course of action at the moment. On the solemn matter of marriage, for example, he chose not to inform his father beforehand. Mencius, in defense of this apparently unfilial act, suggested to his students that allowing the father to mess up the whole affair could have brought about more serious consequences (*Mencius* 1970: 5A: 2). Shun, in Mencius's view, appealed to a personality ideal for guidance which transcends all ordinary rules of civilized conduct and provides ultimate justification for the meaningfulness of any particular rule of conduct in the human community. He was deemed a paradigm of filial piety because, even though he was not submissive and by established convention might even be thought disobedient, his action showed concern and respect for what must have been the wishes of his father's ego ideal. In this sense, Shun never challenged his father's authority, nor did he ignore it; he conscientiously rectified it and thus restored it. The continuous presence of the father, both actual and ideal, in Shun's moral consciousness enabled him to develop his inner strength through a constant symbolic interaction with this significant other. Shun could not have realized his filial love alone. For this, he was grateful not only to his father but also to his stepmother and half-brother.

The legend of Shun can be conceived of as the worst possible case for maintaining that filial piety is a natural expression of the son's spontaneous love and care for his father. The Confucian interpretation stresses the authentic possibility of self-realization even if involved in the most unwholesome dyadic relationship. The moral is clear: we should all be inspired by Shun's example in adjusting himself to an extremely difficult relationship, harmonizing himself with it in his own quest for moral excellence, and using it to transform creatively himself and those around him. Thus the legend of Shun conveys the two-fold message that the father-son relationship is inescapable and that it engenders an inexhaustible supply of symbolic resources for self-cultivation. Implicit in this message is a typical Confucian paradox. The father-son tie is a constraint, a limitation, and a bondage; yet through its constraining, limiting, and binding power, it provides a necessary means for self-cultivation for the father as well as the son. This seemingly arbitrary imposition of the super-ego upon the individual is rooted in a perception of the human condition as one in which the father-son relationship itself implies a transcendence beyond the psychosocial dynamics that envelop it. Shun's ability to follow the dictates of his moral sense clearly shows a realized possibility for the Confucian son to appeal to his father's ego ideal, an appeal which in turn informs his own conscience of the best course of action.

In a thought-provoking essay on "Father and Son in Christianity and Confucianism," Robert Bellah remarks on the "truly heroic loyalty" of an unwavering minister in demonstrating the supreme value of filial piety in political protest as an indication of "the roots of the strength and endurance of a great civilization" (Bellah 1976: 95). However, he also observes that in

"the Confucian attitude toward political and familial authority, there does not seem to be any point of leverage in the Confucian symbol system from which disobedience to parents could be justified. This does not mean parents could not be criticized. When they did not live up to the pattern of their ancestors there was indeed a positive duty to remonstrate, but they could not be disobeyed."

(Bellah 1976: 94)

This observation leads him to conclude:

"[T]he Confucian phrasing of the father-son relationship blocks any outcome of Oedipal ambivalence except sub- mission – submission not in the last analysis to a person but to a pattern of personal relationships that is held to have ultimate validity. An outcome that could lead to creative social innovation as in the Protestant case was precluded by the absence of a point of transcendent loyalty that could provide legitimation for it. In the West, from the time of the Mosaic revelation, every particular pattern of social relations was in principle deprived of ultimacy. In China filial piety and loyalty became absolutes. In the West it was God alone who in the last analysis exercized power. In China the father con- tinued to dominate."

(Bellah 1976: 95)

If we follow Bellah's insightful observation, the Confucian orientation clearly fails to account for the multilayered meaning of the Oedipus complex: the sentiments and pathos of love and fear, respect and guilt, and obedience and rebellion generated in man's relationship to his father. The reason for its alleged failure, however, is quite subtle. As Bellah notes in the beginning of his essay, "in Chinese religious symbolism familial figures are far from central. Though there is no civilization that has placed greater emphasis on the father-son tie, it is not reflected in the ultimate religious symbolism" (Bellah 1976: 78). This apparent asymmetry between social structure and religious symbolism can serve as a reference point for a more focused investigation of the father-son relationship in Confucian thought. Again, it is helpful to take Bellah's essay as a point of departure. "Having sampled briefly some of the implications of the father-son symbolism in Christian belief and ritual," Bellah warns us against a literal reading of the Freudian thesis:

"Nevertheless it becomes obvious upon reflection that the Christian symbolism is not explained by the Oedipus complex. If it were simply a direct projection of the Oedipus complex, then since the Oedipus complex is universal so would be Christian symbolism. But this is clearly far from the case. Christian symbolism is in fact highly unique, emerging from a particular historical context and bearing a particular historical role, a fact that Freud seems to have recognized. The particular qualities of the Christian symbolism emerged in the first instance from the Christian notion of God, around which the whole symbolic structure hangs."

(Bellah 1976:82)

It seems that, in the Confucian perspective, the explanatory power of the Oedipus complex as Freud envisaged it was greatly enhanced by Christian symbolism both as a background under-standing and as a particular manifestation, if not direct projec-tion, of a unique perception of the father-son relationship. To be sure, Christian symbolism can hardly be *explained* by the simple notion of a direct projection of the Oedipus complex. The very fact that the Oedipus complex makes a great deal of sense for the analysis of basic Christian motifs in psychodynamic terms seems to suggest that its own conceptualization may have been deeply influenced by Judaeo-Christian symbolism in the first place. The Oedipus complex may not be as universal as Freud supposed it to be. It is neither "the nucleus of all neurosis," nor the "origin" of the major aspects of human society and culture as he asserted in *Totem and Taboo* (Freud 1952). However, the Oedipal situation, the highly charged emotional ambivalence inherent in the father-son relationship, does appear to have universal significance. The projection theory, however, is too simple-minded a causality to account for the tremendous power and influence that cultural symbolism exerts upon social structure.

Despite the centrality of the family in Confucian society, it is not conceived as an end in itself. The Confucians regard the family as the natural habitat of humans; it is the necessary and the most desirable environment for mutual support and personal growth. The father-son relationship, viewed in this context, is a defining characteristic of the human condition: it is human to have a father. The ultimate purpose of life is neither regulating the family nor harmonizing the father-son relationship, but self-realization. Indeed, only through self-cultivation can one's family be regulated and, by implication, one's relationship to one's father harmonized. Understandably the *Great Learning* takes self-cultivation as the root, and regulating the family, governing the state, and bringing peace to the world as the branches (Chan 1969: 86–7). The implicit logic that self-cultivation can eventually bring about universal peace under heaven, as branches are the natural outcome of a healthy root, need not concern us here. It will suffice to note that, while there is no evidence that cultural symbols such as *t'ien* ("heaven") and *tao* ("way") in Confucianism are projections of familial values, the father-son relationship and the other "five relationships" must be understood in terms of a transcendence that gives meaning to this particular social structure.

Unlike Christian symbolism, which tends to undermine the significance of familial relationships in its soteriology, with Jesus as saviour, Confucian salvation, as it were, takes the basic dyadic relationships in the family as its point of departure. The emphasis is on the concrete path by which one learns to be human rather than on the final goal of self-realization. The idea of the *Analects* that filiality and brotherliness are the bases of humanity, properly interpreted, means that being filial and brotherly is the initial step towards realizing one's humanity (1:2). Mencius, in criticizing the Moist universalism, argues against the ethics of treating people on the street as dearly as one would treat one's father (*Mencius* 1970: 3B: 9). It is not the ethical idealism that bothers Mencius but the impracticality of the whole procedure. If we reduce the richness, including the fruitful ambiguities, of the father-son relationship to the one-dimensional encounters we normally have with people on the street, our good intention of caring for strangers as dearly as we care for our parents may result in treating our dear ones as indifferently as we treat strangers. The insistence that we begin our tasks of self-realization in the context of the immediate dyadic relationships in which we are inevitably circumscribed is a basic principle underlying the father-son relationship in Confucian symbolism.

An equally basic principle governing the father-son relationship is reciprocity (Yang 1957). The impression of the father as the socializer, the educator, and thus the authoritarian disciplinarian is superficial, if not mistaken. It is true that the Confucian son is not permitted to express his rebellious feelings toward his father, but to describe the explosion of age-long repressed aggression of sons against fathers as a central problem in modern as well as traditional Confucian society is misleading. According to the norm, the father should act fatherly so that the son can follow in a manner most appropriate to his self-identification. The son's filiality is conceived as a response to the father's kindness. The father must set an example for the son as a loving and respectable person before he can reasonably expect his son to love and respect him. Indeed, he should, in his son's mind, be seen as an exemplary teacher. On the other hand, he is not encouraged to instruct his son personally for fear that the intimacy between father and son be damaged as a result. Understandably, exchanging sons for formal instruction has been a common practice in Chinese society.

The sternness of the father image in Confucian culture must not be confused with aloofness or indifference. The father is not supposed to be physically close to the son. Physical closeness seems to be a prerogative of mother and son. Nevertheless, the father remains intimate with the son as his constant companion in the most critical stages of his development. The caring father guides the son's education, oversees his maturation, assists in his marriage arrangements and prepares him for his career. The son in turn endeavors to fulfill his father's aspirations by internalizing them as goals in his own life. Reciprocity so conceived seems common in many other societies. A peculiar justification in the Confucian symbolism is that this reciprocal intimacy is not only absolutely necessary but also highly desirable for personal spiritual growth. This is diametrically opposed to the idea that the quest for inner spirituality requires that one transcend or forsake all primordial ties. The centrality of the father-son relationship in Confucian thought can thus be seen as a paradigmatic expression of the Confucian perception that selfhood entails the participation of the other.

Does this mean that since in Confucian symbolism there is no obvious shift of the ultimacy (e.g. "heaven" or "way") from the natural social order to a transcendent reference point (such as God), there is no resultant capacity to ask ultimate questions? If this is the case, Confucian selfhood is, in the last analysis, a category in social ethics and one which does not seem to have any profound religious import. On the other hand, if Confucian selfhood is itself a transcendent reference point, a line of thought I intend to pursue further here, how are we to understand its linkages with ultimate ideas such as "heaven" and "way"?

The answer lies in the Confucian conception of the self not only as a center of relationships but also as a dynamic process of spiritual development. Ontologically, selfhood, our original nature, is endowed by heaven (Chan 1969:98). It is therefore divine in its all-embracing fullness. Selfhood, in this sense, is both immanent and transcendent. It is intrinsic to us; at the same time, it belongs to heaven. So far, this conception may appear to be identical to the Christian idea of humanity as divinity circumscribed. By analogy, Confucian selfhood, or original human nature, can be seen as God's image in man. However, the transcendence of heaven is significantly different from the transcendence of God. The Mencian thesis that a full realization of our mind can lead us to a comprehension of our nature and eventually to an understanding of heaven is predicated on the belief that our selfhood is a necessary and sufficient condition for us to appreciate in total the subtle meanings of the mandate of heaven. To translate this into Christian terms, it means that humanity itself, without God's grace, can fully realize its circumscribed divinity to such an extent that the historical Jesus as God incarnate symbolizes no more than a witness of what people ought to be able to attain on their own. After all, Christ is also called the Great Exemplar. However, this claim exhibits a family resemblance to the notorious Confucian pelagianism: the denial of original sin, the assertion that we are endowed with the freedom of will not to sin, and the avowal that we as human beings have the unassisted initiating power to appropriate the necessary grace for salvation. Besides, the Confucian position does not even consider grace as relevant to self-realization.

Though we do not take transcendence to mean an external source of authority, not to mention a "wholly other," there is still a distinctly transcendent dimension in Confucian selfhood, namely that heaven resides in it, works through it and, in its optimal manifestation, is also revealed by it. Selfhood so conceived maintains a tacit communication with heaven. It is the root from which great cultural ideals and spiritual values grow. Understandably, subjectivity in the Confucian sense is not particularistic and is, paradoxically, the concrete basis for universality.

Since I have elsewhere elaborated on this point (Tu 1976), let us here enquire only into the significance of transcendence in selfhood for the idea of dynamic spiritual development. On the surface, if goodness is intrinsic to human nature, why is there any need for self-realization? A direct response is simply to note that the intrinsic goodness in our nature is often in a latent state: only through long and strenuous effort can it be realized as an experienced reality. In a deeper sense, however, a distinction between ontological assertion and existential realization must be made. Self-realization is an existential idea, specifying a way of bringing into existence the ontological assertion that human nature is good. Precisely because human nature is good, the ultimate basis for self-realization and the actual process of initiating self-cultivation are both located in the structure of the self. Pelagian fallacy notwithstanding, Confucian selfhood contains the necessary inner resources for its own dynamic spiritual development.

There is an implicit circularity in this conception of the self: human nature is good so that there is an authentic possibility for dynamic spiritual development and vice versa. If we accept that the above-mentioned distinction of ontological assertion and existential realization also involves a dialectic relationship, the circularity is no longer a vicious one. Rather, we can well see that inherent in the structure of the self is a powerful longing for the transcendent, not for an external supreme being but for the heaven that has bestowed on us our original nature. This longing for the transcendent, in a deeper sense, is also an urge for self-transcendence, to go beyond what the self existentially is so that it can become what it ought to be. Although we are, in ontological terms, never deficient in our internally generated capacity for spiritual development, we must constantly open ourselves up to the symbolic resources available to us for pursuing the concrete paths of self-realization. The participation of the other is not only desirable but absolutely necessary. For as centers of relationships, we do not travel alone to our final destiny; we are always in the company of family and friends, be they remembered, imagined, or physically present.

The ultimate question for the Confucians then is, how can I, in the midst of social relations, realize my selfhood as the heaven-endowed humanity? The reason that the father-son relationship is so central to Confucian symbolism is itself a reflection of this mode of questioning. Since I can never realize myself as an isolated or even isolatable individual, I must recognize as a point of departure my personal locus with reference to my father among other dyadic relationships. My relationship to my father is vitally important for my own salvation, because if it is ignored, I can longer face up to the reality of who I am in a holistic sense. After all, my heaven-endowed nature can only be manifested through my existence as a center of relationships. For my own self-cultivation, I cannot but work through, among other things, my relationship to my father with all its fruitful ambiguities. The Sage-King Shun certainly had a more difficult task than most, but he, like us, could not bypass his social relationships in order to establish an intimate connection with heaven directly. He was able to reach heaven in the sense of fully realizing his selfhood precisely because he courageously faced up to the challenge of his social relationships near at hand. Social relationships are not in themselves ultimate concerns. They become prominent in Confucian symbolism because they are, on the one hand, rooted in one's depth psychology and, on the other, extended to one's religiosity.

The father-son relationship, in this sense, provides a context and an instrumentality for self-cultivation. It is not because our fathers dominate or because we dare not disobey them that we cultivate our sense of respect for them. We respect them for our own project of self-realization and, with gentle persuasion, they may be convinced that it is also for theirs. Indeed, our ego ideals come into existence as a result of our discipleship, friendship, ministership, brotherhood, and a host of other social roles. The father-son relationship, central as it is, constitutes but one among them. Like Shun, we take our relationships to our fathers as absolutely binding, but we do not submit ourselves to their arbitrary rule. For their own sake as well as ours, we must appeal to our heaven-endowed nature, our conscience, for guidance. After all, it is for the ultimate purpose of self-realization that we honor our fathers as the source of the meaningful life that we have been pursuing. Indeed, there is a sense of a "creative fidelity" (Marcel 1964) in our relationships to our fathers. We are all involved in a joint venture to bring about the good life for our society. We know that we have to rise above the self-centeredness of our limited world views really to appreciate the universal mandate of heaven inherent in our human nature. We take our dyadic relationships absolutely seriously because they, in concrete ways, help us to enrich our supply of internal resources with symbolic content. Filiality, brotherliness, friendship, and the like are thus integral parts of our spiritual development. It is in this sense that Confucian selfhood entails the participation of the other.

Lest we should misconstrue the symbiosis of selfhood and otherness as a still-undifferentiated organismic notion, it is important to note that the Confucian perception of the self, without ideas of original sin and God's grace, is far from being an assertion of prelapsarian naïveté. The lack of a myth of the Fall notwithstanding, human frailty, fallibility and diabolism are fully recognized in Confucian symbolism. The Confucians are acutely aware of the human propensity for self-destruction, not to mention slothfulness, wickedness, arrogance, and the like. Indeed, it is this deep sense of the tremendous difficulty that one encounters in one's self-cultivation that prompts the Confucians to define personal spiritual development as a communal act. However, the idea of a loner trying to search for salvation in total isolation, without the experiential support of a community, is not inconceivable in Confucian society. The more cherished approach, rather, is self-cultivation through communication with and sharing in an ever-expanding circle of human-relatedness. Even at the risk of losing one's individual autonomy, the Confucian chooses fellowship of companionable people, i.e. "like-minded friends," to develop themselves jointly through mutual exhortation. In this connection, the father-son relationship, not unlike the teacher-student relationship, or for that matter the husband-wife relationship, is in the last analysis a "covenant" based upon a fiduciary commitment to a joint venture. Through the significant other, one deepens and broadens one's selfhood. This is the meaning of the Confucian self not only as center of relationships, but also as a dynamic process of spiritual development.

Notes

1 The *Analects* refer to the *Lun Yu*, a collection of maxims by Confucius that form the basis of his moral and political philosophy.
2 The *Book of Rites* or *Li Chi* refers to one of the Five Classics which originated before the time of Confucius. The *Book of Rites* deals with the principles of conduct. It was probably written in the third century BC and discusses the rules of private as well as public conduct. See James Legge, trans., The Chinese Classics, 5 vols. (Oxford: Clarendon Press, 1893–95) for English versions of the *Analects* and the *Book of Rites*.

References

Ahern, E. M. (1981) *Chinese ritual and politics*. Cambridge: Cambridge University Press.

Balazs, E. (1964) *Chinese Civilization of Bureaucracy; Variations on a Theme*. Edited by A. F. Wright. Trans. H. M. Wright. New Haven, Conn.: Yale University Press.

Bellah, R. N. (1976) *Beyond Belief: Essays on Religion in a Post-*

Traditional World. New York: Harper & Row.

Chan, W. T. (trans.) (1969) *A Source Book in Chinese Philosophy*. Princeton, NJ: Princeton University Press.

Erikson, E. H. (1977) *Toys and Reason; Stages in the Ritualization of Experience*. New York: W. W. Norton.

Freud, S. (1952) *Totem and Taboo*. Trans. J. Strachey. New York: W. W. Norton.

Fung Yu-lan (1952) *A History of Chinese Philosophy*. Trans. D. Bodde. Princeton, NJ: Princeton University Press.

Hsü Fu-kuan (1968) *Chung-kuo hsiao-tao ssu-hsiang te hsing-ch'eng yen-pien chi-ch'i tsai li-shih chung te chu-wen-t'i* (The Formation, Development and Historical Issues of Filial Thought in China). In Hsü Fu-kuan, *Chung-kuo ssu-hsiang shih lun-chi* (*Collected Essays on Chinese Thought*). Taichung, Taiwan: Tunghai University Press.

Hsu, F. L. K. (1970) *Americans and Chinese: Purpose and Fulfillment in Great Civilizations*. Garden City, NY: Doubleday.

_____ (1971) *Under the Ancestral Shadow; Kinship, Personality, and Social Mobility in China*. Stanford, Calif.: Stanford University Press.

K'ung-tzu chia-yü (*Sayings of the Confucian School*) (1968) Comp. Wang Su. (Reprint of the Shu edition of the Sung dynasty.) Taipei: Chung-hua Book Company.

Marcel, G. (1964) *Creative Fidelity*. Trans. R. Rosthal. New York: Farrar, Strauss & Giroux.

Mencius (1970) Trans. D. C. Lau. Harmondsworth: Penguin Books.

Munro, D. J. (1969) *The Concept of Man in Early China*. Stanford, Calif.: Stanford University Press.

_____ (1977) *The Concept of Man in Contemporary China*. Ann Arbor MI: University of Michigan Press.

Pye, L. W. (1968) *The Spirit of Chinese Politics; a Psychocultural Study of the Authority Crisis in Political Development*. Cambridge, Mass.: MIT Press.

Smith, H. (1967) Transcendence in Traditional China. *Religious Studies* 2: 185–96.

Tu Wei-ming (1972) Li as Process of Humanization. *Philosophy East and West* 22(2): 187–201.

_____ (1976) *Centrality and Commonality: An Essay on Chung-yung*. Honolulu: University Press of Hawaii.

_____ (1979) Ultimate Self-Transformation as a Communal Act. *Journal of Chinese Philosophy* 6: 237–46.

Weber, M. (1951) *The Religion of China: Confucianism and Taoism*. Trans. H. H. Gerth. Glencoe, Ill.: Free Press.

Wolf, A. P. (1974) *Religion and Ritual in Chinese Society*. Stanford, Calif.: Stanford University Press.

——— (ed.) (1978) *Studies in Chinese Society*. Stanford, Calif.: Stanford University Press.

Yang Lien-sheng (1957) The Concept of Pao as a Basis for Social Relations in China. In J. K. Fairbank (ed.) *Chinese Thought and Institutions*. Chicago: University of Chicago Press.

8

The Changing Concept of Self in Contemporary China

Godwin C. Chu

Introduction

The self is an important concept for understanding social behavior. As a construct, the self is open to diverse definitions, as we have seen in Hsu (1981a), Johnson (1981), and Smith (1981). This chapter takes a look at the changing self in contemporary China through a broad lens. Since empirical data is as yet unobtainable, I shall use whatever information is available to suggest, more as *hypotheses* than as evidence, what I consider to be some of the salient aspects of the changing self of the Chinese today. Further research is required to test these hypotheses.

For my discussion, the self is defined as a configuration of roles expressed in self-other expectations and observable in self-other interactions. This definition largely follows Mead's (1934) notion of the self. The slant in this definition, if any, is not so much on how an individual "sees" himself. Rather, it is on the fundamental behavioral expectations that an individual has of himself when interacting with others. The former takes a cognitive approach. The latter follows a behavioral orientation. While both are important aspects of the concept of self, it is largely through the latter that we make observations and inferences about an individual's self and generalize them to a cultural group. A generalization of this kind can be either sketchy or illuminating depending on the representativeness of the situations in which the observations are made and the individuals who are being observed.

I suggest that the self develops out of interactions with three broad entities in one's environment (Chu 1979). They are: significant others; materials and objects; ideas, beliefs, and values (see *Figure 8.1*):

(a) *Significant others,* individuals in the self's social environment with whom he constantly interacts in various kinds of role relations.

(b) *Materials* and *objects* in the self's physical environment which he relies on for his survival and which, through the extent of technology, support and mediate his social relations.

Figure 8.1 Concept of self in relation to significant others, materials and objects, and ideas

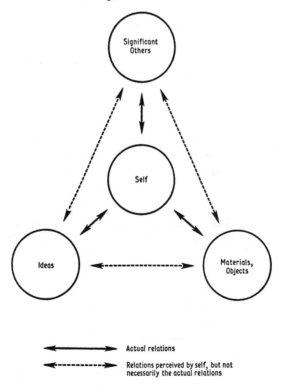

Significant
Others

Self

Ideas

Materials,
Objects

⟵————————⟶ Actual relations

⟵- - - - - - - ⟶ Relations perceived by self, but not
necessarily the actual relations

(c) *Ideas*, including ideology and religious beliefs – both *cognitive* and *evaluative* – which influence the way the self perceives and responds to his social and physical environments, and sets priorities for his social relations and manipulation of materials and objects in his physical environment.

Out of these interactions, a conceptual configuration emerges with regard to oneself, which has lasting implications and guides one's further interactions with significant others, materials and objects, and ideas. Of these three entities, significant others are of crucial importance to the formation of an individual's self. Of course, the significant others in one's environment are themselves the products of the general cultural milieu in which both they, the significant others, and the self live and function. The significant others do not have a totally free hand in influencing the development of an individual's self. However, it is largely through interactions with the significant others that an individual comes to perceive and internalize the ideological content of his society. It is through such interactions that the individual learns to manage and manipulate his material environment for his own survival.

An individual develops a concept of self through interactions with all three entities, which are themselves related to one another. The purpose of our tripartite paradigm is to suggest a *framework of comparative analysis*. We can make observations, either cross-culturally or within one culture over time, as to whether people's interactions with significant others are oriented primarily toward cultural ideas or materials and objects, and which of these entities more strongly shape the nature of the self in a particular culture.

I want to emphasize that there is continuity as well as discontinuity in the very social and physical environments in which the self develops. The discontinuity in a child's maturation process is obvious. Any child must progress from the loving environment of home to the hazards of schooling, the challenge of adulthood, and the responsibility of parenthood. Underlying this process of discontinuity is a thread of continuity that is distinctive of a particular culture. It is on the basis of this continuity that we are justified to speak of the "self" of a cultural group.

Recognizing that the interactions between the self and his social and physical environments have a pattern of continuity within a cultural milieu is not to overlook the importance of change. When there is a major change in any of the three entities, either in the significant others or in the environment of materials and objects or in the ideological underpinnings, we can expect some change to take place in the configuration of the self. We know some of our friends change after they get married, that is, when they acquire new significant others. Losing one's job, especially after middle age when the individual has more or less established a stable relationship with materials and objects, can have a devastating effect on his self-image. We know children brought up in wealthy, conservative families sometimes become radicals when exposed to a different ideology in college. We recognize the significance of these changes. What we want to emphasize is that unless the cultural thread of continuity is forcefully disrupted by external elements, the general nature of self in a cultural group tends to persist even though some individuals may change their self-concepts under particular circumstances. Even when an individual is confronted with the pressure of change, the impact of early experience through interactions with significant others is important because it mediates the way in which the self handles the subsequent interactions with his new social and physical environments.

These two observations – *cultural continuity* and impact of *early experience* – are relevant to our discussion of the changing self in contemporary China. In China since 1949, particularly during the ten years following the Cultural Revolution initiated in the chaotic summer of 1966, the thread of cultural continuity has been forcefully disrupted. Especially in the decade of 1966 – 76, for untold millions of Chinese (more so in the cities than in rural villages) life suddenly lost many of its familiar bearings. Recently it was officially recognized that during those ten years "the standards of right and wrong were reversed. Honor and shame switched places. Civility, courtesy and morality were branded as forms of revisionism. Barbarian behavior of physical violence, destruction and robbery were given the laurel of heroism" (*People's Daily*, 1981). Destruction and cruelty became virtues in the name of revolution as the Red Guards wrought havoc in defiance of traditions. The impact of those years, especially on those who were growing up during that period, could be profound. For this reason, as we shall illustrate later, we believe that the self among the younger generation is quite different from that of the older generation. However, the fact that the Chinese people have survived bears witness to the other observation, namely, the enduring impact of early experience, which is a reflection of the strength of the traditional Chinese self individually and the roots of continuity in the Chinese culture collectively. We shall return to this point later.

In the context of these general observations, I shall discuss four related topics:

(a) What are the nature and source of strength of the self among Chinese of the older generation? An answer to this question will provide a baseline for understanding change.

(b) What is the changing nature of self-other relations with authority figures as an important component of significant others?

(c) What is the nature of self-other relations with marriage partners, who are also important significant others?

(d) What is the impact of three decades of ideological communication intended by the leadership of the Chinese Communist Party to change the nature of the self through internalization of new ideas and values?

I want to stress again that due to the limited information available, my discussion should be viewed as suggestions for further research rather than empirical findings.

Nature and strength of the self

The self is conceptualized here as a configuration of role relations with significant others. What characteristics of this configuration shall we examine in order to understand the self in a particular culture? One characteristic, we suggest, is the *direction* in which the role relations are primarily oriented, whether to the individual or to the significant others. We recognize that in any role relations both orientations are present. The question is one of relative emphasis. Another characteristic has to do with the *primary basis* of defining the self-other relations, whether on cultural ideas or on materials and objects. Again the question is one of relative emphasis as both cultural ideas and materials/ objects are relevant in self-other relations under most circumstances.

A brief look at the American self will provide an illustration by contrast. It seems that in the American culture the primary orientation tends toward the individual self rather than toward the significant others. This point was vividly impressed on me by a story Francis Hsu once told. His three-year-old granddaughter was visiting one day. She was playing with something that annoyed Hsu. Hsu told her to stop. The little girl refused: "Because *I* like it." The self-assertiveness of the Americans apparently begins early in childhood and later permeates self-other relations in adult life.

The self-other relations in the American culture appear to be defined or mediated to a considerable extent by relations with materials and objects. An advertisement taken from an American magazine illustrates this point. Showing a middle-aged couple and two sons riding motorbikes in a resort area, the advertisement pictures a happy American family enjoying its vacation together. The caption says: "We get our money's worth."

Several points are worth mentioning about this advertisement. It emphasizes family togetherness, which is not a prominent theme in American advertising, and thus rather exceptional. In this case, this togetherness is achieved in the exciting activities of a vacation. It seems perfectly natural for Americans to say "We get our money's worth." One wonders what a Chinese family would do to achieve togetherness and whether it would use money to measure the worth of family union.

The American self seems to be characterized by individualism. It tends to assert one's self rather than accommodate others and to strive for a high degree of self-reliance and independence. Materials play an important role in self-other relations.

The traditional Chinese self, on the other hand, appears to be relatively more oriented toward the significant others, rather than toward the individual self. An old saying will illustrate this point: "One's body, hair, and skin are gifts from one's parents. One is not at liberty to do harm to them." Contrast this with the popular attitude among some American teenagers: "This is my life, and I'll do whatever I like with it." The traditional Chinese self exists primarily in relation to significant others. Thus a male Chinese would consider himself a son, a brother, a husband, a father, but hardly *himself*. It seems as if outside the relational context of the significant others, there was very little independent self left for the Chinese. This point can be further illustrated by the position of women in traditional China. Before marriage, a woman followed her father. After marriage, she followed her husband. After the death of her husband, she followed her son. The self had little meaning outside these rigidly defined social contexts. The idea that a woman could stand on her own, and be herself, simply did not seem possible. A person, in this case a woman, measured the worth of herself not by what she had personally achieved, but by the extent to which she had lived up to the behavioral expectations of the significant others as defined by the predominant cultural ideas.

How cultural ideas determined the manner in which the Chinese in the past defined self can be illustrated by the custom of *shou chieh* (守節), or chastity observation. After the death of her husband, a woman was obligated to his family and also to her own family to remain chaste by not remarrying. It is important to note that *shou chieh* was not voluntarily observed primarily because of the woman's personal love for her husband. It was dictated by the two families according to cultural ideas. Monuments were erected as a tribute to young widows who endured years of hardship and brought up sons who later achieved a measure of prominence, either by passing a state examination or by entering the government service. There was a touching story about a widow whose husband died when her son was a baby. The son grew up, passed a state examination, and took a bride.

On his wedding night, the mother called him in and gave him a package wrapped in an old piece of cloth. He opened it and found many coins, all smooth and shiny as the engravings had worn off. He was puzzled. His mother explained:

"When your father died, I was young. I worked hard to bring you up. Many nights I could not sleep. I used to get up and throw these coins on the floor. In complete darkness I crawled over the room until I had found every one of them. Now that you have grown up and are getting married, I want you to remember this."

These examples illustrate that in the traditional Chinese self, seen as a configuration of role relations with significant others, the direction was oriented primarily toward the significant others in a manner defined by predominent cultural values. A self of this nature is not highly assertive, but seeks to accommodate others and in return receives enduring social support.

What is the *strength* of this self?

An answer to this question is relevant if we want to assess the functions of self to an individual and understand the role of self in the behavioral patterns of a culture. In dealing with the social and physical environments, an individual runs into situations of frustration, defeat, humiliation, or even physical abuse. Some experience may damage an individual's sense of self-worthiness, or even the purpose of life. How a person copes with such situations and whether he (she) can survive a devastating experience will be a measure of the strength of self.

A primary source of strength is *significant others*. In time of severe distress, one usually seeks comfort in one's spouse, family members, or close friends; that is, if one can count on them. Another source is *cultural ideas*, including moral values and religious beliefs. Christians in the early days were able to sustain inhuman persecution and torture because of their belief in Jesus Christ. In Chinese history many scholars were undaunted by overwhelming external forces because they had the support of moral conviction. Examples are Wen Tien-hsiang of the Southern Sung dynasty and Szu Ko-fa of the Ming dynasty, to mention but two. *Materials* are another source of the strength of self, perhaps a rather fragile one. The arrogance of the wealthy is too well known to require elaboration.

In most cases, the self derives its strength from all three sources, although some individuals may rely more on one than on the others. It is my hypothesis that among the older generation Chinese the primary strength of the self was derived from relations with significant others as defined by the traditional cultural ideas. A self developed on this basis had both its strength and drawbacks. Because it was built upon relations that were highly enduring and unchanging according to cultural ideas, the traditional Chinese self had a high degree of security. It was not a segment of a lonely crowd. At a time of crisis it did not stand all by itself, but had something solid to fall back on. On the other hand, a self of this kind functioned within a relatively narrow range of relational constraints. The person is not free to do whatever he wants, so to speak. The nature of the social relations and their supportive ideas were so rigidly defined that the Chinese by and large demonstrated a high degree of resistance to innovation and change (Chu 1979).

In the past the self-other relations among Chinese were built on the traditional collectivity of kinship networks and supported by such cultural ideas as loyalty, filial piety, chastity, integrity, dignity, endurance, and courage. In contemporary China, the communist party has been making an effort to replace the traditional collectivity with a new collective unit built around the party structure, based on similar ideas and values. The most important values are loyalty to the party, instead of to the kinship group, and dedication to the party leadership, personified until recently in Chairman Mao, instead of filial piety to parents and ancestors.

The strength of the self among those Chinese who grew up prior to 1949 was put to a severe test during the chaotic years of the Cultural Revolution. Many of them were persecuted, tortured, and paraded on the streets by the Red Guards. Some of those who were party members were able to maintain their selves intact by relying on the strength of their party dedication, according to accounts in the Chinese press following the purge of the Gang of Four.

An example publicized in the Chinese media in 1981 was Shuai Meng-chi, a courageous woman who joined the Chinese Communist Party in the 1920s (Ping 1981). In 1932 she was captured in Shanghai by the Kuomintang. She was tortured in prison, but never yielded. When the Cultural Revolution started in 1966, she was deputy minister of organization of the party. Already over seventy years old then, she was jailed for seven years by the radical group headed by Chiang Ching, Mao's wife. While in jail, Shuai was subjected to various forms of physical punishment. Many times, when the torture was becoming unbearable, she told herself that she must stand firm and that she must not commit suicide. She kept up her spirit by reading the poems of Mao and other old comrades. She wanted to live through the experience and continue to contribute to China's socialist reconstruction.

The more numerous non-party members, particularly the intellectuals, seemed to be able to cling to their enduring family relations despite physical separation, thereby surviving the brutal onslaught by the Red Guards. The fact that the Chinese in the past had accustomed themselves to yielding to external demands seems to have made it less painful for them to tolerate what would otherwise have been intolerable. At the same time, their traditional family relations, which had made demands on them in the past, now functioned as an invisible psychological haven for the Chinese self at a time of crisis.

Relations of self with authority figures

While the self is a configuration of self-other relations in a variety of settings, the relations with authority figures are particularly significant. To use an analogy, if we see the self as a tree, then authority figures are like gusty winds. A tree can bend and seek survival like the willows planted in the barren land in north-western China. Or a number of trees can band up, like a hedgerow, and fight the wind. The relations with authority figures are important because they not only influence the nature of the self, but also shape the contours of society. Hsu (1981b) has characterized the Chinese culture as one dominated by *submission to authority* and the American culture as one distinguished by *self-reliance*. We might interpret this to mean that the Chinese self in the past reflected a high degree of submissiveness, while the American self asserts a considerable measure of independence.

We do not suggest that authorities in China today are not respected. They are. But a variety of evidence, some anecdotal and some documentary, suggests that many Chinese today, particularly those who grew up after the 1949 revolution, treat authorities in a way quite different from the past. One example was the prevalence of writing *tatzupao,* the big character posters, to criticize officials for their errors. The posters were extensively used in 1957, first in the Hundred Flowers movement by the rightists to criticize the party and later that summer by the party to mount a counterattack in what is now known as the antirightist movement (Chu 1977). It was during the Cultural Revolution, especially the summer of 1966, that the big character posters attracted worldwide attention. China was covered by posters put up by Red Guards to attack old customs and traditions as well as party regulars (Chu, Cheng, and Chu 1973). Afterwards, posting *tatzupao* became a recognized means of expressing dissent. A lengthy *tatzupao* posted in Canton in 1974 by three young intellectuals severely criticized the Maoist policies of the party and demanded more freedom and democracy. For days, the poster signed by Li I-che remained intact for thousands of local residents to peruse (Chu 1981). The Democracy Wall in Peking, until it was discontinued in early 1980, was covered with critical posters. The right to post *tatzupao* was written into the 1975 constitution of the People's Republic. This provision has been amended because critical posters are thought to be counterproductive to the current "four modernizations" campaign in China.

Another example of outspoken expression in relation to authorities is the "letters to the editor" column in the official *People's Daily* and other newspapers. These letters often contain harsh criticisms of party officials on a wide range of topics (Chu and Chu 1983). One letter, for example, severly criticized the unruly behavior of police. Another listed in detail the wasteful spending of local officials. Another letter challenged a party policy that prohibited the marriage of party members to certain categories of individuals who were considered undesirable. As a result of that letter, the party removed those restrictions. Such letters would have been unimaginable prior to 1949 when people were awed by the very mention of officials.

How prevalent is the individual assertiveness reflected in the posting of *tatzupao* and the letters to the editor? I tend to think this new assertiveness is quite prevalent. The letters, for example, appear to be a highly popular form of public expression. Each newspaper has a special department to handle the hundreds of letters it receives every day. In October 1978, for example, the *People's Daily* was receiving more than 3,000 letters a day (Chu and Chu 1983). Often after one letter is published, hundreds of readers write to provide support. Other than the letters and the controversial *tatzupao*, I shall mention one anecdote. An overseas Chinese resident in the United States returned to China in the summer of 1979 to see her family. Her niece in China, whom she had met for the first time, accompanied her as she traveled in the country. During a journey by train, her niece, a factory worker, started chatting with another passenger who was an upper-level cadre in a province. They began to talk about some of China's problems. The visitor, who had lived in the United States for more than twenty years, was startled by the blunt words her niece used in discussing the ills of China's bureaucracy. At one point, her niece told the cadre: "You and people like yourselves are largely responsible for the situation China has found itself in." The visitor could not imagine anybody in the past having the nerve to talk to a high-ranking official in that manner. Later she asked her niece to be more careful. Her niece said most young people talked like that, as long as the cadre was not an immediate supervisor.

The riots in the Tien An Men Square in Peking on April 5, 1976, in which close to 100,000 participated, can be seen as another illustration of the newly found assertiveness of the Chinese in relation to authorities. Most of the participants in the riots were young people. They burned trucks and attacked barracks. They defied the municipal authorities and posted many poems to attack the radical leadership, later known as the Gang of Four after they had been purged in October 1976 following the death of Chairman Mao.

The overall impression one gets from these illustrations is that the younger generation Chinese do not submit to persons of authority simply because of their high positions in the way that their elders did in the past. The new Chinese self, if one is emerging, appears to be asserting a degree of independence unknown before.

Relations of self with marriage partner

Another important aspect of self-other relations exists between marriage partners. Of the various relations the self has with significant others, few are more enduring than husband-wife relations. In China in the past, the wife deferred to the husband. Today, on the basis of my personal observations, there seems to be a much greater degree of equality between husband and wife, at least in urban areas.

I would like to use the criteria of *mate selection* to illustrate the concept of self, because the way a person chooses someone to be a lifelong companion reflects both the concept the person holds of himself (herself) and also his (her) general orientation toward others. In traditional China the selection of a marital partner was made by parents, who relied on go-betweens. The main criteria were known as *men tang hu tui* (門當戶對), that is, the doors of the two families should be of similar texture and the houses must face each other. In other words, comparability of family social status was of paramount importance. Whether the young couple were compatible and could get along with each other was of little consequence. In fact, until the early republican years when western influence began to move in, the Chinese bride and groom did not see each other's face until after the wedding ceremony. The criterion of romantic love did not seem to figure in most people's minds.

Today the situation is quite different. Social status comparability is not totally irrelevant, as we occasionally read newspaper accounts of how urban parents opposed the marriage of their daughters to a coal miner or a peasant youngster. Up until a policy modification in 1978, children of the five black social categories (offspring of former landlords, former rich peasants, counter-revolutionaries, rightists, and those designated as bad elements) generally had difficulty if they wanted to marry outside their circles. This policy has now been abolished. Today young men and young women not only see each other, but they also go to school and work together.

Highly revealing about the concept of new Chinese self among the younger generation is a set of ten criteria popularly circulated among urban young women who are looking for suitable mates.[1] These criteria are recited in a verse form and are rhymed in Chinese. Each begins with a number, as follows:

(a) One son of the family (一子當家). That is, there are no brothers or sisters-in-law to bother with. In the past, unmarried sisters-in-law often picked on the bride, who was considered an intruder.

(b) Two parents have gone to heaven (二老歸天). The relations between the bride and the groom's parents were usually ruffled. The bride was supposed to serve her husband's parents, especially the mother, in a totally submissive manner. Mistreatment of the daughter-in-law by the mother-in-law was common. A well-known case became a long epic, "The Phoenix Flies South-east," during the Han dynasty. A young couple were in love after they married, and that displeased the mother-in-law. Despite the pleading of her son, who was an official himself, the old lady ordered the bride to be dismissed. The couple obeyed. She eventually jumped into a river, and he hanged himself. Nowadays, the new Chinese bride wants a husband with no parents.

(c) Three things that turn and one thing that has a voice (三轉一响). These refer to dowry, including a watch, a bicycle, and a sewing machine, which all have some moving parts, and a radio. Only a man of some means can afford all of these. In big cities, a television set is preferred to a radio.

(d) Forty-eight meters (四十八米). Housing is in short supply in China. This criterion requires the groom to provide a living space of forty-eight square meters, or 432 square feet, which is considered to be first-rate accommodation.

(e) Five facial features are well balanced (五官端正). This criterion is self-explanatory.

(f) Six categories of kinship relations are totally ignored (六親不認). The Chinese generally use the term "six categories" to refer to a broad range of relatives by blood and by marriage. This particular criterion was an old saying in the past to refer to someone who had no regard whatever for the important Chinese value of honoring kinship obligations.

(g) Seventy-two yuan (七十二元), a good wage in China.

(h) Eight sides all smooth and slippery (八面玲瓏). This is another phrase taken from the traditional repertory of Chinese sayings. It means that the person is a wheeler-dealer.

(i) Wine (which is pronounced the same way as nine in Chinese) and cigarettes are taboo (酒烟不進). Self-explanatory.

(j) Ten-degree (fully) satisfied to have *me* run the house (十分滿意我當家). The bride should be the boss.

These ten criteria are noteworthy for what they exclude as much as for what they include. There is no mention of family comparability. In fact, family and relatives are totally rejected. There is no mention of love or romance, a continuity from the past. Presumably someone who does not drink or smoke should be in good health. But age is not mentioned as a criterion. Nor are knowledge and scholarly achievements. All the personal qualifications mentioned are materialistic: sufficient dowry, adequate housing, and good income. There is no mention of any moral standard. In fact, the picture one gets is that of a self-centered go-getter who has somehow managed to climb up the social-economic ladder. It is quite different from the ideal image of a selfless party member who is dedicated to serve the people.

Is this the model husband urban Chinese girls are looking for?

Are these the criteria eligible bachelors in China now use to measure themselves? If so, what does it tell us about the self-concept of China's younger generation? Is it possible that the young people are unsure of enduring relations with significant others and are out to take whatever material benefits they can? And if this is indeed the trend, how does one explain the change from the past?

A primary reason, I think, is the impact of the *Cultural Revolution*. While different people came away from the Cultural Revolution with diverse experiences, one point does not seem to be lost on the younger generation. That is, moral principles did not pay. Violence and destruction were encouraged and re-warded. Scholars and party officials who were dedicated to the people were persecuted and tortured. Opportunists like Wang Hung-wen gained power and position fast, if they knew how and where to place their chips. "They rose by helicopter," as the Chinese put it. The impact of this experience appears to be especially significant for those who were of an impressionable age when the Cultural Revolution began in 1966.

Another reason, perhaps a less important one by comparison, is the dwindling *influence of the family*. That is not to say that the Chinese family no longer exerts any influence. It still does, but the influence has diminished for several reasons. First, the traditional kinship network has been dispersed by population migration when people are assigned jobs far away from their hometowns. The social and cultural underpinnings that used to back up the family influence are no longer there. Second, the occupational structure has been changed so that almost every-body now works for the state and receives wages or work points. The family no longer has the financial resources that it used to have. Third, because in most cases both parents now work, they have less time to look after their children. In big cities many children grow up with latchkeys on their necks. There is nobody home when they come back from school, and they need the key to open the door. The process of cultural transmission from one generation to the next has been curtailed.

The seemingly strong preoccupation with material benefits needs to be viewed in a perspective of social change. Traditionally the Chinese were not aggressively concerned with material gains because of the nature of the social structure. Those who belonged to the upper social and economic strata already had a degree of plentitude. They could afford to be casual about material things. The majority of people on the other end of the scale were resigned to their place in society. They acknowledged their fate, so to speak. High material aspirations would be futile and were hardly entertained. As a result, China's limited material wealth did not translate itself into a perception of scarcity.

The situation today is quite different. The total amount of material resources has undoubtedly multiplied. But so have the rising aspirations in the new social structure, not to mention the increasing demands of a growing population. Instead of the old notion of everybody knowing his place, the new ideals propagated by the party encourage everybody to expect a life of sufficiency. Almost everyone feels he or she is entitled to certain material desires, and yet the reality of economic underdevelopment cannot satisfy them immediately.

It is possible that a combination of these factors – the dwindling influence of the traditional significant others, the new ideas of equal opportunity and rising aspirations, and the relatively limited availability of material resources – may have contributed to the formation of a transient self among the younger generation Chinese that is oriented more toward the self than toward significant others and based more on material relations than on commitment to moral values and ideas. This transient self may change as changes occur in these factors.

Impact of ideological communication on the self

For more than three decades the party has been waging a nationwide ideological communication campaign to create what is sometimes referred to as a "new Chinese man," or a new self-concept. This new self is to be characterized by selfless dedication to the cause of building a collective utopia under the leadership of the Chinese Communist Party. The ultimate goal, in the words of Chairman Mao, is to serve the people wholeheartedly. The self should be oriented toward a collective significant other, in a way defined by the ideology of Mao.

Many communication campaigns were launched to help promote this new self-concept. There were: the ideological reform of teachers of institutions of higher education in 1950, the thought reform movement in 1952, the study of Wu Hsun (an altruistic beggar) in the same year, intended to cleanse the bourgeois mentality of intellectuals, the anti-rightist movement in 1957 following the Hundred Flowers movement, the "turn over the heart to the party" movement in 1958, the "four clean-ups" movement in 1964, the Cultural Revolution that began in 1966, and the anti-Confucius movement from 1973 to 1976, to mention some of the highlights. In each campaign, the mass media − newspapers, magazines, radio, and more recently television − set the tone while the population met in their small local groups to discuss their interpretation of the campaign themes and to pledge their support. The intensity of the campaigns varied according to the political climate and the geographical locations. It reached high points during the anti-rightist movement of 1957 and the Cultural Revolution in its initial period. Urban areas, especially big cities like Peking, Shanghai, and Canton, felt the impact more strongly than rural areas. Intellectuals and party members were generally the focus of attention (Barnett 1980).

The overall effects, however, are difficult to assess because of the uneven campaign intensity over time and the diversity in the target groups. For those who grew up before the 1949 revolution, the effects appear to have been less than pronounced. The self that had already developed prior to the revolution seems to have undergone relatively little change. Family-based relations are still important to them in their self-other orientations. Instead of following the party's advice to speak out, they seem to respond with caution, perhaps a reflection of their experience in the ideological rectification campaigns they took part in. One explanation of the marginal effects of the communication campaigns was offered by a Chinese official who was in charge of personnel. Lamenting a trend of *simulation*, the official said:

"When a campaign comes, there are people who would prepare themselves in every conceivable way. They pretend to be progressive and sincere, as if they were really engaged in a relentless struggle against all wrongdoings. At a mass meeting for self-criticism, they would cry, moan, and confess all their mistakes. After the campaign is over, when the 'storm has calmed down,' they are back to their old selves. Their self-criticisms are tossed aside, and they will do whatever they want to do."

(An 1953)

On those who grew up after the revolution, the effects seem to be more apparent. In the past, school children took the new ideology most seriously. As they grew older, the effects of ideological communication seemed to become attenuated. By the time they were about to graduate from high school and faced the reality of finding a job and making a living, frustration set in. "They are afraid of revolution and are trying to escape criticism and struggle" (*Wen Hui Pao* 1968). The seriousness with which the young people took the ideological communication also appeared to be related to the social and political environments at the time. Surrounded by intense political actions, most Red Guards during the Cultural Revolution apparently took the new ideology very seriously. Their disappointment came when they were sent to work in the villages after they had played their role of organization disruption in the initial chaotic periods of that movement.

There was apparently something in the rhetoric of activism and selfless dedication that appealed to the young Chinese who grew up after the revolution. Even today, several years after the purge of the Gang of Four, whose radical policies have been repudiated, after the party has pledged not to wage any more ideological criticism campaigns, there are hints of a lingering predisposition toward the radical past among some of the young people. This predisposition seems to become activated when the material aspirations of the young cannot be expeditiously realized.

The party leadership seems to be aware of this adverse trend and has been initiating *educational campaigns* to restore a sense of morality among the young people.

In February 1981, the Chinese Communist Youth Corps started a movement for the millions of corps members and youth pioneers to emulate the well-known communist martyr Lei Feng (Hsin Hua 1981). The purpose was to set an example for all the young people and to establish a new code of morality, civility, and courtesy according to the ideals of communism. Such a new code is considered essential to both economic development and the political stability of the country.

Shortly afterwards, nine mass organizations in China, including the All-China Federation of Labor Unions, the All-China Federation of Women's Associations, and the Chinese Communist Youth Corps, expanded it into a nationwide movement for all the people in China, with a particular emphasis on the younger generation (*People's Daily* 1981). The movement promoted *five standards* and *four "beauties."* The five standards were: civility, courtesy, sanitation, orderly conduct, and morality. The four beauties were:

(a) "Beauty in heart and spirit" requires cultivation of an upright personality and ideology in support of the leadership of the party and socialism. This beauty is to be demonstrated in patriotism, integrity, and honesty. Any behavior that blemishes national honor and personal dignity or is self-centered and couched in falsehood must be avoided.

(b) "Beauty in language" requires the use of polite language that is harmonious, graceful, and modest, rather than rude and profane. One should not twist words and argue without reason.

(c) "Beauty in behavior" requires diligence, friendliness, discipline, and behavior that will not harm the collective interest but will promote the welfare of the people and society. One must not damage public property nor violate law and other.

(d) "Beauty in environment" requires sanitation and cleanliness in one's home, place of work, and any public gatherings.

It was recognized that this new movement must begin with children in the formative years, from the time they learn to talk. These organizations planned to carry this movement to the families, schools, factories, stores, and any other places where people gather. All the available media of communication, including art, literature, music, drama, dance, and television, were being pressed into service to carry out this movement of civility and courtesy. During a visit to China in May 1981, I saw posters propagating the virtues of the five standards and four beauties almost everywhere I went. The impressions I got from talking to a cross-section of individuals suggest that the campaign, even in these brief three months, had achieved some results. However, if the transient self among the younger generation Chinese is largely a consequence of the social and economic factors we have discussed earlier, then a correction would require changes in those factors rather than ideological and educational campaigns, although the latter can help.

Summary

We shall summarize our discussion into a number of hypotheses.

The self is conceptualized as a configuration of roles expressed in self-other expectations and observable in self-other interactions. The self develops out of interactions with significant others, mediated by materials and objects on one hand and ideas, beliefs, and values on the other.

We hypothesize that the Chinese self prior to the communist revolution of 1949 was distinguished by a continuity having two characteristics. First, the role relations were oriented primarily toward significant others rather than toward the self. Second, the basis of self-other relations was defined primarily by cultural ideas rather than materials.

The thread of cultural continuity among the Chinese has been disrupted in the last thirty years, especially during the Cultural Revolution. Because the self of the older generation Chinese was oriented toward family members as significant others and defined by traditional cultural ideas, they were able to rely on their enduring family relations and survived the onslaught of the Red Guards.

At the same time, in the context of the new social and cultural milieus, a new Chinese self is emerging among the younger generation. The new Chinese self no longer maintains a continuity with the past as closely as the traditional Chinese self did. It is more assertive, less accommodating, and less submissive to authority figures than in the past. The new Chinese self is not as strongly anchored on enduring family relations and traditional values as in the past but leans more toward relations built on what appears to be a utilitarian and material basis.

The new Chinese self is less secure than its traditional predecessor. It has lost some of the security that comes with strong family ties and submission to authority. Submission in the Chinese culture can be rewarding to a person because he will be taken care of by the authorities he submits to. On the other hand, the new Chinese self can now interact with the social and physical environments with a greater degree of freedom to pursue both individual and collective ends. If appropriate structural mechanisms can be worked out, for example, by allowing sufficient room for individual incentives in a general context of collective goal achievement and by replacing familial ties with rewarding occupational group identification, such as the factory or the production work team of a commune, the new Chinese self has the potential of freeing itself from the bondages of the past and contributing to the development of a modern China. If individual material pursuits cannot be realized at a minimal level, then a portion of the new Chinese self may fragment back to a radical collective identity similar to that once advocated by the Maoist ideology.

The emergence of the new Chinese self in its current budding form appears to be largely a result of changes in China's social and economic structures – the dispersion of kinship networks, diminished resources of the family, radical changes in the occupational structure, and rising aspirations in a context of limited resources – rather than the demonstrable effects of ideological communication. As far as the self-concept is concerned, the impact of the many ideological campaigns waged since 1949 has been either marginal or mixed. The one exception is the Cultural Revolution, which seems to have left an imprint on the younger generation in a way quite unintended by its original purpose. The wanton destruction and chaos wrought during the Cultural Revolution has greatly weakened the moral fabric of the new Chinese self, which the party is now taking steps to mend.

Postscript

After completing this paper I came across a survey report in the *People's Daily* (Huang 1981). The first of its kind as far as I can remember, the report revealed some interesting findings about the young people of China. The survey was conducted by three researchers among 987 young respondents interviewed in factories, communes, schools, and residential districts in two provinces, Fukien and Anhui. The researchers used a questionnaire technique, although the methods of sampling and the composition of the sample were not reported. The findings were summarized in five parts.

(a) The young Chinese people overwhelmingly reject the leftist radicalism and broadly support the party's new directions and policies. However, among some of them there exists in varying degrees inadequate understanding of the superiority of the socialist system and insufficient confidence in China's "four modernizations."

(b) The young Chinese people are concerned with the future of China. Their thinking is critical and lively. They demonstrate a greater ability for independent thinking and less inclination for conservatism and traditionalism than the past generation. They are in the forefront of ideological liberation. However, some of them lack a clear-cut direction in their ideology. They lack stability in applying standards of right and wrong. Some even demonstrate certain erroneous tendencies.

(c) The young Chinese people are pragmatic. They are concerned about the economic development of their country. They are concerned about their own realistic benefits. They are enthusiastic about learning science and technology, about acquiring some useful skills. The empty political rhetoric of the ultra-leftists has no following among them. Among some of the young people, however, there is a feeling of boredom about politics. They lack lofty ideals. The stimulation of political activities and the appeals of charismatic leadership are losing ground among these young people.

(d) The young Chinese people are expressing greater and greater demands for the material and cultural life. They show an increasingly strong desire for what is aesthetic and beautiful. They abhor the life of poverty, the material abstinence, and the cultural dictatorship advocated by Lin Piao and the Gang of Four. However, some forms of excessive desire divorced from the reality of China's economic development are gaining ground among some of the young Chinese. They lack a persevering, enterprising spirit. Capitalism and other forms of non-proletarian ideology are still seriously eroding some of the young people.

(e) Moral standards are gradually improving. Many young people have played an exemplary role in establishing a new moral code in society. But the ten years of turmoil (the Cultural Revolution from 1966 to 1976) have diluted legal concepts. The lack of moral cultivation remains to be further remedied. The abnormal psychology among some young people requires further healing.

Our hypotheses about the self's relation with authority figures, the lack of moral fortitude, and the materialistic tendencies among the young Chinese do not appear to be inconsistent with these findings. The campaign against "spiritual pollution" launched in late 1983 can be seen in part as a response of the party to such trends among the young Chinese, short lived as it was.

Note

1 I am indebted to Professor Daniel Kwok of the University of Hawaii for bringing these criteria to my attention.

References

An, T. W. (1953) To Struggle for Eradication of the Passive Attitude and Unhealthy Conditions in Party Organizations. *People's Daily*, February 12. (This was an official report prepared by the Ministry of Personnel for the Study Session of the Central Government Cadres.)

Barnett, A. D. (1980) The Communication System in China: Some Generalizations, Hypotheses, and Questions for Research. In G. C. Wilhoit and H. de Bock (eds) *Mass Communication Review Yearbook*, vol. 1. Beverly Hills, Calif.: Sage.

Chu, G. C. (1977) *Radical Change through Communication in Mao's China*. Honolulu: University Press of Hawaii.

_____ (1979) Communication and Cultural Change in China: A Conceptual Framework. In G. C. Chu and F. L. K. Hsu (eds) *Moving a Mountain – Cultural Change in China*. Honolulu University Press of Hawaii.

_____ (1981) The Current Structure and Functions of China's Mass Media. In G. C. Wilhoit and H. de Bock (eds) *Mass Communication Review Yearbook*, vol. 2. Beverly Hills, Calif.: Sage.

Chu, G. C., Cheng, P. H., and Chu, L. L. (1973) *The Roles of Tatzupao in the Cultural Revolution*. Carbondale, Il.: Southern Illinois University.

Chu, G. C. and Chu, L. L. (1983) Mass Media and Conflict Resolution: An Analysis of Letters to the Editor. In G. C. Chu and F. L. K. Hsu (eds) *China's New Social Fabric*. London: Kegan Paul International.

Hsin Hua News Agency (1981) Peking Is Calling on Young People to Learn from Fei Feng. *Wen Hui Pao Daily*, February 13. Hong Kong.

Hsu, F. L. K. (1981a) *The Concept of Self in Cross-Cultural Perspective*. Paper presented at Second Annual Symposium on Current Topics in Psychology: Culture and Self, University of Hawaii, Honolulu.

_____ (1981b) *Americans and Chinese: Reflections on Two Cultures and Their People*, (rev. edn). Honolulu: University Press of Hawaii.

Huang Chi-chien (1981) How Should We Understand Our Younger Generation? *People's Daily*, February 24. (The survey was conducted by Huang, Cheng Li-hua, and Fan Hsin-ming in 1980.)

Johnson, F. (1981) *A Historical Overview of Self in the West*. Paper presented at Second Annual Symposium on Current Topics in Psychology: Culture and Self, University of Hawaii, Honolulu.

Mead, G. H. (1934) *Mind, Self and Society*. Chicago: University of Chicago Press.

People's Daily (1981) Nationwide Campaign on Civility and Courtesy is Initiated. *People's Daily*, February 28.

Ping Tuan (1981) She Was Never Conquered – An Interview with Old Comrade Shuai Meng-chi. *People's Daily*, February 27.

Smith, M. B. (1981) *The Constitutive Metaphorical Basis of Self*. Paper presented at Second Annual Symposium on Current Topics in Psychology: Culture and Self, University of Hawaii, Honolulu.

Wen Hui Pao (1968) Editorial. *Wen Hui Pao*, September 27.

PART IV

The Self, Adaptation, and Adjustment

9

Culture, Self, and
Mental Disorder[1]

Anthony J. Marsella

Introduction

The purpose of the present paper is to discuss the interrelationships among culture, self, and mental disorder. To address such a broad problem within the confines of a brief paper may indeed be precarious. Yet it is becoming increasingly clear that the mental health professions cannot hope to resolve the problems confronting them without understanding the basic relationships among these three critical variables. It is my hope that this preliminary effort will serve to focus attention on the substantive, pragmatic, and theoretical implications which arise from linking culture, self, and mental disorder.

The paper is divided into four sections. The first section focuses on culture and mental disorders with a specific reference to the development of this topic as a subdisciplinary specialty in both psychiatry and the behavioral sciences. The section emphasizes the emergence of culture as a critical variable for understanding all aspects of mental disorder including its etiology, diagnosis, expression, course, and outcome. This section also calls attention to the self as an important theoretical linkage between culture and mental disorder. The second section discusses the concept of self with special reference to its definition and meaning. The distinction between self as object, self as process, and self as essence is made.

The third section discusses culture and self. The argument is made that culture and self are reciprocally related phenomena.

The self must differ across cultures! Cultural differences in self partially account for cultural variations in both normal and abnormal behavior. The section focuses on cultural differences in the self in terms of individuated versus unindividuated self structures and their relationships to different language systems characteristics (e.g. concrete metaphors versus abstractions) and modes for representing reality (e.g. imagery versus lexical modes). These factors condition "self as object" and, in turn, influence the epistemological orientation which ultimately is "self as process." It is argued these variations in self as object and self as process are inextricably linked to the definition, etiology expression, and treatment of mental disorder. The last section discusses the interrelationships among culture, self, and mental disorders, especially with regard to the influence of the self on different aspects of mental disorders across cultural boundaries.

The fundamental argument of the paper is that culture, self, and mental disorders are interdependent phenomena, and as such, it is logical to expect cultural variations in various aspects of mental disorder. Within the context of this argument, culture emerges as a critical variable in the field of mental health, a variable which must be given the same consideration as biological and psychological variables in our theories.

Culture and mental disorder

Our contemporary interest in cultural relationships to mental disorders can be traced to the words of Jean-Jacques Rousseau, the famous philosopher who, in 1749, woke from a mystical experience on a country path in France and stated, "Man is by nature good, and only our institutions have made him bad" (Durant and Durant 1967: 9). In less than a century, these words became the rallying cry for all social reformers. Culture – society – our way of life, became the target for reformers seeking to ameliorate the growing problem of mental disorder. In 1851, Jarvis, a psychiatrist in New England, observed: "Insanity is then a part of the price we pay for civilization. The causes of the

one increase with the developments and results of the other."
(Jarvis 1851, in Rosen 1969:21).

In commenting on this early situation, George Rosen, the
medical historian, wrote:

"Is insanity on the increase? The problem derived from a
number of sources. For one, there was the nature cult of the
eighteenth century which viewed the present as a degenerate
retrogression from a golden age of natural virtue. Any further
development of civilization was found to increase manifestations of degeneracy. Then, this was also the period of the
early Industrial Revolution with its attendant evidences of
social maladjustment. The alleged increase of insanity was
viewed as another aspect of this situation, and physicians,
philosophers, and others speculated on the question whether
man would be able to adapt successfully to the increasing
complexities of society."

(Rosen 1969:182)

By the late nineteenth century, western researchers journey-
ing to distant lands began to report on mental disorders among
non-western populations. For some, there was interest in the
infrequent occurrence of insanity found in non-western cultures
(e.g. Andrews 1887), while for others, there was a growing
fascination with the so-called "exotic psychoses" like *latah*,
pibloktoq, *malimali*, and so forth (e.g. Van Brero 1885; Musgrave
and Sison 1910). The cross-cultural study of mental disorders
finally emerged as a specific strategy for identifying cultural
influences on mental health when no less a figure than Emil
Kraepelin, the father of modern western psychiatry, was forced
to admit that Indonesian and Chinese patients he had encountered during the course of his world cruise in 1904 had showed
little resemblance to his western patients. Kraepelin (1904)
suggested the name *vergleichende psychiatrie*, or comparative
psychiatry, as the name for those interested in studying mental
disorders across cultural boundaries.

Today there are numerous subdisciplinary specialty areas
such as transcultural psychiatry, psychiatric anthropology, medical sociology, and cross-cultural psychology which are actively

involved in studying relationships between culture and mental disorder via cross-cultural research approaches.

Reviews of the cross-cultural literature on mental disorders (e.g. King 1978; Strauss 1979; Sartorius 1979; Marsella 1979, 1982; Draguns 1981) have unanimously concluded that cultural factors are inextricably linked to the etiology, distribution, manifestation, and course and outcome of mental disorders. Marsella stated:

> "Clearly, there is no reason to believe that cultural variables should have any less influence on deviant behavior patterns than they do on 'normal' behavior patterns. Even if certain biochemical processes may be universally operative in the etiology of mental disorders, it is obvious that the [individual's] appraisal and behavioral response to these processes must be filtered through culturally conditioned experience. Further, the social response to the behavioral pattern must also reflect cultural influences. Certain cultural traditions may, by the response they condition to various behavior patterns, maintain, enhance, and encourage a symptom's development."
>
> (Marsella 1982)

But, though the literature implicating cultural variables in all aspects of mental disorders is extensive, it has not been universally accepted. For many mental health professionals, especially those within the fields of psychiatry, biological and psychological models of mental disorder are still dominant. Aside from the rather obvious reason that these professionals have simply ignored the research literature and thus have failed to benefit from its findings, it is also likely that the absence of a theoretical framework linking culture and mental disorder has prompted the lack of support.

When a clinician is dealing with a patient the biological and psychological variables often appear more suspect than the more indirect cultural variables in which they are embedded, fostered, and nurtured. It is easier to speak of anxiety as mediated by biochemical processes or psychological stressors than to talk of the cultural foundations of the problem. One possible basis for a theoretical model of culture and mental disorder is the introduction of the concept of the self as a fundamental linkage.

Self

There is no other concept in the English language which presents so many definitional problems as "self." It is one of those words which has countless meanings, depending upon how a particular writer or speaker may choose to define it. As a result, "self" has a broad connotative meaning and a limited denotative meaning. The concept of self has been the object of extensive study in western psychology for more than a century. Indeed, it has occupied the attention of some of psychology's foremost figures, including William James (1890) (i.e. the hierarchical self, including pure ego). Others include Cooley (1902), Mead (1934), Goffman (1959), Blumer (1969) in sociology; and Symonds (1951), Snygg and Combs (1949), Koffka (1935), Sarbin (1952), Rogers (1951), Wylie (1961), and one of the authors in the present volume, Smith (1978), in psychology. This list represents but a small portion of the large number of individuals who have been interested in the concept of self within the disciplinary traditions of modern-day behavioral science. Yet, though the list is long, a lack of clarity continues to abound. This is true because of the complexity of the topic. For example, in an attempt to clarify the meaning of "self," Smith (1978) wrote:

> "I am not talking at this point about the Self as a successor to the Soul, or even about the self-concept. Nothing that *thing-like*, substantive, or concrete can ground our consideration appropriately. I am talking, rather, about universal features of being a person, distinctive features that we find fascinating and, when we take them seriously, as mysterious frontiers of cosmology. So: selfhood involves being *self-aware* or *reflective*; being or *having* a body (a large debate here); somehow taking into account the *boundaries of selfhood* at birth and death and feeling a *continuity of selfhood* at birth and death and feeling a *continuity of identity* in between; placing oneself in a *generational sequence and network of other connected selves* as

forebears and descendants and relatives; being in partial *communication and communion with other contemporary selves* while experiencing an irreducible *separateness of experience and identity*: engaging in joint and individual *enterprises* in the world with some degree of *forethought and afterthought* (not just 'behaving'): *guiding* what one does and *appraising* what one has done at least partly through *reflection* on one's performance; feeling *responsible*, at least sometimes, for one's actions and holding others responsible for theirs. I could go on."

(Smith 1978: 1053–054)

Smith's comments are not a definition but an attempt to give meaning to the concept of self. In this respect, he is successful for he calls our attention to the many dimensions of the self. The self is all of the following and more: (a) a super-ordinate organizing tendency which offers structure and continuity to experience, especially as it assumes forms like self-concept or self-ideal; (b) a process by which we come to know about ourselves and the world about us; (c) a set of recurrent behavior patterns which mold and are molded by the socio-environment; (d) a sense of socio-personal identity which is differentiated from the more pervasive object world.

In addition to self as object and self as process, some writers have posited a self which is the essence of all matter and energy in the universe. It is the ultimate reality. This point of view of the self has particularly been a concern of some Asian philosophy and psychology. For example, Yoshifumi wrote:

"when one realizes the real self, one at the same time touches reality itself; to know the real self means, at the same time, to know reality. A thing known as it really exists is nothing other than reality known as it is. To know reality can be nothing other than to know our selves and all the things in the world as they really exist and become."

(Yoshifumi 1968: 80)

Yet another example of this perspective are the words of Nishida Kintaro, who stated: "Our true self is the basic substance of the universe, and when we know the true self, we not only are united with the good of mankind, but merge with the basic substance of the universe and spiritually unite with the divine mind" (Kintaro 1924:180, cited in Yoshifumi 1968:82). Within these examples, what emerges is (a) self as object, (b) self as process, and (c) self as essence. The multiple nature and meanings of the terms have resulted in some confusion which has limited the applications of the concept, especially in the field of mental health.

Culture and self

Cultural variations in the nature of the self have not been extensively studied by behavioral scientists unless, of course, one chooses to allude to the writings of the "culture and personality" perspective in anthropology which dominated much of the 1940s to the 1960s. These researchers, including Benedict, Mead, Linton, DuBois, Kardiner, Gorer, and others, did much to point out cultural differences in personality, and indirectly, in the nature of the self. In more contemporary times, researchers such as Hsu (1963), DeVos (1976), Bharati (1976), Carstairs (1958), and Geertz (1973) have been in the forefront of efforts to understand the relationships between culture and self through empirical study rather than historical or philosophical enquiry and scholarship.

One of the clear findings to emerge from all of these efforts is that the self differs across cultural boundaries. Cultural experience conditions the self as much as it conditions our values, ways of thinking, and social relations. That this is the case should not be surprising. What is surprising is that so little has been written about culture and self; this may be due to definitional and semantic problems. It is difficult to establish linkages between culture and even a simple behavior; when we attempt to show relationships between culture and something as abstract as the self, the problem reaches Brobdingnagian proportions.

My purpose in the present section is to elaborate some of my previous thoughts about the nature of culture and self relationships (e.g. Marsella and Quijano 1974; Tanaka-Matsumi and Marsella 1976; Marsella, 1978, 1979). In the following section, I will attempt to extend these elaborations to the topic of mental disorder across cultures.

Culture is one of the major determinants of human behavior. In conjunction with the physical environment, it represents one of the two major "external" sources which mold human behavior. These two influences also interact with two "internal" sources, biological and psychological influences, to comprise the primary determinants of human behavior. Culture has both external and internal representations. Externally, it is represented by various institutions (e.g. familial, educational, political, religious, economic) and artifacts. Internally, it is represented by various values, belief systems, world views, and epistemologies. All of these forces are in simultaneous interaction and at any point in time, the person is the repository of all these influences, and a reflection of their properties as they have been internalized via biological and psychological codification.

But behavior is not simply a function of the person. The person exists, at any given moment of time, in a situation. No person exists apart from an externally represented configuration of forces. It is the simultaneous interaction of the person and the situation which ultimately yields behavior. Behavior is a continual adjustment to the person-situation interaction as a whole. Within this framework, culture, physical environment, biology, and psychology are all reciprocally related to one another. They are co-existent forces which are represented and coded in one another's modes and ultimately, in some organized way, in the total person, the total situation (for the situation is also a function of these variables), and in behavior. Behavior, whether it is "normal" or "abnormal," is a continual response to person-situation forces and a modifier of them.

In this way, behavior is the ultimate reflection of life. It is change, it is growth, it is differentiation. Behavior is the organism in union with its context in pursuit of its purpose. This purpose may ultimately prove to be the full development of all potential organismic-situational possibilities or variations, of which we actually develop only a limited few, constrained as we

Figure 9.1 Interactional model of behaviour

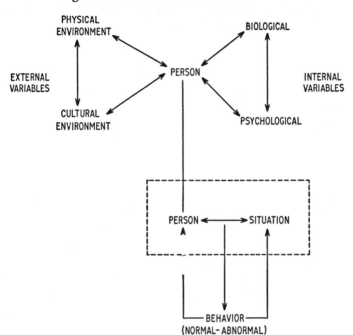

Source: Marsella 1979.

are by the accidents of birth or place. Behavior is ultimately a transformation in energy/matter which is part of the continually changing universe. It is an energy/matter transaction within the context of distinct organizational forms (i.e. organism, environment) which we, through socio-linguistic convention, call a person and a situation. These thoughts are presented in *Figure 9.1*

Thus, culture in union with the other determinants discussed comes to play a major role in shaping the person and the situation. One can speculate that "self as object" and "self as process" are, respectively, differentiated portions of the organismic-environmental unit which are labeled as I, me, or mine, and the epistemological processes (including our models of time, space, causality) by which we label and extract meaning and knowledge from the world. It is not culture alone which influences self as an object or process, but rather, culture in union with the previously discussed forces of the physical environment, biology, and psychology.

Culture and "self as object"

Numerous authors have written about cultural variations in self-structure (i.e. the definition of the self in terms of its incorporated elements and their organization), including Nakamura (1964), Caudill (1964), DeVos (1976), Tatara (1974), Doi (1973), and Tanaka-Matsumi and Marsella (1976) for Japanese; Geertz (1973) and Connors (1982) for Balinese; Constantino (1966), Bulatao (1969), Sechrest (1969), and Marsella and Quijano (1974) for Filipinos; and the splendid compendium of selfhood in the east and west edited by Charles Moore (1968).

A major conclusion of all these writers is that the self of these groups is extended to include a wide variety of significant others. This has been termed a "collateral" self, a "diffuse" self, or an "unindividuated" self. It is of note that while the "unindividuated" self is considered a norm for self-structure in some cultures, western cultures frequently see this as being pathological. The interdependencies in human relations with their consequent deemphasis on individual autonomy and independence are considered to be "immature" because they represent excessive familial ties and prevent "personal" growth, independence, autonomy, and differentiation.

In contrast to "unindividuated" self structures, western cultures, especially American male "WASP" patterns, prize "individuated" self-structures. Independence is valued in the west, and the associated character prototype is separate, detached, and self-sufficient. These two contrasting patterns — individuated versus unindividuated — represent polarities in prototypical self structures. It would be convenient if cultures fell into two neat piles at each of the two poles. Such is not the case!

Although cultural experience, in concert with other forces, conditions particular self-structures to predominate over others, personal observations suggest that there is greater movement across a range of self-structures within a given person and culture than might be expected. For example, our experience of self-structure can vary as a function of altered levels of consciousness in which we switch modes of experiencing reality. During a peak experience or a moment of meditation, we may lose all sense of self. We go beyond being a distinct personal being and social being to a new type of structure in which we are a part of all things. Within all cultural traditions a normative self-structure reflecting the values and goals of the culture, as well as their socio-environmental patterns, may be identified. But there is also room for alterations in this structure.

The forces which mold self-structure or "self as object" in a given culture can be found in the interplay of both the external and internal forces as described in *Figure 9.1*. For example, extended family structures with their mutual pursuit of life activities, mother-child relations which maintain self attachments through continued obligation, and even peer group pressures which enforce certain expected roles and behavior patterns, all contribute to the emergence of a self-structure which is essentially diffused beyond the individual's sense of self.

But self-structure must also be considered within the context of a culture's language and its preferred mode for representing reality (i.e. imagistic versus lexical coding). These two variables are reciprocally related to self-structure in that they both condition and are conditioned by it. Thus what we have is an interplay at the psychological level of analysis of three important factors: (a) self-structure, (b) language, (c) preferred representational mode.

Culture and "self as process"

Let us assume that self-structure varies along a dimension of "individuated" to "unindividuated" and that our representational mode may include imagistic and/or "lexical" preferences. If we add the possibilites of our language being oriented toward concrete metaphorical versus abstract metaphorical alternatives, we now have the opportunity to view the emergence of a culture's epistemological system. Epistemology, or our theory of knowledge or knowing, is essentially "self as process." Given this analysis, "self as object" and "self as process" become inextricably linked to one another. What a person is, is a function of how a person knows; how a person knows is a function of what a person is. Object and process are related. *Figure 9.2* displays some of these relationships. Let me elaborate further.

Self-structure is linked to language and to our preferred mode of experiencing reality. The nature of these relationships is closely allied to the specific pattern of language we use. It is my opinion that many non-western languages can be considered "metaphorically" concrete rather than abstract.

A metaphor functions to extend our comprehension. Marks stated, "Mind follows a metaphorical imperative seeking out relationships that entwine disparate phenomena and events" (Marks 1980: 252). Wallace Stevens, the famous poet, observed, "The proliferation of resemblences extends an object" (Stevens 1951: 78), cited in Lakoff and Johnson 1980: 5).

The use of poetic metaphors as part of everyday language (e.g. "He is an oak tree," rather than "He is strong") condition a different sense of reality because they make frequent reference to concrete and tangible objects which can be readily experienced sensorily. In a previous paper, I stated:

> "In this respect, a metaphorical language provides a rich immediate sensory experience of the world which is not diluted by being filtered through words which distantiate the cognitive understanding from the experience. In a metaphorical language system, the understanding and the language are one."
>
> (Marsella 1978: 10–11)

The use of concrete metaphors thus links sensory experience and thought closely together. One effect of this may be an increased reliance upon imagistic modes of representing reality rather than lexical (i.e. word-based) modes. Imagery, as a mode of representing or experiencing reality, has different implications from lexically mediated representations and experiences.

Figure 9.2 Continuum of objective versus epistemological orientations

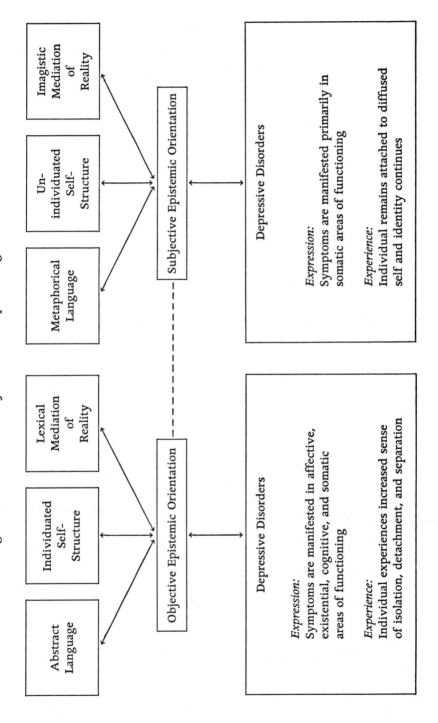

For example, lexical mediation is constrained by both grammatical and semantic aspects of the language. This forces a certain
"logic" on the experience. However, with the use of imagery,
these constraints are limited. Even "normal" conceptions of
time, space, and causality can be superseded because with
imagery, what an individual imagines constitutes a momentary
reality. Lexical mediation produces a different experience – an
experience "one step" removed from a more basic sensory
understanding of an event. In a previous publication, I wrote:
"One outcome of the imagistic mediation of reality is that reality
boundaries become quite subjective and are transcended much
more readily. . . . An experience is permitted to have a private or
personal meaning and does not have to be 'objectified' in words"
(Marsella 1978: 11).

The subjective and private nature of experiencing reality that
predominates among people characterized by imagery, concrete
metaphorical languages, and diffuse self-structure is also related
to a more personalized view of causality. All things have
personal meanings. The fall of a leaf is not a chance event but
rather one laced with personal meaning. In this world in which
phenomenological experience dominates understanding, it
becomes virtually impossible to consensually validate or "objec-
tify" reality. All things become related and intertwined and
assume personal meanings. Science, with its emphasis on detached enquiry (an obvious impossibility) is inappropriate as a
means for understanding. And the type of linear thinking that
accompanies lexical and abstract mediation and a more individuated self-structure is not feasible.

In brief, it is my opinion that there is a reciprocal relationship
among self-structure, language, and representational modes.
Unindividuated self-structures are more closely related to language systems characterized by use of concrete metaphorical
terms and imagery; individuated self-structures are more closely
related to language systems characterized by abstract terms (e.g.
power, synergy, freedom) and lexical representations of reality.
Each of these patterns of relationship are associated with
different epistemological orientations (i.e. subjective versus

"objective") which can be conceived as alternative "self as process" styles.

Ultimately, all behaviors, whether normal or abnormal, are related to the particular pattern of "self as object" and "self as process" which characterizes an individual or cultural group. In the next section, my purpose will be to demonstrate how concepts of mental health, and manifestations of mental disorder relate to self as object and self as process for a particular cultural group.

Culture, self, and mental disorder

Continuity in phenomena

All too often, theorists appear to be content to discuss a given topic horizontally without any reference to the topic's links to proximate levels of analysis. For example, we find theorists quite willing to invoke biochemical explanations of complex human behaviors. However, they are often either unwilling or unable to discuss structures and processes which are related to biochemical functioning at psychological or cultural or even genetic levels. Thus, much of our theory really represents fragmented suppositions which ultimately give mistaken impressions that behavior is a result of molecular processes acting in isolation from other phenomena. There is tremendous discontinuity.

I have noted that this discontinuity creates mistaken impressions that behavior, whether it be normal or abnormal, arises from distinct structures or processes which have little relationship to the totality of the organism and its situational contexts. In the author's opinion, this approach has greatly limited our knowledge and its applications. It should be clear from *Figure 9.1* that any behavior is simultaneously a function of biological, psychological, cultural, and environmental variables acting together. We cannot assume that either the causal patterns or expressive forms of behavior are limited to one level of phenomena. Rather, there is a continuity among all levels. Within this context, culture, self, and mental disorders are interdependent phenomena.

Non-western theoretical orientations have long acknowledged the interdependencies among different levels of phenomena. For example, Needham wrote the following regarding Chinese cosmology:

> "Things behaved in particular ways not necessarily because of prior actions or impulsations of other things, but because their position in the ever-moving cyclical universe was such that they were endowed intrinsic natures which made that behavior inevitable for them. If they did not behave in those particular ways, they would lose their relational position in the whole (which made them what they were), and turn into something other than themselves. They were thus parts in existential dependence upon the whole world organism. And, they reacted upon one another."
>
> (Needham 1962:281)

Similarly, Lock, in discussing the nature of disease within the context of Asian cosmology, stated:

> "Sickness ... [is] due to a pattern of causes leading to disharmony. ... The function of diagnosis is not to categorize a patient as having a specific disease, but to record the total body state and its relationship to the macrocosm of both society and nature as fully as possible. ... Therapy is designed to act on the whole body – removal of the main symptoms is not considered adequate as all parts of the body are thought to be interdependent – in this sense the model is holistic. ... It is believed that the functioning of man's mind and body is inseparable."
>
> (Lock 1976:15–17)

Kitaeff observed a similar position within the healing traditions of India, Nepal, and Tibet. He noted:

> "The total cultural continuity of individual, community, and god, and of sickness, health, and ultimate liberation involves

the whole spectrum of the healing process, – the purification of body, speech and mind. Precise correspondence exists among all these elements, so that the elementary substances in the body are considered a microcosm of divine forces in the universe and the yogic or tantric ceremonies of healing may simultaneously act upon the physical and subtle bodies to achieve spiritual wholeness as well as physical and mental well-being."

(Kitaeff 1976: 2)

All of these examples point out the non-western orientation toward interdependency among seemingly disparate phenomena. All elements are part of a whole and the principle force is harmony among the parts. Contrast this perspective with the more reductionistic and analytical perspectives of the western world in which parts exist in isolation from wholes, in which events at one level of existence have no implication for events at other levels, and in which biology, psychology, and sociology are simply considered separate topics of enquiry. Clearly, within the latter context, it becomes virtually impossible for cultural researchers to convince biological researchers that there is an interdependency between the two levels.

The concept of self offers a mediating link for relating cultural variables to mental disorder, for it is the experiential representation of culture. In the following sections, I want to examine possible interfaces between culture, self, and mental disorder as they relate to the definition and expression of mental disorders.

Culture, self, and definitions of disorder

Let me first address the issue of the definition of mental health within the context of culture and self relationships. Mental health, from a traditional psychiatric perspective, often involves the absence of psychiatric symptoms, much as mental disorder involves the presence of symptoms. These symptoms are frequently perceived to exist in recognizable clusters which are used to diagnose a disorder (e.g. anxiety neurosis, paranoid schizophrenia). This framework reflects a "medical" or "disease" perspective which views the body and the mind to exist in separate substrates. Thus when paranoid schizophrenia is diagnosed, it might be speculated that there is an excess of dopaminergic activity at midbrain levels which produces characteristic delusional behaviors. What is missing, however, is the concept of harmony among biological, psychological, and spiritual levels, the sense of wellness that arises when all parts of the person are working together as a unit rather than in opposition or conflict, a view held both explicitly and implicitly in many non-western cultures.

Human beings function at many levels simultaneously. Can a delusion or hallucination simply be a function of biochemical excess in ten thousand neural synapses in a confined area of the brain? Have we mistaken necessary with sufficient conditions? Even a biochemical process must be interpreted by a psychosocial being; this interpretation must be translated into a behavioral display which is then responded to socially; and the social response to the behavior must then yield a subsequent interpretative response. The individual experiencing a "delusion" does not experience it in isolation from other aspects of his/her functioning. It is the total person, from neural synapse to enlightened self-awareness, that experiences a delusion, and it is the cultural milieu which responds to exacerbate, maintain, or enhance the problem.

In brief, my argument is that the very concept of mental health cannot be separated from either culture or self. Self as object defines a particular set of referents for reality, a particular set of descriptors which define the nature of human nature. For some cultures, these referents emphasize the interdependency of different levels of human functioning and the process by which they are harmonized and transcended into a large whole, a higher order of self. Indeed, in some forms of religious practice, the emphasis goes beyond experiencing the unity of self to experiencing "no self"; this involves achieving a total blending of self with the universe, and with this is experienced "nothingness." For example, Hora wrote:

"Enlightened man transcends his self in 'seeing the truth of what is.' In this process of losing himself he finds that which is real. ... In the experience of understanding, the true nature of reality is revealed. In it there is neither 'self' nor 'other'; there is only the all transcending timeless process manifesting itself in that 'field of phenomena' which man is the medium of."

(Hora 1979:73)

In the west, the definition of mental health may often be more limited because of psychiatric concepts which view mental health in disease metaphors or analogies. In non-western cultures, mental health assumes a different meaning, a meaning which considers the many levels of human functioning as a harmonious blend. Our concepts stem from different notions of self as object and self as process. These factors even influence the range of experience labeled as madness.

Culture, self, and the expression of disorder

From the viewpoint of western psychiatry, mental disorders assume universal forms because they reflect the universal structures of the human body, especially the nervous system. Ethnocultural variations in mental disorders are often denied or given limited attention under the rubric of "culture specific disorders." Yet it is clear that all mental disorders are culture specific because we can never separate culture from mental disorder – because we can never separate culture from self or self from mental disorder. The self provides the bridge between culture and mental disorder, a bridge for understanding why disorders assume certain forms of expression and content.

For example, research on ethnocultural variations in the expression of depression among Japanese-American, Chinese-American, and Caucasian-American people revealed differences in the expression of depression (Marsella Kinzie, and Gordon 1973). In particular, the Chinese evidence a strong somatic dimension, the Japanese a strong interpersonal dimension, and the Caucasians a strong existential dimension. These findings received subsequent support from the work of Kleinman (1977, 1980). In interpreting the findings, we noted:

"What emerges is the possibility of interpreting complaints
... as reflections of self perceived as somatic functioning, as
interaction, as cognitive process, and as an ... existential
process. ... One value of considering complaints within this
framework is that the concept of self provides a rather
interesting and heuristic metapsychological bridge for
examining the influence of culture and individual differences
upon behavior. ... Different cultures may condition their
members to develop particular dimensions of self over
others."

(Marsella, Kinzie, and Gordon 1973: 448–49)

The case of "depression"

The topic of depression is perhaps the best example I can use to
demonstrate my point. There have been considerable studies of
depression among cultures. In virtually every instance, and
regardless of the research strategy employed (i.e. clinical interview, matched diagnosis, factor analysis), the results have
indicated that non-western samples differ in the expression of
depressive affect and disorder (see Marsella 1981). Many non-
western people manifest depression primarily in somatic areas of
functioning and do not present or represent the problems at
psychological levels. Thus there is no articulation of depressed
mood, feelings of inadequacy, guilt, or parallel experiences of
isolation and detachment. In my literature review, I stated:

"If a culture tends to label experience in psychological terms,
then the picture of depression known in the West may
emerge. ... Without psychological representation, it is conceivable that somatic problems may pass more quickly and be
more amenable to direct treatment. ... It is when the
psychological representation occurs that the somatic experience
of depression assumes completely different consequences and
implications. ... 'Depression' apparently assumes completely
different meanings and consequences as a function of the
culture in which it occurs."

(Marsella 1981: 261)

A theoretical reason which may account for these variations resides in the "self as object" and "self as process" distinctions which exist across cultures. Cultures which condition an unindividuated "self as object" and a subjective "self as process" epistemology are more likely to foster somatic representations simply because self is not construed in existential and affective terms. Further, the individual continues to feel they are a member of some larger group rather than becoming isolated, detached, and separated.

A research study I conducted on the phenomenology of depression among Japanese people may help explain this conclusion. Tanaka-Matsumi and I asked Japanese and Caucasians to associate to the word depression (Tanaka-Matsumi and Marsella 1976). In Japanese, the word which we used was *YUUTSU*; this word was derived after considerable studies of connotative and denotative meanings. The results indicated that the Caucasians associated words like "sadness," "despair," "dejection," and so forth. All of these were words reflecting internalized mood referents. But the Japanese responded with words like "storm," "clouds," "mountain" – words which make reference to external objects.

The reason for this is that these words permit the Japanese person to communicate his/her feelings in terms of impersonal emotional referents which do not draw attention to the individual as a unique and distinct being. Thus the person can remain embedded in the larger group or unindividuated reality. We stated:

> "Asserting one's individual emotional state does not comply with the predominant emphasis on the social affinity and collaterality of the Japanese group ... Japanese tend to project their mood to external referents and to avoid individualization of their mood."
>
> (Tanaka-Matsumi and Marsella 1976: 390)

Within this framework, the mood aspects of depression for many non-western groups may be experienced as somatic dysfunctioning and as impersonalized projections utilizing external referents. This eliminates the guilt, self-blame, and existential despair which characterizes western depressive experiences, and so insulates the non-western person from the risks of isolating him/herself from their sense of self. Thus, the non-western individual maintains his social role and is protected from the sense of loneliness and isolation of self that accompanies the depressive experience among westerners. The latter group, by continually referring to their inner states in personalized terms, further distance themselves from a social nexus. This accentuates and exacerbates the problem.

In brief, I am speculating that the experience of depressive affect and disorder is different for non-western people. In particular, I feel that depression has far less crushing implications for the sense of self because the language/thinking process permits the experience to be coded and communicated in either somatic terms or in impersonal external referent terms. This process is functionally related to the socio-cultural context of non-western societies, in which individuality is subordinated to a collective identity through a socialization process which maintains conformity through hierarchically oriented social systems, familial economic systems, and social relationship patterns which stress process rather than product outcomes. These thoughts are represented in *Figure 9.2*.

Disorder and reality

It is obvious that if cultures vary with regard to their conception of reality, disorders which are based on reality contact also may vary. For example, psychotic disorders are by definition a function of loss of contact with reality. In western psychiatry, there are three general classes of psychotic disorders: schizophrenia, manic-depressive psychoses, and paranoid states. The central feature of these disorders is a loss of contact with reality, characterized by delusions, hallucinations, disorientation for time, place, and person, and general confusion.

But among many non-western cultural groups, reality boundaries are not as rigidly fixed as they are in the west. Mystical states, depersonalization, visions, and deviant belief systems are tolerated far more, especially if no one is physically harmed by the individual's behavior. For example, among rural Filipinos with whom I worked, seeing visions, speaking with saints or dead relatives, beliefs in supernatural forces including witches, were all accepted as normal.

Every culture has some standard of acceptable behavior; and, if you exceed this standard, you are likely to be considered a deviant. But it is clear that these standards vary considerably, based upon the culture's concept of reality. In cultures which value more subjective standards of reality (such as those characterized by unindividuated self-structure, imagery preferences, concretized metaphors, and personalized meanings), disorders which we in the west label as psychotic assume a different meaning and have different implications.

In closing, I wish to assert that it is not simply the manifestation of mental disorders that varies across cultures, a fact which the research literature amply supports, but that the entire phenomenon is different. We cannot separate our experience of an event from our sensory and linguistic mediation of it. If these differ, so must the experience differ across cultures. If we define who we are in different ways (i.e. self as object), if we process reality in different ways (i.e. self as process), if we define the very nature of what is real, what is acceptable, and even what is right or wrong, how can we then expect similarities in something as complex as madness?

Culture and self are inextricably linked to both normal and abnormal behavior. The imposition of western psychiatric assumptions on non-western people is not only unwarranted, but potentially dangerous in its implications. Psychiatry, psychology, and cultural anthropology must begin first and foremost with an understanding of the nature of human experience. This requires a knowledge of the self. The self is tied to culture and culture varies across the world. We need to introduce these valuable dimensions into western psychiatric thought and practice.

Note

1 The preparation of this chapter was partially supported by NIMH Grant No. 5 R12 MH31016-05, entitled, "The Determinants of

Outcome for Severe Mental Disorders," awarded to the author for participation in the WHO Collaborative Project on Severe Mental Disorders (Norman Sartorius, M. D., Ph. D., director).

References

Andrews, J. (1887) The Distribution and Care of the Insane in the United States. *Transactions of the International Medical Congress* 5:226–37. (Cited in Rosen 1969.)

Benedict, R. (1934) Anthropology and the Abnormal. *Journal of General Psychology* 10:59–80

Bharati, A. (1976) *The Light at the Center: Context and Pretext of Modern Mysticism.* Santa Barbara, Calif.: Ross Erickson Publishers.

Blumer, H. (1969) *Symbolic Interactionism.* Englewood Cliffs, NJ.: Prentice-Hall.

Bulatao, J. (1969) Westernization and the Split-level Personality in the Filipino. In W. Caudill and T. Lin (eds) *Mental Health Research in Asia and the Pacific.* Honolulu: University of Hawaii Press.

Carstairs, M. (1958) *The Twice Born.* Bloomington, Ind.: University of Indiana Press.

Caudill, W. (1962) Emotion in Modern Japan. In R. Smith and R. Beardsley (eds) *Japanese Culture.* NY: Wenner – Gren Foundation.

Connors, L. (1982) The Unbounded Self and Balinese Therapy. In A. Marsella and G. White (eds) *Cultural Conceptions of Mental Health and Therapy.* Boston: Reidel Press.

Constantino, J. (1966) The Filipino Mental Make-up and Science. *Philippine Sociological Review* 14:18–28.

Cooley, C. (1902) *Human Nature and the Social Order.* New York: Scribners.

DeVos, G. (1976) The Relationship of Social and Psychological Structures in Transcultural Psychiatry. In W. Lebra (ed.) *Culture Bound Syndromes, Ethnopsychiatry, and Alternative Therapies.* Honolulu: University of Hawaii Press.

Draguns, J. (1981) Psychological Disorders of Clinical Severity. In H. Triandis and J. Draguns (eds) *Handbook of Cross-Cultural Psychology, vol. VI: Psychopathology.* Boston: Allyn & Bacon.

Doi, T. (1973) *The Anatomy of Dependence.* Tokyo: Kodansha International.

Durant, W. and Durant, A. (1967) The Story of Civilization, Part X: Rousseau and Revolution. New York: Simon & Schuster.

Geertz, C. (1973) *The Interpretation of Cultures*. New York: Basic Books.

Goffman, E. (1959) *The Presentation of Self in Everyday Life*. Garden City, NY: Doubleday.

Hollowell, A. (1934) Culture and Mental Disease. *Journal of Abnormal and Social Psychology* 29: 1–9.

Hora, T. (1979) Beyond Self. In J. Welwood (ed.) *The Meeting of the Ways: Explorations in East/West Psychology*. New York: Schocken Books.

Hsu, F. (1963) *Clan, Caste and Club*. New York: Van Nostrand.

James, W. (1890) *Principles of Psychology*. New York: Holt, Rinehart & Winston.

Jarvis, E. (1851) On the Supposed Increase of Insanity. *American Journal of Insanity* 8: 333–64.

King, L. (1978) Social and Cultural Influences on Psychopathology. *Annual Review of Psychology* 29: 405–33.

Kintaro, N. (1924) *A Study of Good*. Tokyo: Iwanami-Shoten. (Cited in Yoshifumi 1968.)

Kitaeff, R. (1976) The Healing Spectrum in India, Nepal, and Tibet. Paper presented at International Conference on Religion and Parapsychology, Tokyo.

Kleinman, A. (1977) Depression, Somatization and the "New Transcultural Psychiatry." *Social Science and Medicine* 11: 3–9.

＿＿ (1980) Patients and Healers in the Context of Culture. Berkeley, Calif.: University of California Press.

Koffka, K. (1935) *Principles of Gestalt Psychology*. New York: Harcourt, Brace, and World.

Kraepelin, E. (1904) Vergleichende Psychiatrie. *Zentralblatt für Nervenherlkande und Psychiatrie* 15: 433–37.

Lakoff, G. and Johnson, M. (1980) *Metaphors We Live By*. Chicago: University of Chicago Press.

Lock, M. (1976) Oriental Medicine in Urban Japan: A Harmony of Tradition and Science. Unpublished Ph. D. dissertation, University of California, Berkeley.

Marks. L. (1980) *The Unity of the Senses*. New York: Academic Press.

Marsella, A. (1978) Toward a Conceptual Framework for Understanding Cross-Cultural Variations in Depressive Affect and Disorder. Invited address, University of Washington, Seattle.

＿＿ (1979) Cross-Cultural Studies of Mental Disorders. In A. Marsella, R. Tharp, and T. Ciborowski (eds) *Perspectives in Cross-Cultural Psychology*. New York: Academic Press.

＿＿ (1981) Depressive Affect and Disorder across Cultures. In H.

Triandis and J. Draguns (eds) *Handbook of Cross-Cultural Psychology*, vol. 6, *Psychopathology*. Boston: Allyn & Bacon.

—— (1982) New Directions in Cross-Cultural Mental Health. In A. Marsella and G. White (eds) *Cultural Conceptions of Mental Health and Therapy*. Boston: Reidel Publishing.

Marsella, A. J., Kinzie, D., and Gordon, P. (1973) Ethnocultural Variations in the Expression of Depression. *Journal of Cross-Cultural Psychology* 4: 435–58.

Marsella, A. J. and Quijano, W. (1974) A Comparison of Vividness of Mental Imagery across Sensory Modalities in Filipinos and Caucasian-Americans. *Journal of Cross-Cultural Psychology* 5: 451–64.

Mead, G. H. (1934) *Mind, Self, and Society*. Chicago: University of Chicago Press.

Moore, C. (1968) *The Status of the Individual in East and West*. Honolulu: University of Hawaii Press.

Musgrave, W. and Sison, A. (1910) Mali-Mali: A Mimic Psychosis in the Philippine Islands. *Philippine Journal of Sciences* 5: 335

Nakamura, H. (1964) *Ways of Thinking of Eastern People*. Honolulu: University of Hawaii Press.

Needham, J. (1962) *Science and Civilization in China*. Cambridge: Cambridge University Press.

Rogers, C. (1951) *Client-Centered Therapy*. Boston: Houghton-Mifflin.

Rosen, G. (1969) *Madness in Society*. New York: Harper & Row.

Sarbin, T. (1952) A Preface to the Psychological Analysis of the Self. *Psychological Review* 59: 11–22.

Sartorius, N. (1979) Cross-Cultural Psychiatry. In K. Kisker *et al.* (eds) *Psychiatrie der Gegenwart*. Berlin: Springer Verlag.

Sechrest, L. (1969) Philippine Culture, Stress, and Psychopathology. In W. Caudill and T. Y. Lin (eds) *Mental Health Research in Asia and the Pacific*. Honolulu: University of Hawaii Press.

Smith, M. B. (1978) Perspectives on Selfhood. *American Psychologist* 33: 1053–063.

Snygg, D. and Combs, W. (1949) *Individual Behavior*. New York: Harper & Row.

Stevens, W. (1951) *The Motive for Metaphor: The Collected Poems of Wallace Stevens*. New York: Alfred A. Knopf. (Quoted in Marks 1980.)

Strauss, J. (1979) Social and Cultural Influences on Psychopathology. *Annual Review of Psychology* 30: 397–416.

Symonds, P. (1951) *The Ego and the Self*. New York: Appleton-Century Crofts.

Tanaka-Matsumi, J. and Marsella, A. J. (1976) Cross-Cultural Variations in the Phenomenological Experience of Depression: Word Association Studies. *Journal of Cross-Cultural Psychology* 7: 379–96.

Tatara, M. (1974) Problems of Separation and Dependency. *Journal of the American Academy of Psychoanalysis*. 2: 231–41.

Van Brero, P. (1895) Latah. *Journal of Mental Sciences* 41: 537–38.

Wylie, R. (1961) *The Self Concept: A Critical Survey of Pertinent Research Literature*. Lincoln: University of Nebraska Press.

Yoshifumi, U. (1968) The Status of the Individual in Mahayana Buddhist Philosophy. In C. Moore (ed.) *The Status of the Individual in East and West*. Honolulu: University of Hawaii Press.

Author Index

Subject Index